AF380366

Christian Pacifism for an Environmental Age

In this volume, Mark Douglas offers a new vision of the history of Christian pacifism within the context of a warming world. He narrates this story in a way that recognizes the complexities of the tradition and aligns it with a coherent theological vision, one that shapes the tradition to encompass the new causes and types of wars fought during the Anthropocene. Along the way, Douglas draws from research in historical climatology to recover the overlooked role that climate changes have always played in shaping not only the Christian pacifist tradition but also the movement of traditions through western history. Scholars across a range of disciplines – peace studies, Christian theology and history, environmentalism, and environmental conflict studies – will benefit from this model of critical and charitable engagement with the complex history of Christian pacifism, the resources of which will be important for addressing wars in a warming world.

Mark Douglas is Professor of Christian Ethics at Columbia Theological Seminary. He is the author of *Confessing Christ in the 21st Century* and *Believing Aloud: Reflections on Being Religious in the Public Square.*

Christian Pacifism for an Environmental Age

MARK DOUGLAS
Columbia Theological Seminary

CAMBRIDGE
UNIVERSITY PRESS

CAMBRIDGE
UNIVERSITY PRESS

University Printing House, Cambridge CB2 8BS, United Kingdom

One Liberty Plaza, 20th Floor, New York, NY 10006, USA

477 Williamstown Road, Port Melbourne, VIC 3207, Australia

314–321, 3rd Floor, Plot 3, Splendor Forum, Jasola District Centre,
New Delhi – 110025, India

79 Anson Road, #06–04/06, Singapore 079906

Cambridge University Press is part of the University of Cambridge.

It furthers the University's mission by disseminating knowledge in the pursuit of
education, learning, and research at the highest international levels of excellence.

www.cambridge.org
Information on this title: www.cambridge.org/9781108476485
DOI: 10.1017/9781108568548

First published 2019

Printed and bound in Great Britain by Clays Ltd, Elcograf S.p.A.

A catalogue record for this publication is available from the British Library.

Library of Congress Cataloging-in-Publication Data
NAMES: Douglas, Mark, author.
TITLE: Christian pacifism for an environmental age / Mark Douglas.
DESCRIPTION: New York : Cambridge University Press, 2019. | Includes
bibliographical references and index.
IDENTIFIERS: LCCN 2018045100 | ISBN 9781108476485
SUBJECTS: LCSH: Pacifism – Religious aspects – Christianity – History of doctrines. |
Nonviolence – Religious aspects – Christianity – History of doctrines.
CLASSIFICATION: LCC BT736.4 .D595 2019 | DDC 261.8/7309–dc23
LC record available at https://lccn.loc.gov/2018045100

ISBN 978-1-108-47648-5 Hardback

Contents

Acknowledgments

There is no "I" in "book". As much as spending time hunched over a computer or digging through library stacks are solitary enterprises, good books come about through the work of others: writers who came before us, scholars around the world who now share their wisdom with us, colleagues who gather round us, draft-readers who offer suggestions to us, and friends and family who support us. This brief acknowledgments section notes only some of the more prominent among those who have made this book possible; as such, it functions, synecdochally, as recognition for many. Those who go unmentioned below do so not because they don't warrant my gratitude but because my faulty memory hasn't brought them to mind as I write.

As the afterword notes, this is not the book I had initially intended to write. The changes that the manuscript underwent on the way from moving in one direction to becoming this very different book can be either partially blamed on or significantly credited to a range of conversation partners who not only enriched it but continue to enrich me. Among these I mention Ellen Ott-Marshall, Ted Smith, and Ian McFarland at Emory University, Kim Cobb at Georgia Tech, Kipton Jensen at Morehouse College, Kevin O'Brien at Pacific Lutheran University, and Ernst Conradie at the University of the Western Cape in South Africa. Thanks to all of them.

This book has benefitted from many people who read particular chapters of it in draft form and offered feedback that strengthened it and me. Among them are my colleagues at Columbia Theological Seminary (CTS), especially those who read a version of Chapter 7 one year and a draft of Chapter 8 a couple years later as part of our monthly "Dean's Lunch" gatherings. In that regard, special thanks to my colleague in ethics at CTS, Dr. Marcia Riggs, whose own work on religious ethical mediation is proving helpful to any number of people who study and train in the practices of conflict transformation. Beyond CTS, I shared Chapter 8 with a number of colleagues in Emory University's Graduate Division of Religion, including Liz Bounds and Bryan Ellrod, as well as the aforementioned Ted Smith and Ellen Ott-Marshall and the soon-to-be mentioned Brian Powers. The Reformed Theology Reading Group (James Calvin Davis, Roger Gench, Elizabeth Hinson-Hasty, and Doug Ottati) suffered through rough drafts of Chapters 2 and 5 in order to reduce the suffering of those who now read this book. And comments from the reviewers who read the manuscript for Cambridge University Press were especially helpful in streamlining and strengthening the Introduction and Chapter 6. Thanks to all of them.

Beyond reading and offering feedback, several people labored with me in the book's production. Beatrice Rehl and Eilidh Burrett at Cambridge Press have been wonderful to work with: gracious and thoughtful in the ways of the best editors. Colleagues on the board of Georgia Interfaith Power and Light were constant sources of encouragement. My family – especially my wife, Rev. Lindsay Armstrong, our daughter, Logan Armstrong Douglas, as well as my in-laws, Jim and Bev Armstrong – put up with my crabby periods and celebrated my small victories. Thanks to all of them.

A generous grant from the Nohria Family Charitable Fund allowed me to hire a former student and current colleague, Dr. Brian Powers, to do editorial work on the manuscript as well as compile the bibliography and put together the index. Thanks to the Fund and Dr. Virinder Nohria for their willingness to fund my "War in a Warming World" project and to Brian for his careful and gracious editorial work. Though it is perhaps a bit odd to advertise a book from one press in the pages in another, I would nevertheless encourage readers to buy and read Brian's book, *Full Darkness: Original Sin, Moral Injury, and Wartime Violence* (Eerdman's Press, 2019). It is totally worth it.

Between the time that the first draft of this book was completed and the time of its publication, the world lost a great man: Rev. Dr. David Bartlett. In his career(s) as a pastor and scholar, David exemplified collegiality in its most profound and magically light-hearted ways. To say that he was a friend to many only begins to capture the way David created and built friendships wherever he went. Along with many students and colleagues at

CTS, I was fortunate that he was willing to give up his first retirement from Yale Divinity School and join the faculty at CTS – and that after he retired (again, this time from CTS, and then, yet again, from Trinity Presbyterian Church of Atlanta), the two of us were able to continue to work together on a range of projects and share many and wide-ranging conversations, sometimes with our spouses and/or kids and sometimes just the two of us. In our time together, David was, among other things, a wise mentor, thoughtful colleague, careful editor, willing co-conspirator, easy travel-partner, engaging co-preacher, gracious host, and good friend. I expect his voice will be easy to pick out among all those that compose the rest of the heavenly choir when next we meet. Although his own academic work was in the areas of New Testament and homiletics, David nevertheless manifested in his life and work many of the best practices of peacemaking and peacebuilding that will be so necessary for life in the Anthropocene. I dedicate this book to him.

Climate, Conflict, and the Conventional Narrative of Christian Pacifism

Christianity has a long and profound tradition of nonviolence. The tradition begins in the New Testament church (and extends even further back, in various precursor forms, to the last few centuries B.C.E.) and it continues to the present. The significance of the tradition can be measured, in part, by an influence that extends far beyond not only the peace churches that rest most deeply in the tradition but beyond Christianity itself. Whether in its early anticipation of an immediate eschaton that obviated the need for the use of force, in its growing emphasis on obedience to the nonviolent teachings of Jesus as expressed in the synoptic gospels, in the obligations of those joining religious orders to avoid violence during the Middle Ages, in the development of the "peace churches" – Mennonites, Brethren, Amish, Quakers, and others – during the Reformation, or in more recent work that has been done by important scholars and public intellectuals like Dorothy Day, Martin Luther King, Jr., John Howard Yoder, Stanley Hauerwas, and those whom they've influenced, this commitment to nonviolence has expressed itself in myriad ways that have, nonetheless, always been identifiably connected to the church. In an age in which the capacity to wreak violence has revealed itself on such massive scales – including, potentially, the obliteration of the human race – a set of voices arguing for alternatives to violence is especially worth hearing. Moreover, over the past 150 years, the viability of nonresistance/nonviolence/pacifism/nonviolent resistance[1] as an idea has proven to be an especially powerful force for social change,

---

[1] These terms do not mean the same thing; for now, though, they bear sufficient familial resemblance to each other to be treated alike for my purposes.

generally to the good and often directly connected to actions of the Christian church.[2] While there is still much to be done in a violent world, the church's commitment to and effective advocacy for nonviolence can hardly be understated.

Given its significance not only for Christian communities of faith but for the larger world, this legacy of nonviolence warrants close attention by anyone who would think about matters of war and peace from within the context of Christian theology and ethics, especially during times of rapid change. What role might this tradition of nonviolence play in the twenty-first century as we address war in a warming world?

In this volume, I raise a series of questions about the way those who have advocated nonviolence have understood time and the implications of this understanding for our entrance into the Anthropocene.[3] If the major thesis of this book – that we are entering a new social imaginary[4] shaped by environmental concerns and demanding the reconstruction of our thoughts,

---

[2] See John Mueller, *The Remnants of War* (Cornell, NY: Cornell University Press, 2004) for an argument that the idea of pacifism has, since the U.S. Civil War, led to the end of conventional warfare in most of the world.

[3] "The Anthropocene" is a term popularized by chemist Paul Crutzen at the beginning of the twenty-first century to describe the epoch in which human beings gained the capacity to fundamentally alter the earth's geological and ecological systems. While start dates for the Anthropocene vary – from the dawn of agriculture and animal domestication to the dawn of the widespread use of fossil fuels to the first explosion of a nuclear weapon on July 16, 1945 – most people use the term to describe the time period that human beings are now entering, which will be defined by environmental concerns. Meant to convey the idea of a human-influenced time-period that can be measured on a geological scale, the term is used informally in scientific and popular culture, and neither a firm starting point nor an agreed-upon definition exists for it. When I use the term in this book, I mean it to convey the time period that we are now entering in which environmental concerns are so severe, so widespread, so dramatic, and so impactful of human existence that human beings will increasingly make sense of the world around them through environmental lenses: not only will climate change, the catastrophic loss of biodiversity, growing human populations, the proliferation of waste, and other environmental concerns become problems to which we must attend; they will shape the way we understand and address other problems. In this book, I will use the terms "Anthropocene" and "Environmental Age" as near-synonyms, recognizing that "environmental" is also a politically fraught term within the literatures of those who engage matters having to do with the interactions and interconnectedness of the natural world and human beings.

[4] The term "social imaginary" is philosopher Charles Taylor's. In his book, *A Secular Age,* Taylor writes of the social imaginary as "the way that we collectively imagine, even pre-theoretically, our social life in the contemporary Western world" (146) that is "something much broader and deeper than the intellectual schemes people may entertain" (171) – "that largely unstructured and inarticulate understanding of our whole situation, within which particular features of our world show up for us in the sense that they have" (173). More on Taylor and the secular age will appear later in the book. See, e.g., Charles Taylor, *The Secular Age* (Boston: Harvard University Press, 2007).

practices, and technologies in order to meaningfully address environmentally shaped conflicts – is anywhere near correct, then questions about when we live are every bit as pressing as those about how we live. Understanding our place in time and understanding our conflicts are of a piece. And understanding our place in time theologically means accounting for both the continuities and discontinuities of the human movement through a history in which God is a primary actor, creating and transforming, judging and redeeming, and in which nonviolence has played a significant role.

Yet what is the conventional narrative of the history of Christian pacifism?

I THE CONVENTIONAL NARRATIVE OF THE HISTORY OF CHRISTIAN PACIFISM AND ITS PROBLEMS

The conventional narrative of Christian pacifism's movement through time goes something like this: Jesus and the New Testament writers espoused nonviolence and/or nonresistance, and pacifism would be central to the ethic of the early church until the time of Constantine (and it would be the exclusive ethic of the church from the close of the canon to around 173 C.E.). After Constantine, the church would align itself with Roman imperial power and, as a result, the pacifist ethic would be replaced by one centered around just war thinking, especially after and due to Augustine. This realignment with the state constitutes not only a change but a fall away from fidelity to a Jesus-centered ethics. As a recent and brief rehearsal of this narrative, W. Michael Slattery's text is representative: "For more than one century after the death of Jesus, until around 173 AD, the Church undisputedly, univocally, and consistently was pacifist and remained so in Church teaching of the fathers for two more centuries, but with increasing compromise of its non-ordained followers until Constantine and the later cementing of 'righteous' violence by Augustine."[5]

Within the conventional narrative, after Augustine and until the rise of the peace churches during the Protestant Reformation, occasional persons and particular groups would promote nonviolence but either in ways that allowed violence on the part of most Christians or that the larger church would view as heretical. However, the Protestant Reformation's emphasis on the authority of the Bible (including New Testament commandments to practice

---

[5] W. Michael Slattery, *Jesus the Warrior: Historical Christian Perspectives and Problems on the Morality of War and the Waging of Peace* (Milwaukee, WI: Marquette University Press, 2007), 84.

nonresistance) and the church's realignment with the state (or, more accurately, range of realignments with the state) create space for various communions to shape themselves around the early church's peace ethic. The peace churches (Quaker, Amish, Brethren, Mennonite, etc.), though remaining small, sometimes persecuted, and generally excluded from the Christian mainstream, would choose to reveal an alternative way of living that bore witness to the nonviolent Gospel for both the rest of the church and the larger world. In the twentieth century, as wars grew increasingly violent and unconstrained, as weapons grew increasingly lethal and indiscriminate, as the legacies of the social gospel movement and progressivism found a home within some of the church's range of communions, as nonviolent resistance revealed itself as an effective means for inducing social change, as resources from other faiths came into view, and as the age of Christendom initiated by Constantine came to a close, the wisdom of the peace churches emerged as a means for establishing a viable and faithful Christian ethic[6] across the theological spectrum.[7]

---

[6] Among pacifists who promote such a narrative – in part or whole, with varying levels of apologetics built into their arguments – see Guy Franklin Hershberger, *War, Peace, and Nonresistance* (Scottsdale, PA: Herald Press, 1969); Jean-Michel Hornus, *It Is Not Lawful for me to Fight*, trans. by Alan Kreider and Oliver Coburn (Scottsdale, PA: Herald Press, 1980); C. John Cadoux, *The Early Christian Attitude to War* (London: Headly Bros. Pub., 1982); Roland H. Bainton, *Christian Attitudes Toward War and Peace: A Historical Survey and Critical Re-evaluation* (New York: Abingdon Press, 1960); G. J. Heering, *The Fall of Christianity: A Study of Christianity, the State, and War* (New York: Fellowship Publications, 1943); Geoffrey F. Nuttall, *Christian Pacifism in History* (Oxford: Basil Blackwell, 1958); Edgar W. Orr, *Christian Pacifism* (Ashingdon, England: C. W. Daniel Co., Ltd., 1958); Joseph T. Culliton, ed., *Non-violence – Central to Christian Spirituality: Perspectives from Scripture to the Present* (New York: Edwin Mellen Press, 1982); Dale W. Brown, *Biblical Pacifism: A Peace Church Perspective* (Elgin, IL: Brethren Press, 1986); Dennis Byler, *Making War and Making Peace: Why Some Christians Fight and Some Don't* (Scottsdale, PA: Herald Press, 1989); Marlin E. Miller and Barbara Nelson Gingerich, eds., *The Church's Peace Witness* (Grand Rapids: Eerdmans, 1994); Peter Brock, *A Brief History of Pacifism: From Jesus to Tolstoy* (Syracuse: Syracuse University Press, 1992); Peter Brock, *Varieties of Pacifism: A Survey from Antiquity to the Outset of the Twentieth Century* (Syracuse: Syracuse University Press, 1998); E. Morris Sider and Luke Keefer Jr., eds., *A Peace Reader* (Nappanee, IN: Evangel Publishing House, 2002); and W. Michael Slattery, *Jesus the Warrior? Historical Christian Perspectives and Problems on the Morality of War and the Waging of Peace* (Milwaukee: Marquette University Press, 2007). The first four (Cadoux, Hershberger, Hornus, and Bainton) are especially important in developing this history, as many of the later writers will rely on their research and narratives. One important exception to this narrative is that visible in Michael G. Long, ed., *Christian Peace and Nonviolence: A Documentary History* (Maryknoll, NY: Orbis, 2011), which fills in sources and details that are generally ignored.

[7] I should note that one variation on this narrative comes from some contemporary Roman Catholic sources, who repeat the claims about the early church's commitment to

On such a telling, the discontinuous quality of the history of Christian pacifism is obvious: aside from the time of the early church, the pacifist Christian voice has always been in the minority and vulnerable. As Geoffrey Nuttall expresses it, "[T]o offer a straight narrative history of Christian Pacifism would hardly be possible. The story is too discontinuous, the existence, or at least the appearance, of pacifists and pacifist witness within the Church is too occasional and sporadic."[8] In such a narrative, only persons of heroic faith or inwardly focused and insular communities tended to espouse nonviolence – and such persons and communities come along only sporadically. Yet where such persons and communities exist, we find moral exemplars and visions of a purer Christian/Kingdom ethic than we can find within a wider church that has compromised fidelity to Jesus's commands in order to pursue justice through the use of force and has sacrificed a willingness to live vulnerably in order to protect itself and others.

This narrative is, moreover, reinforced by those who don't necessarily align themselves with the pacifist traditions. So, for example, sourcebooks on world religions, when they address Christianity and conflict, repeat the narrative.[9] Far from simply describing the tradition of nonviolence in Christianity, these sourcebooks reiterate and thereby extend the power of the conventional narrative.

More fascinatingly, many opponents of pacifism repeat a version of this narrative in their own work. While they take exception to the notion that the advent of Constantinianism constitutes a kind of "fall" (arguing, instead, that it initiates a time in which the Christian faith necessarily undergoes revisions in order to bring other important Christian values and

nonviolence and the fall of the church after Constantine but ignore the Radical Reformers entirely on their way to suggesting that twentieth-century Roman Catholics like Dorothy Day and Pope John XXIII (in *Pacem in Terris*) rediscover and/or reclaim the church's pacifist roots. See, e.g., Eileen Egan, *Peace Be With You: Justified Warfare or the Way of Nonviolence* (Maryknoll, NY: Orbis, 1999) and David Carroll Cochran, *Catholic Realism and the Abolition of War* (Maryknoll, NY: Orbis, 2014). Even this peculiar (if not entirely surprising) bit of pacifist silencing, though, doesn't undermine the conventional narrative so much as bring it into higher relief: the distance between the fourth and twentieth centuries is even greater than that between the fourth and the fifteenth.

[8] Geoffrey F. Nuttall, *Christian Pacifism in History* (Oxford: Basil Blackwell, 1958), 1.

[9] See, e.g., Theodore J. Koontz, "Christian Nonviolence: An Interpretation" in Terry Nardin, ed., *The Ethics of War and Peace: Religious and Secular Perspectives* (Princeton: Princeton University Press, 1996): 169–196; John Ferguson, *War and Peace in the World's Religions* (New York: Oxford University Press, 1978): 99–123; Gregory M. Reichberg, Henrik Syse, and Nicole M. Harswell, (eds.), *Religion, War, and Ethics: A Sourcebook of Textual Traditions* (New York: Cambridge University Press, 2014): Chs. 2–4.

virtues, including justice and responsibility, to the fore), non-pacifists still tend to repeat two key claims in the pacifist narrative: that the pre-Constantinian church was pacifist and that the advent of Constantinian Christianity and the project of justifying the use of violence mandated accepting levels of moral ambiguity that the earlier church didn't have to accept. So, for example, a just warrior as eminent as Paul Ramsey would open the Introduction to his classic book *War and the Christian Conscience* with the claim that, "[f]or almost two centuries of the history of the early church, Christians were universally pacifists,"[10] and a Christian realist as prominent as Reinhold Niebuhr would note that Christian pacifism "is not a heresy. It is rather a valuable asset for the Christian faith. It is a reminder to the Christian community that the relative norms of social justice, which justify both coercion and resistance to coercion, are not final norms, and that Christians are in constant peril of forgetting their relative and tentative character and of making them too completely normative."[11] While Ramey, Niebuhr, and their like make strong arguments for just war and/or Christian realism in their work, when they accede to pacifism's conventional narrative, they place themselves in the awkward positions of surrendering not only to a particular reading of New Testament texts and a distinct vision of the early church, but to a kind of idealism. They give up the figurative moral high ground and argue, instead, that trying to live on the high ground is untenable, unachievable, or quixotic. They confuse inspirational and aspirational visions, thereby not only unfairly mixing moral rigor with utopianism but undermining their own commitments to the ideals that inspire their thoughts.[12]

---

[10] Paul Ramsey, *War and the Christian Conscience* (Durham, NC: Duke University Press, 1961), xv. The narrative is repeated by other just warriors in texts such as Arthur F. Holmes (ed.), *War and Christian Ethics: Classic and Contemporary Readings on the Morality of War* (Grand Rapids: Baker Academic, 1975); David L. Clough and Brian Stiltner, *Faith and Force: A Christian Debate about War* (Washington D.C.: Georgetown UP, 2007); Lisa Sowle Cahill, *Love Your Enemies: Discipleship, Pacifism, and Just War Theory* (Minneapolis: Augsburg Fortress Press, 1994); Richard J. Regan, *Just War: Principles and Cases* (Washington D.C.: Catholic University of America Press, 1996); Matthew A. Shandle, *The Origins of War: A Catholic Perspective* (Washington D. C.: Georgetown University Press, 2011). Even James Turner Johnson repeats a version of the narrative in his book, *Just War Tradition and the Restraint of War: A Moral and Historical Inquiry* (Princeton: Princeton University Press, 1981).

[11] Reinhold Niebuhr, "Why the Christian Church is not Pacifist" in Arthur Holmes, ed., *War and Christian Ethics* (Grand Rapids, MI: Baker Academic, 2005), 303.

[12] Perhaps one bit of evidence for this is the generally unhelpful means-versus-ends disagreement within the Christian just war community between those who argue that the

The conventional narrative relies on a particular pattern in history in which post-Constantinian pacifists attempt to retrieve pre-Constantinian wisdom. The retrieval is unsurprising: if the early church exists in a morally Edenic time in which it faithfully obeys Jesus's commandments to turn the other cheek and love even enemies, then the church's choice to align itself with secular political power in order to insure its continued existence and social significance in the fourth century constitutes a kind of fall from grace. After Constantine, particular persons and communities will rediscover the messianic (nonviolent) ethic of the New Testament and enact it in their lives together. This is, in part, due to the predominance of Protestant interpretations of the history of nonviolence; Protestants, after all, have been far more likely to elevate to primacy the authority of the Bible and, particularly, a history-oriented reading of New Testament texts in making sense of the faith. Yet this pattern is about more than an emphasis on the authority of the Bible. After all, pacifists rely not only on the New Testament but on the writings of the early church fathers in defending their vision of the moral life; the fall from grace happens early in the fourth century, not late in the first. Post-Constantine, then, those who advocate nonviolence within Christian thought repeatedly loop back to the pre-Constantinian church as if the temporal distance between the two periods could – and even should – be disregarded. Treating centuries of history as of limited use for their purposes, pacifist communities skip back to a particular period in the early history of the church that they think will be more useful. That is, the conventional narrative expresses a myth of return.[13]

This myth of return, as expressed in the conventional narrative about the tradition of nonviolence in the Christian church, is undergirded by two

---

word "just" in that phrase comes from "justified" and those who argue it comes from "justice." The former emphasize processes for moving forward in morally ambiguous terrain; the latter in seeking after a particular goal on the far side of that terrain. Sometimes lost in the disagreement are deep convictions about fundamental Christian ideals like *agape* that both found processes and fund ends.

[13] I hasten to add that I am not suggesting that the nonviolent church necessarily participates in a "myth of eternal return" à la Mircea Eliade. Indeed, the dominant perspective of the nonviolent church isn't that it should be shaped (morally and otherwise) by its origin but by its conclusion: it attempts to live into the Kingdom of God, which has not yet fully arrived. As such, the nonviolent church expresses a vision of linear rather than cyclical time. The "return" I describe is neither to Eden nor to Golgotha; it is a return to the early church as the clearest model for how to live as a church that stood outside the patterns of behavior shaped by the use of violence and complicity in the coercive power of the state. For more on the myth of eternal return and Christian history, see Mircea Eliade, *Cosmos and History: The Myth of Eternal Return* (New York: Harper and Bros., 1959), particularly Ch. 4.

basic assumptions: that the pre-Constantinian church manifested an ethic closer to that promoted by Jesus in the New Testament than the Constantinian church and that, since Constantine, advocacy of nonviolence has been episodic and discrete to particular persons and minority communities within Christianity rather than continuously expressed within Christian thought and practices. The latter assumption motivates the return; the former provides a place in time to which to return.

I argue against the conventional narrative in order to undermine these two basic assumptions behind it. First, I will argue that voices for nonviolence in the early church are neither as uniform nor as dominant as the conventional narrative suggests. They are, nonetheless, consistently present. Once we better locate them in their own times and vis-à-vis other voices in the church and surrounding cultures, we can recognize how their embeddedness reveals something significant about the church's witness to nonviolence. It can also help us establish patterns of thought and behavior that continue with regularity through the Middle Ages, the Reformation, and up to the present. That is, once those voices become more varied and less dominant, the possibilities of seeing continuities in the witness of nonviolence throughout the history of the church grow. There have been significant figures and communities throughout history giving voice to a priority toward nonviolence, but their voices have been drowned out by earlier voices to whom we have given megaphones when we have over-claimed the emphasis on nonviolence in the early church.

And, second, I will argue that the various motives and visions that shape nonviolent Christian ethics in the early church are not as pure, clear, or faithful as the conventional narrative describes. Even those figures within the early church deemed most significant by the conventional narrative were driven by problematic motives and values, and these problematic motives and values find expression in the types of reasoning they used in emphasizing nonviolence. As such, we need to treat these figures with a greater degree of suspicion and ambivalence. Treating such figures with more ambivalence, however, is not the same as dismissing them. Allowing for these figures' failings – and even forgiving their failings – helps those who would follow after them recognize their own potential for morally troubling behavior (therein potentially shaping a more forgiving space within which to act), identify some of the sources and consequences of those failings (therein recognizing the necessity of shaping such a forgiving space), and either eliminate or compensate for those failings (therein making resources for justice on the far side of forgiveness more possible).

Having argued against these two basic assumptions, I will then be in a position to argue against the myth of return that animates the conventional Christian pacifist narrative and for a different, more human, narrative. That myth, I will argue, displays a reading of history that can bear the weight neither of the historical data nor of a theological vision of God's work in time that is shaped by creation, crucifixion, and resurrection: a vision that can account for both the continuous and discontinuous movements of traditions through time. Ultimately, it is the *myth* that needs to be challenged more than the narrative that it supports because as we enter into a new social imaginary, *return* is the one direction that we won't be able to go, and to attempt to do so will exacerbate many of the most pressing issues surrounding climate-shaped conflict.

To be clear: I intend to undermine these two assumptions and challenge the myth of return not with the goal of undermining the significance of the Christian witness of nonviolence but, instead, of better situating the Christian pacifist traditions in history in order to shape their usefulness as we enter into a new environmentally shaped social imaginary and face conflicts arising out of and being shaped by that new social imaginary. That is, I want to better locate Christian pacifism in the past in order to help carry its wisdom into the future. From the perspective of the conventional narrative, the options for dealing with pacifism are either to leave it and the early church in the past and, therein, risk either leaving behind the strange wisdom of the New Testament (the just warrior's temptation) or to valorize it, claiming the moral wisdom of the early church in continuity with the New Testament but disregarding much of the church's history between the fourth and sixteenth or twentieth centuries (the pacifist's temptation). Again, I wish neither to bury pacifism nor to praise it. Instead, in demythologizing pacifism, I hope to temporalize – and thereby humanize – it. As it is better situated in history (or, more properly, situated within a reflexively attentive theological vision of how traditions move through time), the Christian witness to nonviolence simultaneously expresses greater fidelity to a religious vision shaped by incarnation, crucifixion, and resurrection and offers more relevance to the way that vision expresses its prophetic hope for the future.

More importantly, I argue that the myth of return that drives the conventional narrative fails not only to do justice to the rich, complex, and human tradition of nonviolence in the history of Christian thought but to adequately locate itself within the scope of God's work in time. Having offered a narrative of discontinuity that is sustained by a myth of return, the pacifist tradition struggles to account for divine activity during periods when the tradition seemingly wanes or among non-pacifist communities. In a richer theological vision of God's work in time, we might recognize that every practice and idea – including those associated with the most rigorous of pacifist ethics – is still but a dim expression of life with God and that all practices and ideas remain in need of transformation. The distance between a Christian ethic that allows for violence and one that doesn't is far less than the distance between any Christian ethic and the politics of the Kingdom of God. Because the tradition is human, it is judged and found wanting. And, paradoxically, because God is already at work transforming the world, the distance between a Christian ethic that allows for violence and one that doesn't is far greater than the distance between any ethic and the actions of God, as God works both in and through the persons and communities that live out those ethics. Because God acts through the tradition, it is hope-filled beyond imagining – and it need not, therefore, rely on a myth of return to justify its continued significance.

Yet what is the form of my arguments?

This book walks through the history of the Christian church's advocacy of nonviolence with an eye to how such advocacy and, particularly, the myths that have encrusted it have been shaped by a particular vision of time. This journey occurs in three parts. The first part of this journey will focus on the first several centuries of the church's advocacy of pacifism, ending roughly with Constantine's rise to power. It is to the insights of the church during these centuries that post-Constantinian and contemporary Christian pacifists regularly return as both sources of authority upon which to found their narrative of the pacifist tradition and as evidence for the enduring significance of that tradition for the contemporary church. Whether these centuries can carry the weight placed upon them, though, is a question in need of answer. Chapters 1 through 3 attempt to answer that question. In Chapter 1, I argue that the evidence of the pacifist church before the end of the second century is more ambiguous than the conventional narrative of the history of Christian pacifism will support, but that such ambiguity need not undermine the significance of that period for understanding Christian pacifism. In Chapter 2, I argue that the reasons that at least some portions of the church in the second and third centuries were pacifist are morally troubling but that such moral failings need not function only as an indictment of the early church's pacifism. And in Chapter 3, I argue that the values and visions that would shape the fourth-century church's embrace of war are, in part, the product of the third-century pacifist church's approach to engaging the world, but that such a mode of engagement need not lead us to discount the wisdom of the pre-Constantinian church. Collectively, then, the first part of the book dismantles the conceptual structures that have undergirded the conventional narrative's valorization of the early church. Along the way, I offer reasons that such a dismantling may, in the long run, help Christian pacifism engage the crises of climate-shaped conflict.

The second part of the book traverses the period from Constantine to the present, questioning the conventional narrative of the Christian pacifist tradition and its treatment of this period of history as long and bleak with only occasional pacifist moments of theological integrity and moral clarity. In Chapter 4, I argue that a more capacious understanding of the fourth century generally and Constantine specifically has the potential not only to provide a far greater range of helpful conversation partners for Christian pacifists but offers a cautionary tale about Christian assessments of the state. In Chapter 5, I argue that the 1500-year stretch between the mid-fourth and the mid-nineteenth centuries reveals a complex mix of continuity and disruption to the Christian pacifist tradition that has been submerged in the conventional narrative of the history of Christian pacifism for not only historically but theologically problematic reasons. And in Chapter 6, I argue that the last century and a half of Christian pacifism has witnessed an explosion in the forms of Christian pacifism and the remarkable success of Christian pacifist arguments in carrying political weight. Collectively, then, this second part of the book provides resources for the building up of a revised and resilient narrative of Christian pacifism as it moves into the environmental age.

The third part of this book completes the project of shaping a revised and resilient alternative narrative of the history of Christian pacifism. In Chapter 7, I argue for a more theologically consistent and practically helpful way of understanding the movement of traditions through time and theology of discernment that can include the work of God in that movement. And in Chapter 8, in light of the preceding chapters, I (finally) offer that narrative.

2 CONNECTING CLIMATE TO CONFLICT

This book offers an alternative history of Christian pacifism; it is, I hope, valuable for that purpose alone. But the concerns that motivate proposing this alternative history are not simply about telling better histories. Instead, the driving concerns that have led to this book are related to the way climate change, specifically, and environmental catastrophes, more generally, are reshaping the causes, types, and understandings of war in the twenty-first century. If Christian pacifism is a way of responding to war, then telling an alternative history isn't simply about trying to offer a story that coheres better with the way Christian pacifism has moved through time; it is about shaping a Christian pacifism that can address these new conflicts. The starting point in this is to recognize that natural forces have always shaped war.

In *The Art of War*, Sun Tzu writes that anyone preparing for battle must consider five factors, among them the weather.[14] His wisdom is sound. Weather has played a dramatic role in many important battles: in the thirteenth century, a typhoon so battered the fleet Kublai Khan sent to invade Japan that the invasion was called off. The Japanese called the storm *kamikaze*, "Divine Wind." In 1588, a storm destroyed the remainder of the Spanish Armada sent to conquer England, thereby dramatically changing not only the political configurations of Europe but the shape of exploration and colonization. More recently, D-Day was almost postponed due to a storm in the English Channel (which did cause several supply ships to sink), and sandstorms prevented Saddam Hussein from launching Scud missiles in the first Gulf War and temporarily halted the U.S. invasion of Iraq in the second one.

Climate, too, has played a dramatic if less obvious role in military history.[15] Climate scientists studying European tree-ring samples suggested that the Roman Empire arose during a period of warm, wet summers in Europe of the sort ideal for agricultural productivity and that the decline of that empire due to invasions from the north and internal political turmoil came during a time of extended droughts.[16] Prior to the mid-fifteenth century, England grew its own grapes for wine. However, the arrival of the little ice age ended the possibility of such harvests.

---

[14] Sun Tzu, *The Art of War*, trans. Samuel B. Griffith (New York: Oxford University Press, 1971). The other factors are terrain, discipline, politics, and leadership.

[15] Weather is the state of the atmosphere at any given point in time and space due to variables such as atmospheric pressure, temperature, and water content. Climate is the meteorological conditions that are characteristic of a particular geographic location, determined by factors like latitude, altitude, the earth's spin, and a place's relation to oceans and mountains. That a day is sunny or rainy is weather; that it is summer or that it tends to rain in April is climate. Weather changes on a daily or even hourly basis; climate changes over years, decades, and centuries.

[16] Andrew Curry, "Fall of Rome Recorded in Trees." *ScienceNOW* (January 13, 2011). Accessed on January 14, 2011 at http://news.sciencemag.org/sciencenow/2011/01/fall-of-rome-recorded-in-trees

The colder weather, though, turned out to be quite good for growing stronger yew trees – and with yew bows made from those trees, the English were able to cross the channel and take possession of some of the wine-growing regions in France, thereby quenching their thirst for the fruit of the vine.[17]

Connections between climate and conflict have long been evident. Climate-related issues (drought, migrations to find arable land, desire for commodities like timber and foodstuffs that cannot be found or produced in sufficient quantities in a particular country) have led to violence for as long as there have been structured systems of conflict – as revealed in battles over resources from early agrarian societies through the age of colonial conquest (what was the East India Trading Company but an armed means of moving resources from one climate to another?) to contemporary conflicts in, e.g., the Horn of Africa. Indeed, over the past several decades, an entire field of study – Environmental Security Studies – has emerged to study the relation between the two.[18] And over the past two decades, Environmental Security researchers have been raising questions about whether contemporary, rapid, human-caused climate change might play an increasingly significant role in shaping patterns of large-scale violent behavior.

Whether those questions had a basis in statistical evidence, however, had not been established. After all, gradual climate change of the sort to occur naturally over decades and centuries never, in itself, led to violence: there are always other – and generally more prominent – causes for the resort to arms. Rome rose for a number of reasons (the comparative power vacuum left after the successes of Alexander the Great, the advent of a mix of Stoic and martial state philosophies, the rise of new technologies and battle strategies, etc.), some of which had, seemingly, nothing to do with climate. Likewise, Rome fell for myriad reasons. Tree rings may establish a correlation; they don't establish causation. And the English

---

[17] That there has been a relationship between climate and the stability of any given culture has long been assumed, though little research has been done to explore the nature of that relationship until recently – and most of this research has examined evidence from pre-modern societies in which people were much more clearly at the mercy of the climate. Short not only clearer causative evidence that climactic change can cause social instability but also that social instability is, in itself, a sufficient precondition to induce civil conflict, the relations between climactic change and civil conflict have needed closer attention than the comparatively anecdotal evidence has yielded until very recently.

[18] For a helpful – if already dated – bibliography of some of the more significant works in Environmental Security, see Thomas F. Homer-Dixon, *Environment, Scarcity, and Violence* (Princeton: Princeton University Press, 1999), 241–245.

didn't invade France primarily because they enjoyed wine. Changes in climate, it seemed, *may* help shape occurrences of systemic violence, but were unlikely to be a sufficient precondition for that violence, especially since the advent of modernity.

Indeed, the causal relationship between climate and armed conflict has been so tenuous that as recently as the late 1990s, Nils Petter Gleditsch, in a systematic literature review, could convincingly argue that "[d]espite numerous pronouncements on the relationship between conflict and the environment, there is no consensus on causal mechanisms. Indeed, several writers have questioned the overall argument [that environment can play any causative role in conflict]."[19] There were simply too many analytic problems with the research (lack of definitional clarity, inattention to important non-environmental variables, cherry-picking data, falsifiability of hypotheses, etc.) to justify claims of causation. As such, there may be sufficient anecdotal evidence to suggest that environmental issues may play a factor – albeit a small one – in conflict, but lacking sufficient (and sufficiently precise) analytic data, this is the *most* we can say about the relation between the two.

Or such was the loose consensus of historians, scientists, and Environmental Security experts until a 2011 study by Solomon Hsiang and two colleagues lent statistical support to the claim that climate change and civil conflict can be causally connected, including in the current day. By examining the oscillations in the El Niño/La Niña weather patterns and their correlation to violence in the tropics over the past sixty years, Hsiang and colleagues were able to "directly associate planetary-scale climate changes with global patterns of civil conflict [revealing that the weather patterns] may have had a role in 21% of all civil conflicts since 1950."[20]

El Niño is episodic[21]. The changing global climate is not.[22] The scientific consensus that global climate change is functioning in

---

[19] Nils Petter Gleditsch, "Armed Conflict and the Environment: A Critique of the Literature," *Journal of Peace Research* 35.3 (1998): 383.

[20] Solomon M. Hsiang, Kyle C. Meng, and Mark A. Cane, "Civil Conflicts Are Associated with the Global Climate," *Nature* 476 (August 25, 2011): 438.

[21] "El Niño" and "La Niña" are the names given to weather patterns in the Pacific ocean that alternate on an average of every five years. El Niño is marked by higher-than-average ocean temperatures and higher air pressures above it; La Niña is marked by the opposite. Collectively, they are referred to as the "El Niño Southern Oscillation" or ENSO. Combined with seasonal variations, ENSO affects rainfall and oceanic and atmospheric circulation patterns around Africa, Asia, South, and North America, thereby impacting cyclonic activity and disease outbreaks as well as a wide range of human activities (farming, fishing, building, travel, etc.).

[22] I should be clear from the outset: in these books, I will not take up the debate about *whether* contemporary climate change is being caused by human activity. That debate has

a linear rather than episodic way, however, has only come about quite recently and questions persist about the shape and steepness of that line. As such, the move from evidence that climate plays a causal role in conflict to the claim that anthropogenic climate change is going to play an increasingly significant role in some armed conflicts must resist two temptations. The first is to treat future events in empirical ways. We simply cannot see into the future with sufficient clarity to allow for simple determinate statements. Instead, we will have to speak in terms of probabilities and potentialities – albeit in ways that take seriously the way current data and methods of analysis make statements about the future far more than simply suggestive. The second temptation, though, is to treat probabilistic statements as insufficiently precise to mandate action. At least within the area of security studies, low-probability, high-impact potential events are treated with the utmost seriousness: a five percent chance that a nuclear weapon might fall into the hands of a particular terrorist organization not only will but ought to lead to a significant mobilization of resources toward gathering more precise data and preparing to prevent such an event from taking place.

So what are some of the ways that global climate change might play a causal role in armed conflict and how seriously ought we to take them? The range of climate-related factors that may play causative or partially causative roles in conflict is extensive, but includes at least concerns related to resource scarcity (including basic goods like food and water), disease spread, the movements of refugees, and the pursuit of previously unreachable resources.

Due to the rise in greenhouse gases, much of them created by human activity, the world is not only likely to see more frequent and severe weather patterns, but – if the pattern Hsiang and his colleagues observed holds – increased occurrences of civil conflict as a result. Drought and flooding, combined with the loss of glaciers and overuse of land, will make arable land scarcer, thereby making food more valuable, shortages of food

been settled – endlessly – through evidence supplied in conference after conference, article after article, and book after book provided by climate scientists from around the world. The few who still deny the reality of human-caused climate change compose only a sliver of an overly vocal minority, which has more political power – at least in the United States – than their position warrants. Nor will I take up – at least in any great detail – debates about how much the climate has or will change and what percentage of that change is directly attributable to human activity. Such debates are important but need not be settled for the arguments in this book to have force. (Indeed, in matters of national security or threats of violence, even a slim chance of an event occurring carries sufficient weight for it to be considered with some seriousness.)

more deadly, and the control of food a greater political or military weapon (especially by warlords, terrorists, and others who are willing to ignore the Geneva Conventions). And all this will occur even as the global population – and therein the demand for food – grows. After a century in which major wars were fought mostly over ideological and political differences, we are seeing disagreements over access to natural resources play an increasingly important role among the causes of conflict.

Climate change will not only shape security issues surrounding food grown on land; it's already changing marine habitats that many coastal countries rely on for food and revenue. So, for instance, the loss of marine habitat and the concurrent depletion of fish around the horn of Africa have already helped to turn the vital but struggling Somali fishing industry into the Somali piracy industry, therein exacerbating not only the internal violent problems of that failed state but dragging other countries whose ships pass around the horn into obligations to protect those ships by deploying military to the area. Other countries – especially those that front or are surrounded by the Indian Ocean – may follow in this pattern. And not only will piracy be a problem. Combine unemployment, poverty, migration, and diminished resources with a weakened state and, as Admiral Joseph Lopez of the U.S. Navy notes, "conditions are ripe for extremists and terrorists."[23]

Longer and wetter warm seasons will stimulate the spread of diseases like malaria to areas further north and south of the equator and/or lengthen the seasons in which people must deal with them, thereby draining economic, humanitarian, and political resources from already politically fragile countries. Kenya, for instance, already faces such problems. These low-income and heavily indebted countries may thereby face epidemics they are ill-equipped to handle and, as a result, are likely to have to deal with increasingly restive populations and the potential for violence even as they request international aid to deal with epidemics.[24] What will the new relations between military and humanitarian interventions be?

Rising sea levels will reshape coastal landscapes, degrade water supplies, exacerbate sanitation difficulties, limit the ingress and egress of supplies and support to and from the coast, and drive millions of people

---

[23] Admiral T. Joseph Lopez, USN (Ret.), "On Climate Change and the Conditions for Terrorism," in *National Security and the Threat of Climate Change* (Alexandria, VA: The CNA Corporation, 2007), 17.

[24] This problem is made even more acute when one realizes that three quarters of all wars since 1945 have been within, rather than between, countries: internal crises, rather than external pressures, are the more likely causes of war.

from their homes – a problem made even more acute by the fact that "[a]pproximately two thirds of the world's cities with populations greater than 5 million people are at least partially in a coastal zone, and a higher percentage of developing country cities are located along a coast than those in the developed world."[25] Massive human migrations will drain many countries of manpower, tax the abilities of other countries to take in these new climate refugees, and spur clashes over borders and between ethnicities – as has been evidenced when Bangladeshis have fled to India after flooding. What will the impact of growing numbers of climate refugees be on questions of national sovereignty, identity, and cohesion?

Seasonal arctic melting will lead to new shipping lanes in the north and access to previously unreachable natural resources, thereby forcing the world's northernmost countries – also among the world's most powerful, if not always most irenic, countries – to give new thought to questions about protecting their vast northern borders while struggling to determine who has rights to those resources. At the same time, the new shipping lanes will lead more equatorial countries (Panama, Egypt) to readdress their roles as gatekeepers (or, rather, lock-keepers) and profit-makers between oceans. And if arctic melting is severe enough – particularly if the ice caps covering Greenland melt into the Atlantic – not only will we face rising sea-levels, but some climate scientists speculate that it may disrupt the oceanic currents that help keep Western Europe warmer than its latitude would otherwise allow, thereby exacerbating its needs for energy and food.

As the above paragraphs demonstrate, the connections between climate change and conflict are many, complex, and varied. They are also under-examined. Undoubtedly, this is, in part, due to the fact that climate change snuck up on many of us, at least to the extent that each progressive study has suggested that climate change is not only more likely but more likely to

---

[25] USAID, "Climate Change, Adaptation, and Conflict: A Preliminary Review of the Issues." Office of Conflict Management and Mitigation Discussion Paper No. 1 (October, 2009): 13. The matter of climate refugees is of enormous importance and complexity, even to the point of definitions. Some refugees are clearly the product of climate change (e.g., islanders in the South Pacific whose homes are disappearing under the rising oceans). Others are less clear: the political crisis in Syria is, in part, the product of sustained droughts in the rural areas that drove young men to the cities looking for work – and then to rebellion against the Assad regime. But are the Syrian refugees of the past few years climate refugees or political refugees? And, given the types of political crises occasioned by the influx of Syrian refugees into Europe, what will the impact of such refugees be when their numbers increase perhaps ten-fold?

be more severe than the previous studies had indicated. For instance, in 1990, the first Intergovernmental Panel on Climate Change wrote "The unequivocal detection of the enhanced greenhouse effect from observations is **not likely** for a decade or more." Then, the second IPCC Assessment Report in 1995 wrote "The balance of evidence **suggests** a discernable human influence on the global climate." In 2001, the third IPCC Assessment concluded, "Most of the observed warming over the last 50 years is *likely [2:3 odds]* to have been due to the increase in greenhouse gas concentrations." In 2007, the fourth IPCC Assessment concluded, "Warming of the climate system is unequivocal ... Most of the observed increase in globally averaged temperatures since the mid-20th century is *very likely [9:10 odds]* due to the observed increase in anthropogenic greenhouse gas concentrations."[26] And, in 2014, the fifth IPCC Assessment concluded, "Anthropogenic greenhouse gasses are *extremely likely* to have been the dominant cause of the observed warming since the mid-20th Century."[27] It is difficult to explore the implications of climate change for conflict when the data on climate change keeps changing – though over time, the implications have tended to become more and more dire rather than more optimistic.[28]

This underexamination is also due to the fact that, in an academic atmosphere that promotes disciplinary specialization, very few people have expertise in matters related to both the environment and conflict. The so-called "stovepiping" associated with disciplinary insularity inhibits not only multidisciplinary expertise but even cross-disciplinary conversations. And even when such multidisciplinary work occurred – as, for example, with those who do environmental security – it has been difficult to bring public attention to bear on these issues in a political climate in which both sides of the topic – climate change and conflict – are so burdened by divisiveness, partisanship, and distrust. Not many scholars

---

[26] Citations, collectively, of the IPCC Reports taken from Will Rogers and Jay Gulledge, "Lost in Translation: Closing the Gap Between Climate Science and National Security Policy" (Washington D.C.: Center for a New American Security, April, 2010), 19. Emphases theirs.

[27] United Nations IPCC, *Climate Change Synthesis Report Summary for Policymakers* (2014). https://www.ipcc.ch/pdf/assessment-report/ar5/syr/AR5_SYR_FINAL_SPM.pdf. Accessed on September 16, 2016. Italics theirs; boldface mine to bring the sentence into conformity with previous sentences.

[28] Robert Kaplan's 1994 article "The Coming Anarchy" may be an exception to this rule. Kaplan's vision was so gloomy that many professionals dismissed it. Of late, though, people have been returning to that article, wondering just how prescient Kaplan was. See Robert Kaplan, "The Coming Anarchy," *The Atlantic Monthly* 272.2 (1994): 44–76.

research across the two disciplines; almost none of them do so with an eye to shaping policy.[29]

Fortunately, a few scholars have taken notice and been actively at work in addressing the connections between climate change and conflict at policy levels. The Center for a New American Security, a Washington D.C. think-tank attempting to develop resources for the U.S.'s national security and defense, has published a number of papers on the topic. In 2007, the CNA Corporation brought together a dozen retired U.S. admirals and generals to study the impact of climate change on national security, out of which came "National Security and the Threat of Climate Change," a document that included the recommendation that the "national security consequences of climate change should be fully integrated into national security and national defense strategies."[30] And, most significantly, having already addressed climate change in its 2010 Quadrennial Defense Review,[31] the 2014 Quadrennial Defense Review Report of the U.S. Department of Defense noted the following:

Climate change poses another significant challenge for the United States and the world at large. As greenhouse gas emissions increase, sea levels are rising, average global temperatures are increasing, and severe weather patterns are accelerating. These changes, coupled with other global dynamics, including growing, urbanizing, more affluent populations, and substantial economic growth in India, China, Brazil, and other nations, will devastate homes, land, and infrastructure. Climate change may exacerbate water scarcity and lead to sharp increases in food costs. The pressures caused by climate change will influence resource competition while placing additional burdens on economies, societies,

---

[29] So far as I can find, for instance, there are very few connections being developed between environmental ethics (which typically explores the relationship between people and nonhuman nature), environmental justice (the relation between peoples as mediated by nonhuman nature), and conflict. Indeed, as Mark Woods points out, exploration of an important but comparatively simpler topic like how much attention should environmental destruction get in shaping military strategy has "no proper name" (Mark Woods, "The Nature of War and Peace: Just War Thinking, Environmental Ethics, and Environmental Justice." In Michael W. Brough, John W. Lango, and Harry van der Linden (eds.), *Rethinking the Just War Tradition* (Albany, NY: SUNY Press, 2007), 18). More recently, Michael S. Northcott has begun to move in this direction in, e.g., *A Political Theology of Climate Change* (Grand Rapids: Eerdmans, 2016). However, while that book touches on history and on war, it does neither in systematic nor in developed ways.

[30] "National Security and the Threat of Climate Change," 7.

[31] The U.S. Department of Defense noted that climate change was among the "powerful trends . . . likely to add complexity to the security environment," before devoting five of its 105 pages to this matter alone. See Department of Defense of the United States of America, "Quadrennial Defense Review Report" (February, 2010): iv.

and governance institutions around the world. These effects are threat multipliers that will aggravate stressors abroad such as poverty, environmental degradation, political instability, and social tensions – conditions that can enable terrorist activity and other forms of violence."[32]

Unfortunately, religious scholars – ethicists, theologians, and others – who research and write on matters of war and peace have been less alert. Very few among them have given any thought to such connections – and for many of the same reasons as those among their secular brothers and sisters in the academy. Indeed, the problem of multidisciplinarity is exacerbated by the fact that religious scholars must think across at least three areas of study: environment, war and peace, and religion. This is not to say that religious scholars are even more insular in their work; religious scholars regularly take up either environment and religion or war and peace and religion. But adding a third element makes for dramatically more complexity.

This book begins to fill in that lacuna by shaping a new narrative about the history of Christian pacifism that is attuned not only to the impact climate has had on conflict and the pacifist response to it in the past but the reasons such a new narrative may be necessary as the world enters into a new age, the Anthropocene.[33] Taking up such a new topic and developing a new narrative by which to approach it means the book may reveal that complexity through its failures as much as through its substantive contributions to the new conversations. And, given the complexity of this task, it will rather determinedly ignore detailed analysis of, or recommendations for shaping of policy; it is my hope that future books will build upon this one and move in that direction.

Upon occasion, religious scholars thinking about the environment have mentioned the impact of war on the climate – usually in the context of wars in the Middle East and the demand for oil.[34] And, even more rarely, religious scholars thinking about war and peace have mentioned the environment. But when they do, they tend to fit questions about care for the environment into more established ways of thinking about war and peace: peace is better for the environment; the *jus ad bellum* just war criteria of proportionality might be used to assess whether the impact of

---

[32] Department of Defense of the United States of America, "Quadrennial Defense Review Report" (February, 2014): 8.

[33] Future books will take up the Christian just war and just peacemaking traditions.

[34] See, for instance, James B. Martin-Schramm, *Climate Justice: Ethics, Energy, and Public Policy* (Minneapolis: Fortress Press, 2010).

a particular war on the environment in a particular area might weigh against pursuing that war; intentionally destroying the environment (through, e.g., the use of Agent Orange, of depleted uranium in munitions, or of burning oil fields to cover one's retreat) might be a war-crime.

This book takes up a more radical challenge. In it, I argue that climate change functions as the harbinger of a dramatic shift in the way we understand the world around us and our relation to it – that we are in a time during which our social imaginaries are being reshaped by our changing relationship to the environment. Or to say that a bit differently, the environment will no longer function simply as one issue among the many that we face – an issue that we might give more or less attention to, depending on our interests and needs – but will instead become a lens through which we make sense of all other issues (much in the way that economics has functioned in the modern age and religion functioned before then). And, therein, attention to the environment will fundamentally reshape the way Christians and other persons of faith understand war and peace. This project, then, inverts the move that religious scholars of war and peace have occasionally made, in which they make sense of environmental issues directly connected to war by fitting those issues into established patterns of thought about war and peace. Instead, I suggest that environmental issues – especially climate change – actually change the way we'll need to make sense of war and peace.

This is, admittedly, an audacious claim. Indeed, part of its audacity is that in making it, I intend to skirt some of the very issues of probability and social-scientific validation that I named above. The larger goal of this book isn't to offer a set of likelihoods that some event or another will happen in the future and, therein, to shape policy considerations (though if the arguments here are at all compelling to those readers with the power to shape such matters, I hope the book might at least contribute to such considerations). Instead, the larger goal of this book is to use the potential impact of climate change as a lens through which to examine the Christian tradition of pacifism as it has evolved over time and to argue for the need to move that tradition in a decidedly new direction. More specifically, I want to argue that anthropogenic climate change may serve as a catalyst for rethinking the Christian pacifist tradition so that its rich resources may be brought to bear not only on climate-caused conflict but on the far wider array of conflicts that constitute war in the twenty-first century.[35] Audacity, indeed!

---

[35] It is for this reason, incidentally, that I will not be pursing questions about the impact of war on the environment. Such questions are vital, relatively well discussed in the social-

Of course, the Christian pacifist tradition has long made audacious claims: that fidelity to God means refusing to fight; that not only does God will peace but will bring peace about; that self-sacrifice (and even, sometimes, the possible sacrifice of others) is both a condition and an expression of hopeful living; that a set of first-century C.E. texts from the Middle East can offer normative wisdom on practices for very different times and places. Such audacity has not only funded the tradition; it has shaped the tradition's profundity.

scientific literature, and freighted with policy implications for a transitional time on a fragile planet. They are not, though, my questions. For those interested in these questions, see Woods, "The Nature of War and Peace," 17–34, esp. footnote 5 on p. 31.

PART I

THE CHURCH AND NONVIOLENCE BEFORE CONSTANTINE

Defense and the environment is not an either/or proposition. To choose between them is impossible in this real world of serious defense threats and genuine environmental concerns.

Secretary of Defense Dick Cheney, 1990[1]

[N]either security, as we have traditionally understood it, nor environment, as we have usually taken it for granted, can continue to be interpreted or acted upon in traditional ways if either environmental change or security is to be thought about or made a political priority in useful ways for the majority of humanity or other species in coming decades.

Simon Dalby, 2009[2]

One of the most original cultural products of our century is our awareness of the power of organized nonviolent resistance as an instrument in the struggle for justice. One characteristic of this instrument is that its operation is often informal and decentralized. By the nature of the case, it does not create institutions of great visible power. Therefore, it is not easy for historians to account for nonviolent resistance as in the telling of stories of military battles and the changing of regimes.

John Howard Yoder, 2010[3]

---

[1] Dick Cheney, "Defense and Environmental Initiative" Forum, Sept. 1990. Quoted in William D. Palmer, "Environmental Compliance: Implications for Senior Commanders," *Parameters* (Spring, 1993): 81.

[2] Simon Dalby, *Security and Environmental Change* (Malden, MA: Polity Press, 2009), 4.

[3] John Howard Yoder, *Nonviolence: A Brief History*, ed. by Paul Martens, Matthew Porter, and Myles Werntz (Waco, TX: Baylor University Press, 2010), 17.

The Silences of the Second Century

The conventional narrative about Christian pacifism begins with the New Testament texts. For some pacifists, it also ends there. But for others, those texts shape a trajectory for the early church that is evident in the writings of Christians in the late first through mid-second centuries, and this trajectory is foundational to the myth of return upon which the conventional narrative hangs. This conventional narrative tells us that "the New Testament promotes an unwavering commitment to pacifism and the church of the first century and a half after Jesus' resurrection adhered to that commitment." Furthermore, it states that "even as things grow more complex after 173 C.E., that commitment funds the pacifist convictions that have continued since then." Yet how accurate is this conventional narrative? Are things as clear as the narrative suggests?

Barrels of ink have been spilled on the subject of nonviolence and the New Testament texts; I have no intention of spilling too much more of it here. Significantly less has been written about the conventional narrative's interpretation of the ninety or so years that precede 173 C.E. Yet to the degree that advocates of that narrative rely on second-century churches as a basis for their telling of history, that period warrants far more attention – and, I will argue, far more circumspection – than it is typically given. The witness of the early churches is undoubtedly significant for those who would seek to follow Jesus in a violent world; it just doesn't signify what the conventional narrative says it does.

Attending to the significance of the second century C.E. within the Christian pacifist tradition begins by attending to the churches of the first century and their texts. While there were any number of epistles and gospels floating through the Middle East at the close of the first century, the second century – largely informally – was an important time of sorting through texts and advancing arguments for some, but not all, of these texts to become central to the Christian faith. Among the informal criteria in discerning which texts would become the New Testament, there is a noticeable emphasis on particular forms of morality and politics: the New Testament may not be univocal with regard to the moral life, but neither is it infinitely flexible. At least two things become clear upon reading through the texts of the New Testament with an eye to morality and politics. First, there is a marked emphasis on living peaceably with others. Both Paul in his epistle to the Romans and Jesus in the Gospel of Matthew advocate nonresistance in the face of violence. The author of Luke and Acts recognizes conflicts both within the community and also against external forces, but such conflict is to be addressed by argument and transformation, not force of arms. Later New Testament epistles call for Christians to live peaceably with their neighbors. The meek inherit the earth, peacemakers are called children of God, and everyone is supposed to turn the other cheek. While there is not a developed argument anywhere in the New Testament against participating in military violence or insurrections, there are passages (Jesus saying he brings not peace but a sword, the commendation of a centurion, the obligation to obey authorities) that certainly complicate any attempt to treat the texts of the New Testament as uniformly advancing a way of nonviolence. It is nevertheless the case that the moral New Testament writings lean toward pacifism.[1]

---

[1] See, e.g., Richard B. Hays, *The Moral Vision of the New Testament: A Contemporary Introduction to New Testament Ethics* (San Francisco: Harper San Francisco, 1996): Whether with regard to rules like "turn the other cheek" found within New Testament texts, the more generally formulated norms found there ("love your enemies"), the paradigm of reconciliation through crucifixion and resurrection, or the symbolic worldview in which struggles are not against flesh and blood but principalities and powers, "the evidence accumulates overwhelmingly against any justification for the use of violence" (p. 340). To be clear, my argument that New Testament writings lean heavily toward nonviolence is a weaker position than Hays takes. Moreover, the distance between the first century and the twentieth shows through in Hays's reliance on theologians like Yoder and Hauerwas who – as this book hopes to make clear – import theological and philosophical arguments into their defense of pacifism through reference to the New Testament that are, themselves, foreign to the first-century context. For a strenuous criticism of Hays's view and use of the New Testament in his rejection of violence, see Nigel Biggar, "Specify and Distinguish! Interpreting the New Testament on 'Non-Violence'," *Studies in Christian Ethics* 22.2 (2009): 164–184 and then Hays's response, "Narrate and Embody: A Response to Nigel Biggar, 'Specify and Distinguish'," in the same volume, pp. 185–198. Working through those two essays reveals at least two things. First, Biggar and Hays, though both excellent exegetes, rely on different hermeneutical presuppositions

Leaning toward pacifism and uniformly advocating pacifism are not the same thing, however: the texts are not univocal or unequivocal on matters of violence. New Testament writings are more diverse and, collectively, less coherent than a single vision with nonviolence at its center will allow. Jesus's exhortations in Matthew not to kill (5:21) and to turn the other cheek (5:39) are countered by the nonjudgmental way Matthew describes Jesus's dealings with Roman soldiers (8:5–13) and the way Roman soldiers recognize Jesus as the Son of God even when his disciples do not (27:54). When Jesus says, "Do not think that I have come to bring peace to the earth; I have not come to bring peace, but a sword" (Matthew 10:34), the sword is almost certainly metaphorical. When Jesus drives the moneychangers out of the temple with a whip (John 2:15), the whip almost certainly isn't. Paul's statements about living peaceably with enemies in Romans (Ch. 12) are countered by his call to submit to secular authorities who "do not bear the sword in vain" (Romans 13:4). When Jesus rebukes Peter for cutting off a soldier's ear and warns him that "all who take the sword will perish by the sword" (Matthew 26:52), we are left wondering what Peter might have been doing with a sword in the first place and how long he's been carrying it.[2]

My goal here is neither to enter too deeply into the fray over the extent of the New Testament's espousal of nonviolence nor to treat the two sides as having equal numbers of passages and arguments on which to draw in defense of their respective positions. The former are fights for other people, and the latter quickly bogs down into interpretations that reveal exegetes' biases as much as texts' meanings. Instead, my goal here is simply and briefly to recognize that the writings of the New Testament are diverse, that they don't all agree with each other, and that treating the books of the New Testament as providing a single position on violence always risks betraying the integrity of the texts so that interpreters may maintain the integrity of their narratives. Based on my own readings of the

---

and starting points that lead them to miss each other's arguments in places. Second, Hays isn't simply doing exegetical work, but letting a theology that has been shaped by trends in late twentieth-century theology shape his thought.

[2] Having named Hays above – and given the preponderance of texts from pacifists in a chapter on nonviolence in the church – I would point to Nigel Biggar, *In Defense of War* (Oxford: Oxford University Press, 2013), esp. Ch. 1, and Despina Iosif, *Early Christian Attitudes to War, Violence and Military Service* (Piscataway, NJ: Gorgias Press, 2013) as significant attempts to wrest the New Testament away from those who argue that nonviolence is central to a New Testament ethic. Whether one agrees with their arguments or those of, e.g., Hays, their work certainly displays sufficient exegetical subtlety to be taken seriously as viable readings of New Testament texts.

texts and commentaries, it seems that, collectively, the New Testament texts lean toward nonviolence. Their varied reasons for doing so and the weight they put into such leaning reveal complexities about Jesus's purposes, teachings, actions, and the implications of those things for the church take us far beyond debates about violence.

The second thing that becomes clear in a thoughtful reading of the New Testament is that its texts are framed by eschatological visions. Most of the writers of the New Testament and the Christian communities to whom they wrote anticipated the return of Jesus at any moment. This eschatological emphasis strongly shaped their moral character: because Jesus's return was considered to be imminent, Christians needed to spend their energies preparing for his arrival and avoiding the very types of distractions – including, even, persecution – that so often lead to violence. The writers of the New Testament remain coy about the timing of this return,[3] but almost all the gospels and epistles refer to its imminence. A set of particular interpretations about time was already at work in shaping Christian ethics even during the first century, and these interpretations themselves tend to be problematic.

Neither advocacy of nonviolence nor the idea of an eschaton is unique to the New Testament writings, as reference to both can be found in the Hebrew Scriptures.[4] Each of these ideas, however, was elevated in importance in the earliest churches. Moreover, nonviolence and the eschaton were conceptually linked in the minds of early believers: in the face of Roman power, about which they, themselves, could do very little, the promised coming of the Kingdom of God was enough to support a way of life that did not involve a resort to arms.[5] As Lisa Sowle Cahill has noted, the promised coming of the Kingdom of God founded an eschatological ethic that is clearly visible in the

---

[3] Luke 21:32 is a possible exception, as it suggests that the Kingdom of God will come in all its fullness within the lifetimes of those original readers.

[4] See, e.g., Walter Brueggemann, *Peace* (St. Louis: Chalice Press, 2001) on nonviolence in the Old Testament or Kevin J. Madigan and Jon D. Levinson, *Resurrection: The Power of God for Christians and Jews* (New Haven: Yale University Press, 2008) on eschatology in the Old Testament.

[5] This eschatological basis for the call to nonviolence helps explain the degree to which the first-century church also promoted obedience to the governing authorities: submitting to them was simply an expression of waiting them out. Chapters 12 and 13 of Paul's letter to the Romans – promoting both nonviolence and obedience to Rome – are coherent only in this context, and the difficulty that Christian exegetes have had historically in reconciling the two passages mostly just reveals their distance from that early church and its fervent belief in an impending eschaton.

major moral writings of the New Testament, particularly in Matthew's Sermon on the Mount.[6]

Yet even the New Testament writings bear witness to an increasingly thorny question: why is this promised Kingdom taking so long to arrive? As the days and years drew out, the early church was left with a complicated project: to maintain fidelity to its eschatologically shaped commitments such as nonviolence while also promoting the kind of patience necessary in waiting for a Kingdom that could seem very distant. Although neither the church's general commitment to nonviolence nor its vision of the coming eschaton disappeared – and for many communities remained as fierce as ever – the commitment and the vision were increasingly uncoupled. As a result, the vision of the eschaton would be reconceived in increasingly spatial rather than temporal terms. In other words, rather than wondering when the Kingdom would return, churches increasingly wondered where it was – including, perhaps, whether it was being revealed in the church over against the larger world. As a result, the church's commitment to nonviolence would go searching for new arguments that could justify it since waiting out a violent world seemed an increasingly unviable approach. So what visions might sustain the commitment to nonviolence?

On the one side, the guiding vision of the coming Kingdom of God was increasingly reshaped through varied practices and ideas that came into prominence after the first few generations of Christians had died. Different passages of Scripture were emphasized. Influenced, in part, by Greco-Roman thought, the Kingdom moved away from being an inbreaking physical reality toward being an essentially spiritual reality that could be entered only after death: the Kingdom became less immanent. New Testament statements about the pace of its arrival were read typologically or allegorically as a way of deferring questions about timing: the Kingdom became less imminent. The guiding vision of the coming Kingdom of God was replaced by an emphasis on the church itself: the Kingdom became domesticated and institutionalized. St. Cyprian could claim *extra Ecclesiam nulla salus* because it had become synonymous with *extra regnum Dei nulla salus*. And through all this, the earliest church's assumptions and claims about the world's transformation, based as they were on an empirically falsified vision of time and its moment in it, were being revised.

---

[6] Lisa Sowle Cahill, *Love Your Enemies: Discipleship, Pacifism, and Just War Theory* (Minneapolis: Fortress Press, 1994), pp. 15–38, esp. 26ff.

These revisions weren't thought-out decisions reached by churches in conversation with each other so much as spasmodic arguments made by small communities of faith feeling comparatively isolated from each other, confused about their relationship to their Jewish roots and neighbors, and vaguely (and occasionally not vaguely) threatened by Roman power. Marcion, for example, read both the Hebrew Scriptures and the various circulating gospels and epistles and came to the conclusion that the God described in the Old Testament could not be the one described in the New. In his vision of time, the age of the false God of the Hebrew people had been replaced by the age of the true God, incarnate in Jesus, to which the New Testament bore witness. Marcion's attempt to put together the texts upon which he thought Christians should base their faith achieved at least two ends: it launched a growing movement to establish an agreed-upon canon and led the early church to conclude that he was a heretic. The two testaments might not describe God in identical sets of terms, but the prevailing sentiment was that the God witnessed to in both was the same God. The relation between the covenant described in the Old Testament – particularly as it related to the establishment of the states of Israel and Judea – and the covenant described in the New would continue to be contested, but after Marcion the center of the church would explicitly refuse to divide either its sacred texts or its ordering of time into two parts.

On the other side, in light of the seeming delay in Jesus's return, new reasons for being nonviolent came to the fore and grew in prominence. Foremost among them was a straightforward reading of New Testament texts. Jesus said, "Blessed are the peacemakers"; therefore, be peacemakers. Paul said, "Bless those who persecute you; bless and do not curse them"; therefore, bless persecutors. Sentences whose imperative weight had been founded in the indicative claims about the coming Kingdom increasingly found their new weight in obligations of obedience to Jesus. Of course, in an age when no group of Christians was likely to be able to use violence strategically against Roman occupation and, due to differences in social status and class, very few individual Christians were likely to be in any position to take up the sword in the first place, these claims were straightforward and coherent, both theologically as well as politically.

By the latter half of the second century C.E., though, Christianity had spread into the military, albeit not always comfortably. Unsurprisingly, questions about Christian commitments to nonviolence grew increasingly acute during the latter half of the second century and the next. Those who espoused nonviolence engaged in increasingly complicated and illuminating projects in which they attempted to maintain fidelity to the developing canon of New Testament literature, including obedience to its teachings and interpretations of the coming Kingdom of God described there. One way to read the developing theologies of nonviolence, then, is as products of the complex theological task of undergirding a particular set of New Testament commands with a developing vision of a Kingdom that is located in distinctive spaces (those occupied by the church, as an alternative polis to the Roman Empire) more than tensive time (which lies between the inaugurated and the consummated Kingdom of God).

Time, though, has a way of sneaking back into conversations about space. After Jesus, the questions "Who are we?" and "When are we?" are necessarily linked for Christians; as such, a developing and distinctive vision of time and the church's place in it grew increasingly clear. Rather than living *between* Jesus's first coming and his second, churches increasingly identified themselves with the community that lives *after* Jesus's crucifixion and resurrection – and, at least compared to "between," "after" can be a subversively and troublingly freighted term. Lacking the immediate constraints of dealing with something bigger than itself that is yet to come, the church could spread into conceptual space that had been reserved for the inbreaking Kingdom of God, which it did. As such, the church's sense of its proper place in time, which never had been entirely clear, became even less so.

I DIVERSE COMMUNITIES BEHIND SINGULAR NARRATIVES

Before making further sense of this shift from "between" to "after" and the implications that would follow from it, though, I need to take up the matter of the church's perspective on violence from the close of the New Testament to around 173 C.E. The conventional narrative argues that between the close of the canon and around 173 C.E., churches were nonviolent. As Roland Bainton writes,

From the end of the New Testament period to the decade A.D. 170–180 there is no evidence whatever of Christians in the army. The subject of military service obviously was not at that time controverted. The reason may have been either that participation was assumed or that abstention was taken for granted. The latter is more probable.[7]

---

[7] Roland Bainton, *Christian Attitudes Toward War and Peace*, 67–68.

This part of the narrative has been taken for granted not only by pacifists but by the wider scholarly community for the past century, as Paul Ramsey's assertion, "[f]or almost two centuries of the history of the early church, Christians were universally pacifists,"[8] makes clear. As much as more recent scholarship has contested the role of violence and military service in the churches since 173 C.E., it has remained largely mute on the time prior to 173.[9]

One reason for the power of the conventional narrative has to do with the response that pacifist scholars gave to Adolph Harnack's work, *Militia Christi*, which was the first great (if problematic) modern text to take up the relation of the early churches to war and the military. In that book, Harnack wrote,

What position Christianity took with regard to the military profession before the year 170 must be determined exclusively by conjecture based on later information. It is only from the time of Marcus Aurelius on [~161–180 C.E.] that we possess direct sources which enlighten us about the actual relationships and how they were judged. The Christian documents of the earlier time are almost entirely silent. This silence, however, is meaningful and instructive... If a "military question" is completely lacking, there arises the well-grounded supposition that there was no such question at all in the Christian congregations at that time. The absence of the question, however, can have diametrically opposed grounds. It was either because Christians on occasion served as soldiers without blame, or because the military service was self-evidently forbidden for Christians. Which is correct?[10]

In the absence of clear documents suggesting otherwise, Harnack relied on a few passages of Scripture that portray neutral or ambivalent attitudes toward military service in general as well as speculations about the way Christians might have participated in this service in order to argue for the former answer.[11] He was almost immediately challenged by C. John Cadoux and, shortly thereafter, by Jean-Michel Hornus, whose scholarly abilities and pacifist commitments showed through their texts.

---

[8] Paul Ramsey, *War and the Christian Conscience* (Durham, NC: Duke University Press, 1961), xv.

[9] With good reason, as there simply are no resources available upon which to build arguments.

[10] Adolph Harnack, *Militia Christi: The Christian Religion and the Military in the First Three Centuries*, trans. by David McInnes Gracie (Philadelphia: Fortress Press, 1981), 65–66.

[11] Harnack's passages include those describing the responses of various centurions to Jesus and the early church, John the Baptist's answer to soldiers in Luke 3:14, and Paul's call for persons to "remain in the condition in which you were called" in 1 Cor 7:20.

Cadoux and Hornus took issue with Harnack's conclusion on several grounds. First, they argued that Harnack unduly minimized the regularity with which church fathers such as Tertullian and Origen, writing in the late second through third centuries, advocated nonviolence. They further contended that Harnack had disregarded alternative interpretations of other ancient texts that should have lent themselves to more caution in his conclusions, and finally that the theological center of the early church grows out of a strong distinction between serving Caesar and serving Jesus: one must choose between the two, and Christians, almost by definition, must choose the latter. More importantly, they argued, Harnack must ignore the bulk of the New Testament writings on nonviolence and nonresistance to suggest that Christian involvement in the military was so non-problematic as to warrant silence on the part of witnesses to the early churches. Any attempt to argue one's way out of Jesus's commandments would have been just that, an argument – and that argument would have shown up in the early writings. Indeed, Cadoux uses Harnack's own words against him:

[Harnack] gives a useful enumeration of the various features of military life, which could not have failed to thrust themselves on the Christian's notice as presenting, to say the least, great ethical difficulty. The shedding of blood on the battlefield, the use of torture in the law-courts, the passing of death-sentences by officers and the execution of them by common soldiers, the unconditional military oath, the all-pervading worship of the Emperor, the sacrifices in which all were expected in some way to participate, the average behavior of soldiers in peace-time, and other idolatrous and offensive customs – all these would constitute in combination an exceedingly powerful deterrent against any Christian joining the army on his own initiative.[12]

It is instructive that in this debate between Harnack and Cadoux/ Hornus, both sides appeal to the same authorities to fill in the silence of the hundred or so years that precede 173 C.E. They all appeal to New Testament passages and Tertullian. They offer various theological arguments about militarist metaphors, idolatry, and military service during that period. They suggest continuity between the New Testament texts and the writings of the church fathers that arose more than one hundred years later. They advance abstracted visions of the early church as if it were a singular thing and there were no regional, cultural, class, or status variations to deal with. Both sides present either/or positions: either military service was problematic or it wasn't, as if all churches and Christians everywhere during this time period dealt with the issue in the same way or even felt the need to deal with the issue at all.

---

[12] C. John Cadoux, *The Early Christian Attitude to War*, 105.

The similarities in those appeals and the troubling quality of their contents are signs worth interpreting. Given the silence of the churches on matters of violence during the period, the fact that both sides in the debate draw on the same sources both before and after the period, and the degree to which both sides are using exegetical and theological arguments that align with their predetermined conclusions, choosing sides in the debate tends to devolve into merely choosing the side one wants to win and then ordering the argument to allow for this. Arguments about violence and the second-century churches thus constitute something of a theological Rorschach test: people see what they want to see. Rather than treating the debate as such, I propose a more chastened response to the argument: that in the absence of further evidence, we allow silence to be silence.

This is not to suggest that there is nothing to say. In light of continued research (and silence) on the matter, I would suggest that among the things the two sides should agree upon are the following points:

- There are soldiers named in the New Testament, including soldiers who seemingly join the church. Further, the New Testament texts (e.g., Cornelius in Acts 10; Paul's jailer in Acts 16) do not address the possibility that their church membership necessitates their departure from the military. There are also New Testament texts in which soldiers behave as agents of an empire that stands over against the Kingdom of God (e.g., who mock and crucify Jesus; soldiers guarding the tomb in Matthew 28).
- As of approximately 173 C.E., there are Christians serving in the military. There are also strongly voiced arguments against Christian participation in the military and killing more generally being delivered by prominent Christians of the day, most notably Tertullian.
- We don't have firsthand accounts or arguments about Christians in the military during the period between the close of the New Testament canon and 173 C.E. We do know that this is a time of rapid expansion by Christianity and that various churches across the empire engage that empire in different ways.
- In the writings of several of the earliest church fathers (e.g., Justin Martyr [100–165 C.E.]; Athenagorus [?–160 C.E.]), we read of an early Christian ethic marked by "mildness and gentleness and . . . [a] peaceful and kindly attitude toward all."[13] These texts do not, however, explicitly call for a prohibition either against killing or against

---

[13] Athenagorus, "A Plea Regarding Christians," in Long, *Christian Peace and Nonviolence*, 17.

Christian participation in the military, and often their language-use is clearly more metaphoric than literal: "we who were filled with war, and mutual slaughter, and every wickedness, have each through the whole earth changed our warlike weapons – our swords into ploughshares, and our spears into implements of tillage – and we cultivate piety, righteousness, philanthropy, faith, and hope."[14] Given their vagueness and comparative rarity, these few sources neither offer definitive guidance on questions about violence and military involvement nor can they be construed as representative of the church at the time.

- As will be discussed later in the book, the most prominent church fathers who advance pacifist visions of the church between 173 and 315 C.E. cannot be taken as representing the breadth or center of the church's theological vision; they regularly turn out to be marginal figures in the churches of the time, even if they have come to be regarded as outsized figures in the history of the church since then. Nor, given the pace of change and growth in the church during its first one hundred or so years, can their arguments be taken as representative of the churches that existed prior to 173 C.E.

- After 173, the early churches' reasons for avoiding military service and pursuing nonviolence vary and relate to each other in complex ways even according to the prominent church fathers. Opposition to killing, concerns about idolatry, maintaining good political relations with some neighbors, and distinguishing themselves from other neighbors all play roles in their writings.

- Archeological and literary evidence reveals a wide range of settings in which the church existed, and within that range of settings, Christians dealt with relations to the state and to their immediate (Jewish and Gentile) neighbors in a variety of ways. In other words, there was no

---

[14] Justin Martyr, "Dialogue with Trypho" in Long, *Christian Peace and Nonviolence*, 16. Slattery claims that Justin Martyr "forbade baptism of a catechumen who entered the military" (Slattery, *Jesus the Warrior*, 88) but without citing a source. If this is true, it would be the strongest argument about the church's pacifist mandate during the period in question. However, I can find no evidence for this claim either in Justin Martyr's writings or in secondary literature on him. More importantly, Justin Martyr's statements on military service and killing in war are not only fairly rare but, compared to other arguments he makes about the witness of the Christian moral life, fairly insignificant. Throughout his apologies, he evinces far more concern about sexual ethics and wealth, for instance, than killing in war – and at several points in his arguments when he could bring his convictions about killing and the military to bear on the topic, he does not do so. That is, a balanced reading of either his *First Apology* or his *Dialogue with Trypho* makes it hard to sustain any argument about the centrality of pacifism for faithful Christian living.

single understanding of "church" that was operative, let alone normative, during its first decades of existence (or at any point beyond, for
that matter).

- As will also be discussed in coming chapters, recent scholarship has
  reemphasized the role that not only Hebrew Scriptures but, more
  centrally, Hebraic ways of understanding those Scriptures, had in helping the early churches make sense of themselves. Those texts and those
  hermeneutics include a range of perspectives on violence and empire
  that are wider than those of the texts that were in the process of
  becoming the New Testament, which display considerable variety
  themselves.

- Archeological and literary evidence reveals a wide range of roles
  played by soldiers in the Roman military, not all of which
  involved fighting. While it is unlikely that soldiers were able to
  choose from among possible assignments, it's also possible that
  churches would be able to reach some soldiers more easily than
  others. The evidence also suggests that Rome recruited its soldiers
  from places and classes that overlapped with but were not identical to the places and classes from which the church gained its
  members.[15]

- The church was in a period of rapid geographic and conceptual growth
  and transition during the first hundred or so years of its existence and,
  given the rates of growth and transition, arguments from periods either
  prior to New Testament writings or after 173 C.E. are underdetermined.

---

[15] John Helgeland – who is no friend of the pacifist narrative – has argued that "the army
had a religious structure that informed nearly everything it did." (Helgeland, Daly, and
Burns, *Christians and the Military*, 48). One reason for this argument is that it undergirds
his claim that Christians avoided military service because of concerns about idolatry
rather than nonviolence. Religion was almost certainly ubiquitous in the military, but this
shouldn't be surprising. In a pre-secular age (to adapt Charles Taylor's language), religion
was ubiquitous, not just in the military. The question at hand really needs to be how
Christianity, as a particular version of religion, related to other particular versions of
religion it encountered, including those to be found in the Roman army. And scholarship
from the day suggests that the ways these particular versions of religion related to each
other are multiple and contextual. Given the range of versions of religion and religious life
operative at the time and knowing that there were Christians in the military by the
late second century suggests that syncretism or (more likely) syncretisms were inevitable.
This, again, suggests that contemporary debates between the anti-idolatry and anti-
violence camps are misplaced: they are overlapping religious arguments. None of this is
to suggest that there aren't also early Christians who are attempting to strongly resist
syncretistic moves; it is only to note that it is difficult to treat such early Christians as
representative of the church on all such matters.

• Arguments from silence are, by nature, evidentially weak and, in this context, are notoriously so as we have so few Christian documents or external sources that refer to Christians and the churches from this period. As such, these arguments tend to reveal the biases of interpreters far more than the quality of the evidence.

At the very least, all of this suggests that nobody is in an especially good position to claim this ninety-year[16] stretch of silence as evidence in support of his or her position. Whether or not the church was largely pacifist between ~80 C.E. and ~170 C.E. – and if so, what the reasons for that pacifism might have been – thus far remains a question that lies beyond anyone's ability to offer a definitive position. In respect to this period of time, then, the conventional pacifist narrative cannot bear the weight placed on it. Maybe the church was pacifist. Maybe it wasn't. Maybe some churches were and some weren't. Maybe there were Christians in the military. Maybe there weren't. Maybe there were Christians in the military in some places and not in others. That's all we can say; any narrative that says more isn't trustworthy, and the conventional pacifist narrative overclaims when it states that the church was pacifist until after 170 C.E.

2 BREATHING SPACE FOR AMBIGUITY

Scholars on all sides have worked to eliminate the ambiguities we face in understanding the early churches' relationship(s) to violence. While there is certainly reason to seek greater understanding about those relationships and to seek wisdom in light of such understanding, projects in eliminating ambiguity can conceal wisdom rather than lead to it. The presence of ambiguity is itself a sign in need of interpretation; attempts to either eliminate or quarantine ambiguity risk ignoring real and significant challenges of interpretation. Lacking conclusive resources that collapse the ambiguities of history, ambiguous evidence is best treated as ambiguous

---

[16] Debates about dating the later epistles continue – as do those about the dating of Christian participation in the Thundering Legion (173 C.E. being a likely year for the Legion's conflict with the Sarmatians on behalf of Marcus Aurelius). I have no interest in entering them. I've chosen the dates 80 and 173 C.E. not as historically precise but as a convenient way of setting rough boundaries for the period of silence between the last New Testament text being written and the earliest evidence of Christians serving in the military. Clearly, moving the dates of composition of the later epistles forward in time, perhaps into the early second century, will impact the length of the silence but not the existence of this silence.

rather than evidence in support of one's position. Where primary accounts are absent and other available data is ambiguous, secondhand accounts, especially those driven by clear ideological motives, should be treated with a good deal of suspicion. Overstatement may be useful in promoting the myths that shape traditions, but when contexts change, the narratives that shape traditions may need to change as well. Otherwise, those myths become treated as history and get in the way of those necessary changes.

One of the temptations that historians (and scholars of all stripes) face is the urge to resolve the questions that sent them into their research in the first place. It feels neat, complete, and compelling to be able to answer important questions. Moreover, the ability to offer compelling answers to important questions is one way that historians stake their claims in a given area of study and therein make names for themselves. When articles and presentations are subject to peer review, one of the standards against which they are tested is whether the answers given in a particular article or presentation are better than alternative answers. History moves forward through such an approach.

As important as such resolutions are, however, the temptations toward achieving them are worth at least temporarily (if not permanently) resisting as they foreclose on the possibilities that we might learn from ambiguity. Treating ambiguity as the sign of a problem that needs to be eliminated discounts the possibility that ambiguity may, itself, be what needs to be studied. Ambiguity in the historical record can signal many things: lack of data, conflicting data, disagreement on how to interpret data, failure to attend to the temporal (and, often, spatial) distance between subject matter and interpreter, the failings of contemporary narratives within which data is presumed to fit, the blind spots of those who created the data, the power of earlier interpretations to shape current ones, or even (theologically) the incompleteness of all things this side of eternity. Some of these sources of ambiguity may be resolved when new and compelling data arises, or when disagreements between interpreters are resolved or simply fade from relevance. However, some of these sources of ambiguity must simply be endured. For example, no historian can fully overcome temporal distance, and all master narratives are marked with lacunae and incoherences as they smooth over rough patches or exclude outlying data. Indeed, some of these sources of ambiguity are the self-referential signs to which they point: the limits of perspective within the contexts of the sources of data and the historians who have studied that data throughout history become reminders of historians' need to become more alert to their own perspectives.

The causes of ambiguity – which, given their pluriformity, themselves are likely to be ambiguous – ought to become data in and of themselves for responsible historians. Is this likely to be the type of ambiguity that will go away with new data? Is it likely to be the type of ambiguity that is shaped by the various motives and interests that drive historians to research and needs to be accounted for? Is it the type of ambiguity that serves to point to the varied motives and interests of those who initially produced the data? Or is it the type of data that signals a need for patience as we await new narratives within which such data may cohere? Whether ambiguity is to be overcome, accepted, learned from, or abided with is too important a question to submit to the temptations of resolution. At least with regard to the ambiguous qualities of the data about pacifism in the second century, honoring that ambiguity simultaneously becomes a way of recognizing temporal distance, admitting to researcher motives, signaling the comparative absence that questions of physical force played in structuring the wisdom of the early churches, and revealing the need for and possibilities within new (albeit contextually specific) narratives that have not yet risen to prominence.

Just as ambiguity is a sign in need of interpretation, so is silence. The Christian narrative is silent on the role of pacifism between the end of the first century and the back half of the second. That silence invites caution in how we talk about the place of nonviolence in the early churches; after all, silence can mean many things as we attempt to make sense of history. The telling of any history, as Haitian historian Michel-Rolph Trouillot reminds us, always faces at least four points of silencing: the point at which persons decide what data to record and what data to ignore (how many stories and arguments were written down in the predominantly oral culture of the early church?), the point at which persons decide which bits of recorded data to archive and which bits to leave behind (how many of those written stories and arguments are still available to us?), the point at which persons selectively retrieve data from archives in order to construct a particular narrative (who has drawn from these texts and what are their purposes in doing so?), and the point at which particular narratives are given retrospective significance in order to offer a coherent history (how are these historical documents or parts thereof being used to advance particular arguments about violence and nonviolence?).[17] None of these points of silencing need be driven by

---

[17] See Michel-Rolph Trouillot, *Silencing the Past: Power and the Production of History* (Boston: Beacon Press, 1995).

malicious intent. Instead, they can be shaped by the pressures of busy lives or overwhelming amounts of data, attempts to provide coherence in the face of complexity, and the desire to justify or explain even virtuous actions or attitudes.

Moreover, as scholars like Diarmaid MacCulloch have pointed out, silence can, itself, be a subject of historical interest.[18] As MacCulloch argues, in the first and second centuries C.E., silence – whether vocal or in print – was a virtue for a church that was learning to live with Jesus's continued absence. They were not rushing to fill in that absence with noise but, instead, were allowing silence to serve political, spiritual, and even mimetic purposes. Staying silent became a way of staying safe in some dangerous contexts, a way of ordering internal ecclesial structures (e.g., women remaining silent in church), a method of recognizing the insufficiency and impossibility of words to describe the holy or the unnecessity of language for the Holy Spirit to understand human needs, and a tool with which to integrate Christianity with Hellenistic philosophies that favored silence and apophatic sensibilities.

Sometimes silence is imposed. Sometimes silence is the product of an oversight. Sometimes silence is a good that is intended. Sometimes silence is a sign that we do not yet have the conceptual and/or political resources to produce coherent speech. And the forces that lead to such impositions, oversights, intentions, and confusions vary. All of these factors are operative in the second century C.E. and warrant attention, particularly given the silence of the period on matters of violence. Silence in the second century, then, is itself an ambiguous sign; it is potentially the product of any number of causes. Making sense of silence mandates not only caution but careful exploration of possible reasons for silencing and considerable methodological humility.

Histories – including the history I'm developing here – do more than recover the past and tell stories to the present. They make arguments and advance agendas. Those arguments will be imperfect because the complexity of the past always swamps univocality. Those agendas will be only partly virtuous because they come from people who are never wholly virtuous and who are unlikely even to be fully aware of the things that motivate them. These facts, in themselves, should not be overly troubling. In fact, to the degree that they disrupt grand narratives that are not only untrue but also the cause of suffering, attention to these facts can be helpfully democratizing. But they also mandate a degree of

---

[18] Diarmaid MacCulloch, *Silence: A Christian History* (New York: Penguin Books, 2013).

circumspection about the strength of our claims and a willingness to ask questions about them, about those who offer histories, and about our own motives that ought neither to be ignored nor downplayed. The conventional pacifist narrative about the history of Christian nonviolence during the first two centuries C.E. claims far too much. Questioning that conventional narrative, though, need not undermine the significance of nonviolence for the early church so much as lead to new narratives for new contexts, including the context of the environmental age.

Moreover, practicing a kind of historiographic patience in the face of silence and ambiguity has the potential to provide the conceptual space within which new narratives may eventually arise as new resources become available and as new needs stimulate fresh research. In the context of this project, for instance, the elision of an early Christian emphasis on living peaceably with others and a slightly later Christian emphasis on being pacifist may be the product of various virtues (e.g., nonresistance) and values (e.g., distinct communal identity) that are neither identical to nor necessary for Christian pacifism. Rather, they simply arose at a time when they were necessary to sustain Christian witness within the context of Roman imperialism, were reinforced during the splintering of the church during the Reformation, and are favored within modernist narratives that emphasize individual agency.

Yet as the world transitions into an environmental social imaginary that may be shaped by connectedness more than distinctiveness, such an elision may no longer be advantageous. Where crises are not only global but the causes for such crises are diffused and the responsibilities for such crises are universally albeit unevenly distributed, it won't be helpful to emphasize one's own or one's community's moral rectitude. As perhaps never before, we will necessarily be all in it together. In such a time, virtues and values that can be identified only with a few will carry less and less weight. As such, current ambiguities and silences about the churches' understandings of violence during the time immediately after the writing of the New Testament texts may find address within a time shaped by new virtues and values. Living with ambiguity and silence until then may be the investment we make in a future for Christian pacifism in an environmental age until the time when new narratives shaped by those new virtues and values arise.

2

Mixed Motives and Conflicts Over Conflicts in the Second and Third Centuries

Where most of the second century's silence on matters of nonviolence undermines the conventional narrative about the history of pacifism by revealing how tenuous arguments from silence are, the cacophony of voices from the end of the second century and the third century undermines it by revealing just how varied (in range, motive, and significance) the church's commitments to nonviolence are. Where the conventional narrative draws from and valorizes the arguments of a few theologians of the age (most notably Tertullian and Origen) in order to underline the pre-Constantinian church's commitment to nonviolence, further scholarship reveals a wider range of perspectives and far more troubling motives on the part of the central characters in that narrative. If pacifists are going to resource Christian approaches to violence in the environmental age, they will need to address the problems of the conventional narrative of pacifism in the second and third centuries.

Certainly, these issues do get more complicated and more interesting after 173 C.E., as we do have growing numbers of documents and accounts that address the matter. Moreover, it is also to the second to fourth centuries C.E. that historians of Christian pacifism have regularly turned to find the patristic sources of their positions. Indeed, aside from regular returns to New Testament texts, no set of writings plays more prominence in the history of Christian pacifism than those of the church fathers who write after 173 and before around 300 C.E. Thus, C. John Cadoux's *The Early Christian Attitude to War,* Jean-Michel Hornus's *It Is Not Lawful for Me to Fight,* Guy F. Hershberger's *War, Peace, and Nonresistance,* and Roland Bainton's *Christian Attitudes Toward War and Peace* all look back on these centuries and the writers that lived in them as essential resources for any understanding not only of pacifism but more broadly of the Christian faith.[1] These historians have particularly highlighted Christian opposition to participation in warfare and military service as evidence that the earliest church's opposition to violence remained strenuous through the first several centuries of its existence.

Of course, these arguments from twentieth-century pacifists – as powerful as they have been – demand caveats and at least two qualifications. The first caveat, already suggested above, is that the reason we know that prominent members of the second-century church were opposed to Christians serving in the military and participating in war is that they were writing against Christians who were serving as soldiers in the Roman legions.[2] So this emphasis on nonviolence must be placed within a backdrop in which some Christians, at least by around 173 C.E., were in positions in which they may have been called to act violently.[3] The second caveat, also hinted at above, is that it is dangerous to presume that the opinions of a few early Christians who wrote on the subject can be taken as representative of the possible range of opinions held by the growing numbers of Christians spread throughout the empire and beyond it. Indeed, the two most prominent third-century Christian writers to oppose military service and speak against violence – Tertullian and Origen – could hardly be treated as representatives of the majority position(s) of the church at that time. Both have been condemned as heretics and both wrote with particular rhetorical purposes in mind that would complicate generalizing from their writings. This caveat is further

---

[1] See C. John Cadoux, *The Early Christian Attitude to War*, Guy F. Hershberger, *War, Peace, and Nonresistance,* Jean-Michel Hornus, *It Is Not Lawful for Me to Fight,* and Roland H. Bainton, *Christian Attitudes Toward War and Peace.* The first book was originally published in 1919, the second in 1944, the third and fourth in 1960.

[2] Most notably, the so-called "Thundering Legion" (the *legio XII fulminata*), which included Christians in it who, during Marcus Aurelius's campaign against the Quandi in 174 C.E., supposedly prayed for rain at a time when the legion had been weakened by the lack of water, and the resulting thunderstorm not only refreshed the Romans but caused their enemies to panic. Not all stories of Christian participation in the Roman army end happily for Christians, though: there are repeated examples of Christian soldiers who were martyred for refusing to participate in various (non-Christian) religious military ceremonies.

[3] Whether Roman soldiers were likely to engage in combat is a different question. As historian Ramsay McMullen has noted, many soldiers spent their careers as functionaries, accountants, messengers, and managers and never saw combat. See Ramsay McMullen, *Soldier and Civilian in the Later Roman Empire* (Cambridge: Harvard University Press, 1963).

reinforced by the fact that Christians of the second and perhaps even early third century could not simply access the body of writings we now recognize as the New Testament for support of their positions. There was no such thing, and some of the gospels that did not make it into the canon but that floated around the church of the time, such as the *Infancy Gospel of Thomas*, include stories of a violent Jesus.[4]

In terms of qualifications, the first is that human motives are complex and varied, so the reasons that second- and third-century Christians may have opposed military service and violence are likely to be complex and varied as well. Reading Tertullian and Origen (as well as Arnobius, Lactantius, and others), it is clear that they are motivated, at least in part, by opposition to violence. That said, scholars like John Helgeland have raised serious questions about emphasizing this point to the exclusion of other driving motivations (concerns about idolatry, for example). Early Christians, they argue, avoided military service because participation in the military carried with it obligations to worship other gods.[5] James Turner Johnson has argued that after the failure of the Kingdom of God to arrive immediately, historical evidence from the second and third centuries suggests a growing variety of positions and attitudes with regard to military service and increased attention to the legitimate good that force of arms could achieve.[6] Johnson goes so far as to suggest that the eventual establishment of a just war tradition within Christianity in the fourth and fifth centuries does not reveal a disruption or break with early Christianity

---

[4] Thanks, in part, to the power of Adolf von Harnack's *Militia Christi: The Christian Religion and the Military in the First Three Centuries*, which examines martial rhetoric in the New Testament, those on all sides of the debate about whether Christians participated in the military have paid a great deal of attention to what such rhetoric reveals about Christian attitudes about war. Recognizing the power of language to shape practices, I would, nonetheless, argue that such attention is overblown. Language may shape practices, but it does not do so in simple ways, and most people are fully capable of distinguishing between the symbolic and literal referents of words, especially when those words so clearly signal their symbolic emphases: very few people would confuse "belt of truth" and "breastplate of righteousness" with a real belt or breastplate.

[5] See John Helgeland, "Christians in the Roman Army, A.D. 173–177," *Aufsteig und Niedergang der römischen Welt* II.23.1, 724–834 and Helgeland, R. J. Daly, and J. Patout Burns, *Christians and the Military: The Early Experience* (Philadelphia: Fortress Press, 1985).

[6] On the diversity of perspectives (shaped by geography, ecclesiastical office and/or order, church and secular politics, etc.), see Alan Kreider, "Military Service in the Church Orders," *Journal of Religious Ethics* 31.3 (2003): 415–442. Kreider's account, to which I will return later in this chapter, surfaces many of the range of causes that led to the historic diversity of church positions on violence after 173 C.E.

so much as a gradual synthesis that occurs over a long period of time and predates the Constantinian settlement by hundreds of years.[7]

It is neither surprising nor, in itself, disturbing that the past should prove more difficult to corral than a single particular theological vision can manage. Pacifists are hardly unique in either picking and choosing while interpreting or bumping up against data that won't support their theses. My point in complicating the relationships between the church's witness and its advocacy of nonviolence is simply to highlight the difficulty of capturing the vagaries of events, ideas, and relationships that arise when we closely attend to historical detail.

Moreover, even if Helgeland and Johnson's theses are correct – that the early church was neither so universally opposed to military service nor so driven by a commitment to nonviolence as Cadoux, Hornus, or Bainton suggest – their modifications to that nonviolent narrative still turn on motives and ideas that are, themselves, meritorious. Opposing idolatry and pursuing justice are, after all, commendable goals and actions from within a Christian worldview.

I ANTI-JEWISH SENTIMENT AND EARLY CHRISTIAN PACIFISM

Yet there is also one underexamined motive that seems to have driven the early opposition to military service and violence more generally and it is much less commendable. It serves as the basis for the second qualification to the narrative that the pre-Constantinian church was nonviolent because of its obedience to Jesus's commands: opposition to violence was shaped by anti-Jewish[8] attitudes of the early church fathers. As it is both under-

---

[7] See, among others, James Turner Johnson, *The Quest for Peace: Three Moral Traditions in Western Cultural History* (Princeton: Princeton University Press, 1987). For an excellent examination of the range of contemporary scholarship on the early church and military service, see David G. Hunter, "A Decade of Research on Early Christians and Military Service," *Religious Studies Review* 18.2 (April, 1992): 87–94. Even Yoder recognizes that the vision of the church's engagement with its larger political surroundings that he calls "Constantinianism" predates Constantine, perhaps by centuries. See John Howard Yoder, *The Jewish-Christian Schism Revisited*, ed. by Michael G. Cartwright and Peter Ochs (Waterloo, ON: Herald Press, 2008), 37 n. 22; 20.

[8] The phrase "anti-Jewish" though imperfect (making, as it does, an implicit claim about the possibility of naming a single vision or understanding of the world that can be characterized as definitively "Jewish" in spite of the fact that Judaism, even and perhaps especially of the first few centuries C.E., was a diffuse faith whose adherents held to a range of beliefs and engaged in a variety of practices that would be hard to reconcile with each other and, in the process, ignoring the degree to which Christianity's relationship to Judaism is

examined and morally troubling, this qualification needs much further development.

Begin with the fact that the two church fathers most identified with nonviolence – Tertullian and Origen – are also the two fathers most identified with anti-Jewish polemics. As just a single example, note this statement by Robert Michael in "Antisemitism and the Church Fathers":

> Christ-killers was *the* essential Christian accusation against contemporary Jews throughout the patristic period. Tertullian accused the Jews of deicide in twenty passages in ten of his works. Origen, the third-century exegete, regarded the tragic fate of the Jews as due to punishment for their deicide, the culmination of a history of crime, rebelling against God, blindness, hard heartedness, carnality.[9]

Given that this passage begins by recognizing "Christ-killer" as "*the* essential Christian accusation," it's worth noting that the only two Christians named in the passage are Tertullian and Origen. Many Christians and non-Christians of the day spoke against the Jews; that these two stand out at least suggests something of the level of vitriol in their texts.

Of course, they are hardly alone. Jews are referenced negatively in a wide range of pagan and Christian sources from the second and third centuries, though Greek and Roman attitudes tended toward derisiveness rather than opposition, as nothing in particular hung on rejecting Judaism for non-Christians.[10] And the fact that Tertullian and Origen are both known for opposing violence and condemning Jews could simply be a matter of rhetorical coincidence that is especially apparent since the two of them are so prominent generally. Tertullian barely mentions the

markedly complex) is still a clearer term than the even more cipher-like "anti-Semitic" and will be used throughout this book in spite of the greater popularity of the latter term.

[9] Robert Michael, "Antisemitism and the Church Fathers," in *Jewish-Christian Encounters Over the Centuries: Symbiosis, Prejudice, Holocaust, Dialogue*, ed. by Marvin Perry and Fredrick M. Schweitzer (New York: Peter Lang, 1994), 104. Emphasis his. For another extensive treatment of anti-Jewish sentiment in Tertullian and Origen, see David P. Efroymson, "The Patristic Connection," in *Antisemitism and the Foundations of Christianity* ed. by Alan Davies (New York: Paulist Press, 1977): 98–117.

[10] See J. N. Sevenster, *The Roots of Pagan Anti-Semitism in the Ancient World* (Leiden: E. J. Brill, 1975) or, more recently, Lee Martin McDonald, "Anti-Judaism in the Early Christian Fathers," in *Anti-Semitism and Early Christianity: Issues of Polemic and Faith*, ed. by Craig A. Evans and Donald A. Hagner (Minneapolis: Fortress Press, 1993), 215–252, esp. 220–225. And this anti-Jewish rhetoric precedes Tertullian in the church. Justin Martyr, for instance, says, "you [Jews] are a ruthless, stupid, blind, and lame people, children in whom there is no faith" (Justin Martyr, *Dialogue with Trypho*, 27, trans. by Thomas B. Falls [Washington D.C.: Catholic University of American Press, 2003], 42).

Jews when arguing against violence on the basis of the Christian obligation to behave like Jesus, and when he does mention (some of) them, in *On Patience*, the connection isn't entirely clear:

… He to whom, had He willed it, legions of angels would at one word have presented themselves from the heavens, approved not the avenging sword of even one disciple… He who set before *Him* the concealing of Himself in man's shape, imitated nought of man's impatience! Hence, even more than from any other trait, ought ye, Pharisees, to have recognized the Lord. Patience of this kind none of *men* would achieve.[11]

To be clear: Tertullian was explicitly anti-Jewish in *On Patience*, arguing that the Old Testament consistently connects Israel's sins (idolatry, the murder of the prophets, the murder of Jesus) to impatience. It is Tertullian's position, David P. Efroymson writes, that "it is somehow Jewish to be impatient, just as it is Christian to be patient."[12] But, as Efroymsom also notes, this particular passage is ambiguous. Tertullian was not writing to Jews; hence, Tertullian's use of "ye" would suggest that he is using the term "Pharisees" symbolically, rather than with reference to a particular group of first-century Jews. The statement can be understood, then, to treat impatience as a human, rather than a Jewish, failing.

Origen presents an even more complicated case. In arguing against Celsus, a philosopher who has attacked Christianity, Origen repeatedly quotes Celsus in order to then refute him. Among Celsus's criticisms is that Christianity is a revolt within Judaism. Origen argues against this by reference to nonviolence:

The assertion that "certain Jews at the time of Christ revolted against the Jewish community and followed Jesus" is not less false than the claim "that the Jews had their origin in a revolt of certain Egyptians." Celsus and those who agree with him will not be able to cite a single act of rebellion on the part of the Christians. If a revolt had indeed given rise to the Christian community, if Christians took their origin from the Jews, who were allowed to take up arms in defense of their possessions and to kill their enemies, the Christian Lawgiver would not have made homicide absolutely forbidden. He would not have taught that his disciples were never justified in taking such action against a man even if he were the greatest wrongdoer.[13]

---

[11] Tertullian, "On Patience" in *Christian Peace and Nonviolence: A Documentary History*, ed. by Michael G. Long (Maryknoll, NY: Orbis, 2011), 23. Emphasis his. Patience is among the more prominent of Christian virtues advanced by the church fathers in the second through fourth centuries. Given that patience connotes a certain way of relating to time, the emphasis on patience is a sign worth interpreting.

[12] David P. Efroymsom, "Tertullian's Anti-Jewish Rhetoric: Guilt by Association," *Union Seminary Quarterly* 36.1 (Fall, 1980): 27.

[13] Origen, *Against Celsus* in Long, 24.

Origen's argument at least moves beyond rhetorical coincidence. For some Christians, being nonviolent also meant, explicitly, being non-Jewish. There is, though, a marked difference between being not Jewish and being anti-Jewish, and Origen's argument – at least here – has as much to do with distinction as with opposition. That said, the fact that Tertullian and Origen both draw distinctions between "Jewish" and "Christian" ways of addressing and using violence, when combined with the more explicit anti-Jewish screeds in others of their writings, leans far enough toward linking their pacifist and anti-Jewish arguments to underwrite the mandate to ask further questions about historical and conceptual connections between pacifism and anti-Judaism in the first several centuries of the church's life.

Christians and Jews lived in complex relationships with each other, and the nature of these relationships varied widely across the first several centuries C.E. and according to geography. On the one hand, both Christians and Jews of the first several centuries were in the process of distinguishing themselves from each other. Jewish visions of Christians as heretics mesh with a series of Jewish arguments of the day in which Jews also condemned Samaritans, Pharisees condemned Sadducees, and Essenes condemned Pharisees. In this context, Jewish arguments against Christianity sound more like a family quarrel.[14]

Though Jewish desires to distinguish themselves from Christianity are significantly more muted than early Christian desires to distinguish themselves from Judaism, there were multiple reasons for Jews to pursue such a project. Some Jewish communities were likely to have treated early Christians with antipathy because, at least in some parts of the Roman Empire, Jews had gained some political power and privileges from Rome that were contingent upon the continued ability of Jewish communities to be identifiably Jewish. To do so would involve, in other words, maintaining a certain connection to the law and continuing an emphasis on circumcision that Christian understandings of grace and the inclusion of gentiles made difficult.[15] In other places, Roman persecution of Christians

[14] The cursing of Christians as the nineteenth benediction in the Eighteen Benedictions said by Jews – the *birkat haMinim* – that came out of the supposed Council of Jamnia in 90 C.E. may or may not refer to Christians probably did not come about this early, and is unlikely to have been the results of a council decision (especially since it isn't entirely clear that the Council of Jamnia, which supposedly shaped the canon of Hebrew Scriptures, is a historical event). And rabbinic condemnations of Christianity would come far later in history.

[15] On "privileges" accorded to some Jewish groups in the empire, see Andrew S. Jacobs, "Jews and Christians," in *The Oxford Handbook of Early Christian Studies* ed. by Susan Ashbrook Harvey and David G. Hunter (New York: Oxford University Press, 2008).

would encourage de-identification of Jews with Christians for purposes of self-protection. And after the destruction of the Second Temple and the failed *Bar Kokhba* revolt, the Jewish Diaspora forced Jews to re-think a faith that could not be grounded in Jerusalem and Temple worship and a concomitant concern not only with the shape of the faith but the permeability of its boundaries. For Jews of the second and third centuries, avoiding confusion of their identity with Christians was a matter of not only religious purity, but significant political import.

Likewise, during the first few centuries of its existence, the Christian church's desire to distinguish itself from Judaism grew more pronounced. Increasingly, Judaism represented not only a distinct faith but, from the perspective of the Church fathers, a failed one: having been given the opportunity to recognize its Messiah, it denied him. Having been given release from the constrictions of the law, it refused it. Having been provided with new ways to interpret the Scriptures, it rejected them. Indeed, many in the early church took the failure of the Jewish rebellion against Rome (66–73 C.E.), the destruction of the Second Temple in 70 C.E., and the near genocide of the Jews after the Bar Kokhba Revolt in 132 C.E. as evidence that God had rejected Israel and now favored the church. Yet as long as Jewish communities continued to exist – and, even after Hadrian's death in 137 C.E., to find favor in the empire – this failure was disturbingly hard to see. Whether due to actual conflicts with Jewish communities, confusions about why God would still allow Jews to exist after the new dispensation brought by Jesus, or mimetically based fears that potential Christians would prefer to convert to Judaism, Christian opposition to Judaism took on the vitriolic character of a group that feels threatened by the existence of the other. Moreover, in contexts in which Jews, too, faced persecution by Rome after the destruction of the Second Temple and several failed revolts, it is likely that Christian communities interested in their own preservation may have been pulled toward behaving more like Romans and less like Jews. Certainly by the end of the first three hundred fifty years of the church's existence, it had moved from being identifiably related with Judaism to being identifiably related to the empire. It was undoubtedly safer to identify with the powerful than with the embattled.[16]

---

[16] Whether these distinctions were as pronounced on the ground as they were in the writings is a different question. Given archeological evidence of Jews and Christians living in near proximity to each other and recognition that neither "Christianity" nor "Judaism" are monolithic terms – not to mention the fact that the apologists of either side are unlikely to have represented the opinions of most adherents – it is likely that there were many degrees of differentiation and, therein, opposition between Jewish and Christian communities of

The growing distinctions between Judaism and Christianity shaped a range of complex relationships between Jews and Christians. On the one hand, some Christians believed that being a faith distinct from Judaism was not enough. Increasingly, Christians opposed Jews and argued against Judaism, so much so that an entire genre of literature, the *adversus Judaeos* tradition, arose. While that tradition is most closely associated with John Chrysostom (349–407) and his sermons, many of which blamed Jews for Jesus's crucifixion and argued against Christian and/or Jewish Christian participation in Jewish rituals, the tradition precedes him by centuries. As Rosemary Radford Reuther pointed out in her landmark book, *Faith and Fratricide*, not only were Christian communities imbued with anti-Jewish sentiment, but from its beginning Christian theology itself was as well.[17] While Reuther's arguments – exegetical, historical, and constructive – have come under scrutiny over the past several decades, the dangers and damage she helped name in 1974 continue to warrant concern.

On the other hand, recent scholarship on Jewish-Christian relationships during the first several centuries C.E. does strongly suggest that Jews and Christians continued to live amicably (or at least quasi-amicably) with each other. As Annette Yoshiko Reed and Adam H. Becker highlight in the introduction to their edited volume, *The Ways that Never Parted: Jews and Christians in Late Antiquity and the Early Middle Ages*,

Our literary and archaeological data ... suggest that developments in both traditions continued to be shaped by contacts between Jews and Christians, as well as by their shared cultural contexts. Even after the second century, the boundaries between "Jewish" and "Christian" identities often remained less than clear, consistent with the ambiguities in the definition of both "Jew" and "Christian." Likewise, attention to the entire range of our extant evidence suggests that the continued diversity of Judaism and Christianity found expression in the variety of ways in which Jews and Christians interacted in different geographical, cultural, and social contexts.[18]

the day. For a solid summary of complexity of Jewish-Christian relations during the first several hundred years' existence of the church and the early growth of rabbinic Judaism, see Andrew S. Jacobs, "Jews and Christians," in *The Oxford Handbook of Early Christian Studies*, ed. by Susan Ashbrook Harvey and David G. Hunter (New York: Oxford University Press, 2008), 169–185.

[17] Rosemary Radford Reuther, *Faith and Fratricide: The Theological Roots of Anti-Semitism* (New York: Seabury Press, 1974).

[18] Adam H. Becker and Annette Yoshiko Reed, eds., *The Ways That Never Parted: Jews and Christians in Late Antiquity and the Early Middle Ages* (Minneapolis: Fortress Press, 2007), 2.

Yet if the literary and archeological data suggest such blurred boundaries, why has the dominant narrative so emphasized a fierce parting of the ways? Daniel Boyarin has argued that "'heresiology,' the extraordinary practice of anatomizing, pinning down, making taxonomies of Christians who are not somehow 'in,' was an integral part of the answer to the question, 'What kind of thing will Christianity be?'"[19] Even at facile levels, this seems the case: the need to define/anatomize/distinguish is more pronounced in early anti-Jewish Christian writings than it is in early Christian thought in general. We shouldn't undervalue this detail. If the literary and archeological data support blurring, then we have an obligation to read anti-Jewish writings not as representative of the wider church's relations to Jewish neighbors but as exceptions to those relations. In other words, the *adversus Judaeos* tradition represents a departure from the wider Christian tradition(s) of the times – one that may eventually become dominant, but isn't so in the first several centuries of the church's existence. Additionally, we shouldn't read those who initiate the *adversus Judaeos* tradition as tacitly expressing the broader opinions and practices of the church. Rather, we should read them over and against those opinions and practices, as explicitly choosing to shape a trajectory for the church that pushes it further from its Jewish origins.

Unsurprisingly, this need to define/anatomize/distinguish is also pronounced in early anti-violence Christian writings. In these writings, Justin Martyr, Athenagorus, Tertullian, Origen, and others are marking out a distinct way of living in the world of the Roman Empire that distinguishes the church from the surrounding culture as a way of expressing its distinct sense of mission. Certainly, it could be the case that these particular writers, who happen to address both Christian relationships with Jews and Christian relationships with the empire, are simply using the same rhetorical strategies to address both sets of relationships because that's how this particular set of writers thinks and writes, in which case their anti-Jewish and anti-violence concerns are only related incidentally. Perhaps there is no necessary relationship between being anti-Jewish and being opposed to violence. However,

---

[19] Daniel Boyarin, *Border Lines: The Partition of Judaeo-Christianity* (Philadelphia: University of Pennsylvania Press, 2004), xi. Boyarin notes, moreover, that this was not a one-way process: "The Rabbis, in those same centuries, produced an analogous response, a discourse as well of the pure and authentic opposed to the impure, the contaminated, the hybrid, the *min*" (Boyarin, xii).

there should now be enough uncertainty about the relationship to warrant further investigation.[20]

Having demonstrated a connection between nonviolence and anti-Jewish rhetoric in the second- and third-century church and having situated that connection historically and politically, the time has come to further explore the theological relation between nonviolence and anti-Jewish rhetoric. If anti-Jewish sentiment funds the early church's theological commitment to nonviolence, then getting the relationship between the two right matters a great deal for how we examine later pacifist movements. After all, if those commitments or their underlying structures continue to carry weight with contemporary pacifist movements, then any use of the resources of nonviolence needs to carefully weigh not only the salutary arguments of the tradition but its pernicious ones as well. If both the anti-Jewish sentiment and the church's theological commitment to nonviolence after the close of the first century CE are expressions of a problematic way of locating the church in history, then we need to be doubly wary of the possibility that this problematic way has continued to find expression in arguments in defense of Christian pacifism.

Begin this exploration with Scripture. When Marcion argued that the false god of the Old Testament was different from the God that Jesus called "Abba" and with which he (Jesus) identified himself, he placed the church in an awkward position. On the one hand, the church wanted to strongly affirm that something new and remarkable had happened in the person and work of Jesus, the Messiah. From this perspective, the Law had been replaced by grace and gentiles had been welcomed into the fold without asking them even to uphold the commitments of the Noachic covenant.[21] The Messiah they had all been expecting had come, had died and been resurrected, had sent the Holy Spirit, had commanded them to

---

[20] Another piece of evidence: Augustine – long thought of as the "father" of a Christian Just War tradition that can only exist as the result of a reframed way Christians could understand the relationship between the church and the larger world as he described it in his magisterial *City of God* – understood Christian-Jewish relations in quite different ways from pre-Constantinian Christian scholars. As Paula Fredriksen has argued, Augustine develops a historicizing hermeneutic that links all events of the biblical past with salvation history: from creation forward, history is a continuous narrative about God's work in the world, and that work includes God's giving of the law to the Hebrew people. And as Jews serve as carriers of and pointers to that law, they had *and have* a distinctive and important role to play in witnessing to the work of God. See Fredriksen, *Augustine and the Jews: A Christian Defense of Jews and Judaism* (New York: Doubleday, 2008).

[21] In this tension, Paul's epistle to the Galatians would be treated as superseding Luke's description of the Council of Jerusalem in Acts 15: 19–21.

make disciples in his name, and had promised to return. On the other hand, the God that Jesus called "Abba" was the very God who had created the world, called Abraham, spoken to Moses, established a kingdom, and sent prophets. The church's Scriptures, though expanding to include new letters and gospels, still included the Old Testament. How could the church simultaneously say something transformationally new had happened while maintaining faith with its tradition of thousands of years?

The developing solution to this problem, at least on the part of those who were defining/anatomizing/distinguishing Christianity, was to say that God – the one attested to in both the Hebrew Scriptures and in the person of Jesus, the Christ – had determined that one age (the one before Jesus) would be shaped by one vision and ordered by one set of laws and that the new age (the one Jesus inaugurates) would be shaped by a different vision and ordered by a different set of laws. Jesus comes after the Law and the church comes after Jesus. Jesus's life and teachings replace (or complete) the Law, and the church's obligation is to that life and those teachings. Jesus transforms things – including the church and its members – and that transformation means Christians must not only understand themselves differently but interpret Scripture differently and live their lives differently.

Through it all, the ascendance of "after" language, described above as exemplifying a shift in the way the early church thought about its place in time, is reinforced. Not only does the church come after Jesus's crucifixion and resurrection, Jesus's work described in the texts of the New Testament comes after the work of God described in the Hebrew Scriptures (rather, e.g., than being in continuity with or tensively related to God's work in those texts). A vision of history in which the current time period comes after and replaces its predecessor reinforces tribal self-centeredness ("we represent a new way of doing things") and permits a kind of collective amnesia ("we need not attend to the history"), both of which fund the *adversus Judaeos* tradition and devalue the wisdom of the past. Perhaps an even more significant factor from a Christian perspective, the ascendance of "after" language tacitly favors a kind of realized eschatology in which the future, as *future,* ceases to maintain its prophetic and chastening character. Attention to the possibility that there might still be an infinite distance between "what is" and "what will be," traversable only by the power of divine grace, recedes from prominence and the vacuum it leaves behind quickly fills with an ethic of obligation.

This separation of time between before Jesus and after him recurs constantly in the writings of the church fathers on pacifism:

Those who once rejoiced in fornication now delight in continence alone; those who made use of magic arts have dedicated themselves to the good and unbegotten God; we who once took most pleasure in the means of increasing our wealth and property now bring what we have into a common fund and share with everyone in need; we who hated and killed one another and would not associate with men of different tribes because of [their different] customs, now after the manifestation of Christ live together and pray for our enemies and try to persuade those who unjustly hate us, so that they, living according to the fair commands of Christ, may share with us the good hope of receiving the same things [that we will] from God, the master of all.[22] *Justin Martyr*

To His Excellency, Diognetus: ... You want to know, for instance, what God [Christians] believe in and how they worship him, while at the same time they disregard the world and look down on death, and how it is that they do not treat the divinities of the Greeks as gods at all, although on the other hand they do not follow the superstition of the Jews. You would also like to know the source of the loving affection that they have for each other. You wonder, too, why this new race or way of life has appeared on earth now and not earlier.[23] *Letter to Diognetus*

But to the question of whether a member of the faithful can become a soldier... [T]here can be no compatibility between an oath made to God and one made to man, between the standard of Christ and that of the devil, between the camp of light and the camp of darkness. The soul cannot be beholden to two masters, God and Caesar. Moses, to be sure, carried a rod; Aaron wore a military belt and John had a breastplate. If one wants to play around with the topic, Jesus, son of Nun [i.e., Joshua], led an army and the Jewish nation went to war. But how will a Christian do so? Indeed, how will he serve in the army even during peacetime without the sword that Jesus Christ has taken away?[24] *Tertullian*

To those who ask about our origin and our founder we reply that we have come in response to Jesus' commands to beat into plowshares the rational swords of conflict and arrogance and to change into pruning hooks those spears we used to fight with. For we no longer take up the sword against any nation, nor do we learn the art of war anymore. Instead of following the traditions that made us "strangers to the covenants" (Ephesians 2:12), we have become sons of peace through Jesus our founder.[25] *Origen*

Unless those carnal wars [i.e., of the Old Testament] were a symbol of spiritual wars, I do not think that the Jewish historical books would ever have been passed down by the apostles to be read by Christ's followers in their churches ... Thus, the Apostle, being aware that physical wars are no longer to be waged by us but that our struggles are to be only battles of the soul against spiritual adversaries,

---

[22] Justin Martyr, "First Apology" in Long, 15–16.
[23] "Letter to Diognetus," in Long, 18.
[24] Tertullian, "On Idolatry" in Long, 20.
[25] Origen, *Against Celsus* in Long, 24–25.

gives orders to the soldiers of Christ like a military commander when he says, "Put on the armor of God so as to be able to hold your ground against the wiles of the devil" (Ephesians 6:11).[26] *Origen*

And the list could go on to include Cyprian, Lactantius, and others. Collectively, even these five passages are revealing. First, note the emphasis on a "new ethic" at work in these texts (with the obvious implication that this new ethic displaces an old ethic). The language of replacement and displacement proliferates. Actions that used to be allowed are no longer. Laws that used to apply have been replaced by new laws. Though in the twentieth century the term "dispensationalism" has been commandeered to apply to a particular mode of evangelical thinking most closely connected with John Nelson Darby and the Schofield Bible (and linked to the anti-Semitism of supercessionism), the meaning of the term – that God relates to human beings in different ways during different periods of time – clearly applies here. While other theologians throughout history – including the likes of Augustine of Hippo, Joachim of Fiore, and the Divines who wrote the *Westminster Confession of Faith* (none of whom espoused nonviolence) – have offered their own approaches to dividing time into periods with particular sets of rules applying to each time period, this before/after vision of time with an ethic unique to each time period is particularly indicative of the pacifists of the first several centuries C.E. Provided we can shear the connotations of some expressions of modern evangelicalism from the term, "dispensationalist" is adjectivally accurate.[27]

---

[26] Origen, "Homilies on Joshua" in Long, 26.

[27] I do not intend to dismiss the significance of the problem that the Old Testament presents for those who would affirm nonviolence, nor for that problem to be resolved in ways that reinforce dispensationalist readings of history and supercessionist understandings of Christianity vis-à-vis Judaism. Note, for instance, the patronizing approach to the law (and, implicitly, Judaism) – even as he rejects a more troubling view of covenant theology – in Guy F. Hershberger's preface to the first edition of his authoritative text on nonresistance for the Mennonite Church:

The Mennonite view has always emphasized a covenant theology which recognizes a permission for war under the covenant of the Old Testament, and a prohibition of war under the covenant of the New Testament. It is the author's view that God has provided one fundamental moral law which has been and is valid for all time. This view holds that the Ten Commandments embody the essence of the moral law, and that the life and teachings of Jesus are its authoritative interpretation and fulfillment... [and] assumes that the lower standards of the Mosaic civil code represent a temporary concession on the part of God to the lowered moral state and spiritual immaturity of that time. (Guy F. Hershberger, *War, Peace, and Nonresistance* (Scottsdale, PA: Herald Press, 1944), vii–viii.)

It is for this reason, incidentally, that the disagreement between Christian pacifists, on the one side, and scholars like John Helgeland and James Turner Johnson on the other, about whether it was problematic for Christians to serve in the military because they might take life or because they might commit idolatry is misplaced.[28] Questions about

It is worth noting that in spite of updating and issuing several new editions to the text, Hershberger never rejects the perspective on display here. It is also worth noting that Hershberger took his approach in order to reject even more explicit expressions of dispensationalism within the Mennonite church; unlike many of his conversation partners, Hershberger argued that God commanded the Hebrew people to wage war only because they had rejected the (pacifist) values that God preferred as a way of overcoming enemies. That is, to avoid the standard dispensationalism of his church, Hershberger advanced a vision in which the Hebrew people got it wrong (unlike the Mennonites). Trying to relieve a theologically problematic way of reading history, he exacerbates a morally problematic one. Note, moreover, that Hershberger's text is, in the words of Theron F. Schlabach, "[a]rguably ... the most influential statement of Mennonite social ethics in the twentieth century... Ethicists and commentators who dealt with pacifism, whether approvingly or not, often treated *War, Peace, and Nonresistance* as if it were the definitive statement of Mennonites' pacifist thought." (Theron F. Schlabach, "Guy F. Hershberger's *War, Peace, and Nonresistance* (1944): Background, Genesis, Message" in *Mennonite Quarterly Review* 80 [July, 2006]: 293–4.)

The other three great historians of Christian pacifism – Cadoux, Hornus, and Bainton – say relatively little about the implications of the Old Testament for advocates of nonviolence, preferring to report on what early (and, for Bainton, later) Christian advocates of nonviolence had to say about it or to summarize those sayings. Bainton is representative:

These passages in the Old Testament were very troublesome for the pacifist church fathers. Doubly so because Christians in the army appealed to these examples for their own justification. The fathers had two methods of disposing of such texts. The first was chronological. War belonged to a former historical dispensation... The other escape was by way of allegory... declaring that the disciples of the peaceful Christ would never have been permitted to read the historical books of the Old testament unless the horrible wars there recounted were to be spiritually understood.

(Bainton, 82). Later in the book Bainton also recognizes a dispensationalist sensibility on the part of Anabaptists (see pp. 153ff). Whether the absence of attention to dispensationalist tendencies and their implications constitutes a mark in their favor or not is beyond the scope of this project to assess. Again: although anti-Semitism in the Christian pacifist tradition certainly warrants careful and critical attention, that is not the focus of this project. Instead, I want to explore the vision(s) of time and history operative in the Christian pacifist tradition that shape not only the anti-Jewish attitudes therein, but other conceptual and moral problems for the tradition as well.

[28] The debates were probably already misplaced, as the "ethics-vs-theology" sensibility that drives them suggests a divisibility between ethics and theology that owes more to a modern social imaginary than a premodern one. The connection to anti-Jewish sensibilities offers a causal mechanism – a reason for linking the two reasons to oppose violence – that clarifies how the debates are misplaced.

how to act and how to believe are so deeply linked as to be inseparable, and both sets of questions turned on a presumption about why violence is forbidden: because the new law, which is part of the new faith, makes it so and to think otherwise is to practice the kind of heresy that Jews practice. In the new dispensation inaugurated by Jesus, affirming the old covenant and behaving in ways permitted or commanded by the Old Testament (which is to say, behaving and thinking like Jews) were both immoral and idolatrous.

Second, note the way Scripture is used in such passages. *Contra Marcion*, the Old Testament and God, as described therein, continue to play a role in the rhetoric of nonviolence. Yet Old Testament texts are primarily meant to be read allegorically or typologically, not straightforwardly. Tertullian, who wrote books against both Jews and Marcion, is particularly interesting in this regard. In his *Against Praxeas*, he emphasized the hermeneutical principles that straightforward interpretations are better than allegorical or typological ones (because heretics allegorize) and that Scripture should be used to interpret Scripture. Numerous scholars have noted that those two principles not only can sit in tension with each other, but that Tertullian was quite inconsistent in his application of them.[29] So in his *Adversus Judaeos*, Tertullian "sketched the gradual

---

[29] So, for instance, J. H. Waszink notes this inconsistency and attributes it, first, to Tertullian's training in a range of rhetorical strategies and, second, to the fact that Scripture, itself – and exegesis of it – was, at that point in time, in transition: "it is evident, first, that Tertullian could not yet produce an exegesis of Holy Scripture for its own sake (in the Roman world this activity begins with St. Hilary and St. Jerome); secondly, that he drew upon the achievements of the Greek apologists and upon his own rhetorical and legal training" (J. H. Waszink, "Tertullian's Principles and Methods of Exegesis" in *Early Christian Literature and the Classical Intellectual Tradition: In Honorem Robert M. Grant*, edited by William R. Schoedel and Robert L. Wilken [Paris: Editions Beauchesne, 1979], 18). Geoffrey Dunn, on the other hand, argues that Tertullian employed what we might call a pragmatic hermeneutic, using whatever hermeneutic will best help him make his case. "I would see it as a deliberate rhetorical technique employed to win a variety of different arguments, each technique being used depending upon what an opponent had first put forward" (Geoffrey D. Dunn, *Tertullian* [New York: Routledge, 2004], 22). Without wading too far into arguments about Tertullian's hermeneutical strategies, I would note that Tertullian scholars, who have largely and understandably been especially occupied with Tertullian's audiences, have not paid nearly enough attention to the sources of the scriptural texts he uses. Allegorical and typological interpretations proliferate in his use of Old Testament texts because the primary role that the Old Testament played was to point to Jesus, which mandates non-straightforward readings of the Torah and Prophets, especially. New Testament texts, though – especially those that are not already shaped for allegorical readings (e.g., the parables) – are much more likely to be read in a straightforward way, especially those in which commands are being issued.

revelation of God's law in the Old Testament *and its replacement by the New Covenant*: circumcision, observance of the Sabbath and the ancient sacrifices belong to the past. And he sought to prove, principally from Daniel, that Jesus was the Messiah."[30] His arguments against Marcion in *Adversus Marcionem* aren't so much against a hermeneutic that excludes the Old Testament and rejects the ethic described there as against Marcion's decision to posit two gods, rather than one.

What shows through in these passages, then, isn't that a particular interpretation (or set of interpretations) of Scripture determines how to understand history but, rather, that a particular dispensationalist understanding of history determines *processes* for scriptural interpretation. Answers to the question, "When are we?" drive answers to the question, "How is Scripture authoritative for us?" The significance of this way of ordering these questions will continue to bear close examination as the pacifist tradition moves beyond the pre-Constantinian church, especially given the weight that Scripture carries as an authority for those communions within the tradition.

Finally, note the growing influence of Greco-Roman ideas throughout: Jesus is "unbegotten," dualisms (light/dark, body/soul) recur, and analogical and figurative reasoning replaces literal meanings ("rational swords of conflict and arrogance"). Indeed, in Cyprian's letter to Donatus, we hear loud echoes of Platonic thought:

But in order that the characteristics of the divine may shine more brightly by the development of the truth, I will give you light to apprehend it, the obscurity caused by sin being wiped away. I will draw away the veil from the darkness of this hidden world. For a brief space conceive yourself to be transported to one of the loftiest peaks of some inaccessible mountain, thence gaze on the appearances of things lying below you, and with eyes turned in various directions look upon the eddies of the billowy world, while you yourself are removed from earthly contacts – you will at once begin to feel compassion for the world, and with self-recollection and increasing gratitude to God, you will rejoice with all the greater joy that you have escaped it.[31]

It is unsurprising that Christians in the second and third centuries are influenced by Greco-Roman culture, which was, after all, everywhere after Alexander the Great's Hellenizing project. Yet not only does the inclusion of Greco-Roman thought reveal the lie behind Tertullian's

---

[30] Timothy David Barnes, *Tertullian: A Historical and Literary Study* (Oxford: Clarendon Press, 1971), 106. Emphasis mine.
[31] Cyprian, "To Donatus" in Long, 26–27.

famous question, "What has Athens to do with Jerusalem?"[32] but it highlights the inescapable reality that cultures and the views of the world that arise out of them are never so monolithic or separable as they seem[33]. It follows that claims about a pure gospel, a Christian ethic, or a distinct Christian community of believers should be viewed with suspicion.[34] Moreover, when later pacifists emphasize the difference between pre- and post-Constantinian thought and suggest that the Constantinian church became captive to Greco-Roman-influenced concerns that were foreign to its identity (e.g., the qualities of Being in the Trinity, the natures of Jesus and their origins, the source of the Holy Spirit, the ordering and defining of proper belief, etc.), they must ignore substantial sections of the pre-Constantinian church, including sections from the writings of their own heroes.

2 IMPLICATIONS FOR AN ENVIRONMENTAL AGE

I raise these three matters (a dispensationalist and often anti-Jewish vision of history given voice by prominent representatives of the pacifist tradition, a hermeneutic used for scriptural interpretation that is derived from that vision, and the significance of Greco-Roman influences on pre-Constantinian Christian pacifism) in order to undergird my claim that arguments for nonviolence are inextricably linked to anti-Jewish perspectives in the early church and to highlight the dangers of building conceptual walls between congruent time periods. I also raise them to make a few broader points.

First, every telling of a tradition carries implicit claims about how to interpret history. Later defenses of pacifism will not carry nearly so pronounced an anti-Jewish sensibility, though we need to be alert to anti-Semitism where it raises its foul head, including in pacifist thought. A tradition that rejects violence can still do harm. One reason for this is that as the pacifist tradition moves through time, it will increasingly

---

[32] After all, even Tertullian relied on his training in rhetoric to argue for the sufficiency of Scripture over against Greek philosophies and, implicitly, appropriated the Attic insistence on definitional clarity in order to distinguish between ideas and groups.

[33] For that matter, the idea that Hebraic and Greco-Roman thought can be placed in a conceptual centrifuge and spun until they have separated from each other – an idea that I am (weakly) promoting here – may be heuristically helpful but is ultimately untenable.

[34] For a thoughtful exploration of how Christians might understand cultures and their unavoidable entanglements – and one that influences me here – see Kathryn Tanner, *Theories of Culture: A New Agenda for Theology* (Minneapolis: Fortress Press, 1997).

distinguish itself from other Christian visions of moral living rather than from Jewish visions of moral living. That is, dispensationalism will recede from prominence not because the nonviolent church decides to reject anti-Semitism, but because Jewish thought and ethics recede from the minds of present and potential members as a preoccupying concern or significant alternative. Rabbinic Judaism and Christianity both grow out of a common source during the first several centuries C.E., but once they are established, their family resemblance grows increasingly obscure. However, *something* will fund the way the pacifist tradition interprets history (or, rather many things that may share similar and divisive features: suspicion of ecumenical relations; accusations of heresy; rejections of the full catholicity of the church, etc.). These things, though seldom named and even more rarely connected to the witness of pacifism, usually arise as a reaction to a perceived threat to the pacifist church's coherence, and to the degree that the church universal is the one body of Christ, they are never innocent.

It follows that as Christian pacifism in an environmental age attempts to narrate its own tradition, it should give close attention to the more troubling tendencies that have haunted its past. To the degree that schismatic tendencies have been passed down through its generations, and – more maliciously – that such tendencies have been rooted in judgments against and condemnation of other politically weak, marginalized, and/or oppressed communities, the need for Christians pacifists to be especially alert to such tendencies should not be understated. In an environmental age, careful and realistic appraisals of such tendencies may help Christian pacifists pursue common cause with disparate others in dealing with climate-shaped conflict.

Second, interpretations of history shape particular hermeneutical strategies. In the case of pacifism, the continued return to the New Testament and Jesus's teachings therein as its fundamental authority not only shape a series of messianic ethics but display a nostalgic "myth of return" in which the New Testament and pre-Constantinian churches exhibit a kind of authority that masks cultural differences between both those times and later ones but also neglects the less laudable aspects of those early churches. In other words, in order for the New Testament and pre-Constantinian churches to maintain their normative authority in the pacifist narrative, pacifists will favor particular passages and interpretations over others and, in doing so, will replace the underlying cultural and theological assumptions of the New Testament writers' *Sitz im Leben* with those of their own. As anticipation of an imminent Parousia receded as a driving force in shaping an ethic of nonviolence, it was replaced by obligations to be obedient to a "new law" that replaced Torah and was revealed in particular New Testament texts. And as the existential urgency of relating the new law to the old law receded from prominence, other pressing concerns would shape hermeneutical assumptions that would, themselves, need closer and more critical analysis.

To what texts will Christian pacifists turn in an environmental age? Perhaps rather than turning to those (predominantly New Testament) texts that emphasize a new creation and the distinctive moral shape of that new creation, they might turn to creation stories and a universally shared morality embedded in the universe. Traditions of Christian natural law teachings – mostly foreign to Christian pacifist traditions – may grow in prominence or find fresh expression in Christian pacifism.[35] To what hermeneutical strategies will Christian pacifists turn in an environmental age? Perhaps rather than emphasizing the church as a distinct community that is shaped by a text that is morally authoritative because it is the church's text,[36] Christian pacifists will increasingly attend to the variety of readers and reading strategies within the church and the way that variety blurs all boundaries between "church" and "world." Pluralizing reading strategies rather than pursuing the "right" strategy will not only open the church to other voices but to other texts as well, including those arising in the environmental age.

Third, it follows that chronologies of persons, events, and ideas are messier than narratives about them, especially when those narratives are intended to carry normative weight. Cultures blur into and blend with each other. Demarcations in time may be heuristically helpful but the endings and beginnings they are meant to demarcate seldom separate themselves so cleanly. Historians approach the ordering and narrating of the past with their own ideological concerns and conceptual blinders. The inevitable multiplicity of narratives reveals confusions, lacunae, and

[35] Indeed, to the extent that Christian pacifism constitutes a way of aligning one's life "with the grain of the universe" (to quote Stan Hauerwas's description of John Howard Yoder's ethic), such a turn may already be underway. See Stanley Hauerwas, *With the Grain of the Universe: The Church's Witness and Natural Theology* (Grand Rapids: Brazos Press, 2001). Hauerwas's approach here still may overemphasize distinctness, albeit by grounding it in epistemology (what the church distinctively knows about common morality of the world) rather than morality (what the church distinctively does on the basis of its unique moral vision).

[36] Again, see Stanley Hauerwas, "The Moral Authority of Scripture: The Politics and Ethics of Remembering," in *A Community of Character: Toward a Constructive Christian Social Ethic* (Notre Dame: University of Notre Dame Press, 1981): 53–71.

a range of perspectives that compete with each other for attention and dominance. Traditions are most resilient over long periods of time when they include such matters in their self-understandings: a minority perspective during one point in time may offer insights that make it more dominant at another point in time. As a rule of thumb, though, any narrative that is either too clear or too meritorious has likely succumbed to temptations to essentialism, often resulting in unjustifiable distinctions and boundaries.

Far from being a sign simply of moral failure, the imperfect and sometimes malicious motives that drive Christian pacifist narratives can also signal the reality of the contending and overlapping narratives out of which Christian pacifists shape the stories they tell about themselves and their history. Relieved of the burden of telling the single right/moral/ideal story of themselves, Christian pacifists can pursue projects of moral and theological bricolage in self-aware ways. As the world shifts more dramatically into the social imaginary named "Anthropocene," capacities for such bricolage will grow increasingly important. This side of such a shift, naming the narratives and parts of narratives that will be useful, coherent, and faithful to Christian pacifist witness necessarily involves a significant degree of guesswork and prognostication. It is undoubtedly better, however, to be aware of the range of Christian pacifist resources lying around us awaiting use and to participate in experiments in putting those resources together than to insist that there is an ideal Christian witness – let alone a Christian pacifist witness – to which we must adhere in an environmental age.

Finally, locating any religious or theological tradition through attention to a select group of writers or through attention to written texts in general undervalues the manifold ways that actual adherents behave and the reasons they do so while also unduly honoring writers and their perspectives. Basing one's arguments solely on texts has the effect of reinforcing the perspectives and prejudices of those who have been raised with the ability and resources to write, have been taught to express themselves in written form, and have been energized enough by particular matters to focus that energy into writing texts. Treating Tertullian, Origen, and others as prominent members of and theologians for the church is one thing. Treating them as representative of the church, however, is quite another. Confusing prominence with representation risks reinforcing unjustified and theologically problematic distinctions between persons of faith and leads to supercilious posturing.[37] More significantly,

---

[37] Cadoux, *The Early Christian Attitude to War*, 254. Take, for example, Cadoux's patronizing argument that members of the early church who either participated in or did not feel

it turns particular and complex human beings, each of them *simul justus et peccator*, into heroes shouldering more weight than they can carry. Narratives about traditions are always especially vulnerable when and/ or where they revolve around the distinctively praiseworthy attributes of particular persons.

Because climate change is a global phenomenon, the means by which we address it will arise from the globe as well. This is not to say that climate change will lead to a single global community; indeed, the existence and range of current and potential climate-shaped conflicts belies such a suggestion. It is, though, to suggest that communication between disparate communities that approach such issues in distinct ways will be vital in preventing some climate-shaped conflicts, mitigating or constraining them as they occur, and ameliorating their consequences. As such, varieties of modes of communication are likely not only to be the rule, but subordinated modes of communication (including oral and visual modes) are likely to be necessary.[38]

These four points are generalizable beyond an assessment of the pacifist tradition, particularly as combined with the points in the previous chapter regarding the responsibility of arguments made on the basis of inadequate data or silence to be held tentatively. Just warriors and just peacemakers need to attend to them, as does anyone attempting to use historical data in support of a particular vision, ethic, or ideology. The purpose of making them here is thus twofold: First, I want to complicate the early history of Christian pacifism in comparison to the conventional narrative about its centrality and univocality. I do this not in order to reject, undermine, or otherwise build a case against the tradition of nonviolence in Christian thought but to historicize and humanize it. A slightly humbler vision of the tradition is more resilient than the vaguely idolatrous aura that surrounds the conventional narrative, as I hope this book will reveal. Second, I want to gesture toward a few broadly applicable concerns to which anyone

strongly one way or the other about military service are immature. Their positions, he argues, "arose largely from the immaturity of the problem and of the minds that had to solve it." On the other hand, according to Cadoux, arguments against military service in the early church were given expression by "the mature and deliberate judgment of men long familiar with the ins and outs of the question" (Cadoux, *The Early Christian Attitude to War*, 254). To his credit, Cadoux at least recognizes the problems that the wars of the Old Testament raise for early Christians (see pp. 170–179). His assessment of their solutions, though, is itself problematic.

[38] In this regard, see Willis Jenkins's arguments in *The Future of Ethics: Sustainability, Social Justice, and Religious Creativity* (Washington D.C.: Georgetown University Press, 2013).

writing about the movement of any tradition through time needs to attend. We all fall prey to the temptations of overstating our case and therein undermining our credibility and/or usefulness. The more, though, that we can be alert to these temptations, the lower the height from which we will fall and the easier it will be to rebound. In a conflict-torn environmental age, such resilience is vital.

3

Church, State, and a "Constantinian Fall"

The conventional narrative of the Christian pacifist tradition describes an abrupt and distressing change in the church's relationship to power when Constantine comes to power in the early fourth century. It describes this change as a major shift in ecclesial self-understanding and moral vision. As a result of its rapid transition from being an unapproved religion[1] to being a legal one under Constantine in 315 C.E. (and, by 380 C.E., the official religion of the empire by decree of Theodosius I), the church compromised its most deeply held beliefs and practices. Within the conventional narrative, then, the church of the fourth century is marked by two dramatic shifts: the abrupt shift into legality and the alarming shift from identifying itself with the ethic of Jesus to identifying itself with the ethic of empire. Without discounting the significance of the changes the church went through during that century, the descriptions of both shifts within this narrative are reductionist and, for that reason alone, deeply problematic.

Begin with the abrupt shift into legality. In theory, it happens between the Battle of Milvian Bridge (October, 312 C.E.) and the Edict of Milan (February, 313 C.E.).[2] The shift is so rapid that Roland Bainton begins his chapter on the rise of the Christian Roman Empire thusly: "The accession of Constantine terminated the pacifist tradition in church history. A change apparently so abrupt prompts a doubt whether the earlier

---

[1] "Illegal" may carry too many connotations to be accurate across the history of the church up to that point, though at times it certainly was treated as illegal – and persecuted – during that period.

[2] Exact dates may be contested, but only by days or months.

65

pacifism had actually been as widespread and profound as here portrayed."[3] Bainton goes on to suggest the change had been on the way for perhaps twenty years – which still seems to vastly underestimate this time period, but certainly presents a greater willingness to entertain the idea of a longer-term shift than some versions of the narrative. Hershberger writes, "[I]n A.D. 313 a startling thing happened. Constantine, the Roman Emperor, declared himself a Christian and recognized Christianity as a legal religion. From this point on a great change came over the Christian Church."[4] Hornus argues that "[t]he year 314 represents a compromise, a bargain which the Church struck with the emperor in exchange for his protection."[5] Or Cadoux: "It is generally thought that, with the accession of Constaninus to power, the Church as a whole definitely gave up her anti-militarist leanings, abandoned all her scruples, finally adopted the imperial point of view, and treated the ethical problem involved as a closed question. Allowing for a little exaggeration, this is broadly speaking true."[6]

It is certainly the case that the church in 200 C.E. looked different from the church in 400 C.E. It is also the case that the church's relationship with the state changed as a result of Constantine's rise to power. However, the change was neither so abrupt nor so dramatic as the conventional narrative suggests. For almost its entire existence, the church had been in a range of complicated relationships with the Roman military throughout the empire. During a roughly concurrent period of time – the end of the second and beginning of the third century – but writing from different places, Tertullian argued that Christians should not serve in the military or kill, but could provide service to the empire through their prayers, and that Christians should pray for the emperor and his empire. Hippolytus argued that Christians can serve in the military but a "soldier in command must be told not to kill people; if he is ordered to do so, he shall not carry it out. Nor should he take an oath"[7] and Clement of Alexandria told Christian soldiers to remain in the military and behave honorably by obeying orders.[8] Moreover, the military constituted only one part of the

---

[3] Roland Bainton, *Christian Attitudes Towards War and Peace*, 85.

[4] Guy F. Hershberger, *War, Peace, and Nonresistance*, 70.

[5] Jean-Michel Hornus, *It Is Not Lawful for Me to Fight*, 177.

[6] C. John Cadoux, *The Early Christian Attitude to War*, 256.

[7] Hippolytus, *Apostolic Tradition*, in Long, *Christian Peace and Nonviolence*, 30. Bear in mind here that soldiers served a wide range of roles in society, only some of them having to do with actual participation in battle.

[8] Clement of Alexandria, *Exhortation to the Greeks* X.100.2, in Louis J. Swift, *The Early Church Fathers on War and Military Service* (Philadelphia: University of Pennsylvania Press, 1983), 52.

means by which Rome ruled, even if that was a part about which the church fathers were especially interested.[9]

Perhaps even more significantly, the Roman Empire was undergoing significant change during the first several centuries of the church's existence. As Peter Brown has pointed out, the Roman Empire was a "fragile institution" during that period, and its "inhabitants thought of themselves less as subjects of an empire than as members of a uniquely privileged 'commonwealth of cities.'"[10] In this setting, the empire was governed not from on high but "through collaboration with an empire-wide upper class, drawn from the elites of the cities" whose rules were enforced by the Roman military.[11]

When Christians prior to around 250 C.E. engaged "the state," then, they were primarily engaging a locally governed apparatus controlled by the upper classes who took the maintenance of the cities and the collection of taxes (a good portion of which went to supporting the military) as their primary responsibilities. Christians were included in this class and were involved in a range of these obligations: Marcia was an influential concubine to Commodus; Bardaisan was an important scientist and philosopher; Sextus Julius Africanus was a historian who helped the emperor set up a library in the Pantheon, and there are any number of inscriptions that recognize other Christian gentry during the time and throughout the empire.[12]

All of these roles were wrapped in religious trappings since all of life at the time was wrapped in such trappings. In Roman societies, the gods were everywhere and always involved in human affairs such that all such affairs carried distinct obligations and connotations associated with proper worship. It is a sign worth interpreting, then, that even those church fathers most opposed to killing and to Christians in the military have far less to say about the various interactions between church and state than about the church's engagements with other religious groups and philosophers. This is not to say that violence and military service weren't of significant concern; it is simply that they were not preoccupying concerns in comparison to the many other matters with which the church fathers dealt.

---

[9] A primary part, but not the only part. The church fathers reflect on taxation, on the way Rome distributes wealth and favors, on the philosophical and theological underpinnings of imperial power, and on the infrastructure necessary to maintain power.

[10] Peter Brown, *The Rise of Western Christendom: Triumph and Diversity, A.D. 200–1000*, *Tenth Anniversary Edition* (Oxford: Wiley-Blackwell, 2013), 55.

[11] Peter Brown, *The Rise of Western Christendom*, 55.

[12] See Peter Brown, *The Rise of Western Christendom*, 63ff.

On the one hand, this may highlight the degree to which violence and military participation are distinctly and morally problematic. It also suggests, tangentially, that Helgeland, Johnson, et al.'s claim that Christians avoided military service out of concern with idolatry is too simple: while a Christian emphasis on monotheism shaped a direct challenge to the religious rituals of local polytheisms, this challenge would have existed in all aspects of society, including those in which Christians regularly participated. On the other hand, their attention to killing and the military and their comparative neglect of other state roles within the empire suggests that the church fathers weren't nearly as interested in developing a systematic and oppositional way of thinking about church-state relations as later pacifists would claim. The military was not the whole of the empire and opposition to the military wasn't tantamount to opposition to the empire.

And these relationships to the empire grew more complex over time as Christianity grew in numbers and spread throughout the empire such that as much as ten percent of citizens were Christians by the middle of the third century.[13] Many were serving in varying capacities in public roles and, seemingly increasingly if not necessarily easily, in the military. Even attempts to demarcate pre-Constantinian Christian attitudes toward war and military service according to periods of time founder in the face of such complexity, unjustifiably tending to pull out a few voices as representative of the entire period.[14] As Alan Kreider has argued, there is a growing consensus that "attitudes and practices probably varied

---

[13] This percentage seems to be only a guess by historians, albeit one that has been repeated throughout a range of scholarly texts about Christianity in antiquity.

[14] See, e.g., David G. Hunter's division of the time into three periods: 50–150 C.E., 150–250 C.E., and 250–400 C.E. (David G. Hunter, "The Christian Church and the Roman Army in the First Three Centuries" in Marlin E. Miller and Barbara Nelson Gingerich, *The Church's Peace Witness* [Grand Rapids: William B. Eerdmans, 1994]: 161–181). One problem with this – and any such temporal division – is that it must ignore the fact that the church changed rapidly during its first three hundred years partly because it was expanding into a wide range of cultures in the empire, and the variety of ways the church engaged those cultures shaped internal tensions within the wider church that would not be addressed in any authoritative way until Constantine began calling for ecumenical councils. That is, the cacophony of voices across the empire shaped the movement of the church through time. The other is that it must treat certain prominent voices – namely, in this instance, those that were recorded and preserved – as representing the "center" of Christianity as if Christianity could have a historico-theological essence to it. On the larger theological problems of thinking of Christianity as having a center and periphery, especially in the way it engages the wider cultures in which it exists, see Tanner, *Theories of Culture*.

according to geographical location. Antimilitarist sentiment was strongest among Christians in the imperial heartlands and weakest on the borders... [allowing for] a degree of messiness and inconsistency in early Christian thought... No serious scholar can again write, as Hornus did, about 'The Christian Attitude'."[15]

Further complicating the matter is the fact that the empire's relationship with the church varied over time and across space as much as the church's relationship with the empire did. Periods of peace and benign neglect were mixed with occasional periods of localized persecution. In some parts of the empire, the church tended to go ignored or was even viewed favorably compared to other religious traditions; in other parts of the empire, it was more consistently viewed with suspicion. Where it was viewed with suspicion, however, this tended to be the result of suspicions driven by the category error of gentiles (i.e., pagans) who were converting to Christianity but staying gentile/pagan – and therein becoming deviant pagans rather than either good Roman citizens willing to worship the emperor or good Jews whose place was comparatively safe in the empire. Until the mid-third century, these persecutions were, as Paula Fredriksen has argued, "random, sporadic, and local. The absolute number of Christians who suffered this abuse was probably not large."[16] In other words, the empire as a whole didn't feel especially strongly one way or the other with regard to Christianity until the persecutions at the end of the third and beginning of the fourth century, so it is hard to make the argument that these persecutions played much of a role in shaping Christian resistance to participation in the empire.

I MARTYRDOM AND PURITY IN A CHANGING EMPIRE

Perhaps even more importantly, the Roman Empire was undergoing marked change during the third and start of the fourth century, and these changes were occurring largely independent of anything the church was or was not doing. As Peter Brown has argued, at the beginning of the third century, the Roman Empire was in its own period of dramatic transition. Its fragility had been demonstrated through a series of embarrassing military defeats in the first several decades of the third century, the Persian empire had grown in prominence, and the various cities' connections to Rome had become much more tenuous: "Between 238 and 270,

---

[15] Alan Kreider, "Military Service in the Church Orders," 417.
[16] Paula Fredriksen, *Augustine and the Jews*, 88.

bankruptcy, political fragmentation, and the recurrent defeats of large Roman armies laid bare the weaknesses of the old system of government."[17] Christianity flourished during the time up to the latter half of the third century, in part, because it appealed to those whose confidence in the power of the empire had been shaken and who were looking for another basis upon which to found their faith and maintain law and order.

In the latter half of the third century and especially over the two decades in which Diocletian ruled (284–305 C.E.), however, the empire struck back. As Diocletian centralized power, the authority of the various cities was reduced and the obligations to serve and be loyal to the emperor and his servants increased. The ideological commitments of the empire became more intrusive, and the sense of crisis growing out of these commitments shaped the empire's recommitment to the gods and its antipathy towards the church. Beginning in 250 C.E., the persecution of Christians became more organized, culminating in the "Great Persecution" of 303.

The most common vision of the post-New Testament church - marked by persecution and martyrdom and in contrast to Rome - plays a significant role in the conventional narrative of Christan pacifism. Yet this vision comes not from the church's first several hundred years of existence but from this period:

In 312, Christianity had been in existence for over 250 years. The world of Jesus of Nazareth and of Saint Paul was as far distant from contemporaries of Constantine as is the age of Louis XIV from ourselves. Christians presented their Church as having been locked in unchanging and continual conflict with the pagan Roman empire. But this was a myth. In reality, the period after A.D. 250 represented a new situation. Both empire and Church had changed. [The Great Persecution] marked the coming of age both of the new empire and of the Christian Church.[18]

It was, moreover, during the period between 250 and 314 that the church began to more formally attend to its ecumenical reach throughout the empire (mirroring the empire's own centralization of identity), establish a recognizable hierarchy (increasingly necessary as it had expanded throughout the empire), regularize and order its canon into codices, systematize its worship practices and spaces, and strongly identify itself as a contrast society with a polity that was marked by its differences from and opposition to Rome.

[17] Peter Brown, *The Rise of Western Christendom*, 56.
[18] Peter Brown, *The Rise of Western Christendom*, 62.

It was also this period that not only saw more Christians in the military but the fame of Christian military martyrs such as Marinus in Palestine (d. 260), Maximilian (295) and Marcellus (298) in north Africa, Julius (303/ 4), and the legendary Theban Legion (the "Martyrs of Agaunum"), supposedly in 286. These persons, all serving in the military, were martyrs, giving their lives and/or their testimony to a faith that called on them to stand over against their commanders and the practices of the Roman military for reasons related to both violence and idolatry.[19]

The focus on martyrdom is one sign of a larger shift in Christian self-understanding that began in the middle of the third century. Christians had been martyred since the middle of the first century, and Tertullian had earlier remarked that Christians "become more numerous every time we are hewn down ... the blood of Christians is seed."[20] Yet their lives had not been the focus of the church's teaching about how to live. Instead, "the vehicle of moral instruction [was] the *precept*,"[21] to which the examples were sometimes appended. Even here, however, the examples were either specific instances of behavior or of particular persons treated as types: Abraham was faithful, David was courageous, etc. Only Jesus was truly a model for living, and Christians modeled their lives on what he taught far more than what he did.[22] Yet toward the end of the third century and beginning of the fourth century, hagiography began to take hold, including – perhaps especially – the lives of the martyrs and their willingness to hold to the faith in the face of persecution.[23] Martyrdom, as an alternative

---

[19] See Louis J. Swift, *The Early Fathers on War and Military Service*, 71–79. It was also this period that saw the development of the *Apostolic Tradition* (also known as the *Anaphora of the Apostolic Tradition*), which attempted to provide instructions for Christians to serve in the military but not fight.

[20] Tertullian, *Apology* 50, in *Tertullian: Apologetical Works and Minucius Felix Octavius*, trans. by Arbesmann et al. in The Fathers of the Church Series (Washington D.C.: The Catholic University of America Press, 1950), 125.

[21] Robert L. Wilken, *Remembering the Christian Past* (Grand Rapids: Eerdmans, 1995), 125.

[22] So, e.g., Clement of Alexandria would state, "Our tutor Jesus exemplifies the true life and trains the one who is in Christ... He gives commands and embodies the commands that we might be able to accomplish them" (Clement of Alexandria, quoted in Robert Wilken, *Remembering the Christian Past*, 127).

[23] In her provocative book, *The Myth of Persecution: How Early Christians Invented a Story of Martyrdom*, Candida Moss charts the explosion of martyrdom stories in the third and fourth centuries, distills from the many fictional stories six accounts with historical credibility (*The Martyrdom of Polycarp, The Acts of Ptolemy and Lucius, The Acts of Justin and Companions, The Martyrs of Lyons, The Acts of the Scillitan Martyrs, The Passion of Perpetua and Felicity*), and then dismantles each of those accounts to reveal how each was altered for a range of particular purposes of the church.

to violent resistance, therein becomes an example of how to live nonviolently in a violent world,[24] and even a way to signal one's nonviolent opposition to the state in general.[25]

In these hagiographies, the martyrs weren't treated as examples of the human capacity to withstand or endure violence, though. Nor were they simply pointing to Christ and Christ's power. Instead, the martyrs were portrayed as being caught up in and possessed by that power: as identifying themselves with Jesus. As Brown notes, "Christian accounts of martyrs never emphasized (as we might do) their purely human courage. Rather, the martyrs were presented as men and women possessed by the power of Christ. They had a mighty God in them, and by their heroic deaths, they trumped the power of the ancient gods of the city."[26] Martyrs are baptized (i.e., joined to Christ) in blood (e.g., Saturus). They are crucified (e.g., Blandina). Origen writes of their ability to forgive the sins of others. They are "resurrected" (e.g., Sanctus in Eusebius's *The Martyrdom of Lyon and Vienne*). They see visions of themselves defeating Satan (e.g., Perpetua – who, as in stories of other female martyrs, is masculinized, reinforcing connection with Jesus[27]). They share in Christ's victory over death (e.g., Pothinus). Felicity told her jailers that she would not be suffering alone because Christ would be suffering with her even as she was suffering for him. The story of Polycarp's martyrdom is replete with Christ-like imagery, making him a "sharer of Christ." As Paul Middleton highlights, "identification with Christ forms a crucial

I have no interest in wading into the debates surround Moss's work. Here, I simply note that martyrdom stories need to be read not as history so much as attempts to advance particular social, political, and ecclesial purposes. Martyrdom stories, especially in their accounts of the various martyrs' purity, serve the purpose of elevating the virtue of purity for the church that was telling their stories. See Candida Moss, *The Myth of Persecution: How Early Christians Invented a Story of Martyrdom* (New York: HarperOne, 2013).

[24] See, e.g., Everett Ferguson, *The Early Church at Work and Worship, vol. 2: Catechesis, Baptism, Eschatology, and Martyrdom* (Eugene, OR: Cascade Books, 2014), Ch. 17, for a brief exploration of the relationship(s) between martyrdom and nonviolent protest.

[25] See, e.g., Lawrence Cunningham, "Christian Martyrdom: A Theological Perspective" in Michael L. Budde and Karen Scott, eds., *Witness of the Body: The Past, Present, and Future of Christian Martyrdom* (Grand Rapids: Eerdmans, 2011), Ch. 1. We need to be cautious here: the primacy that some contemporary scholars give to martyrdom as a way of opposing empire can say as much about such scholars' theologies as the early martyrs. That many of the early martyrs did think that saying "Christ is Lord" was incompatible with saying "Caesar is Lord" is certainly the case. That they thought of the confession "Christ is Lord" primarily as a rallying cry by which to resist the empire is another.

[26] Peter Brown, *The Rise of Western Christendom*, 66.

[27] See L. Stephanie Cobb, *Dying To Be Men: Gender and Language in Early Christian Martyr Texts* (New York: Columbia UP, 2008).

element in the self-understanding of the martyrs, and dramatically influenced the way their stories were told."[28]

If the accounts of martyrdom of the later third century are notable for their identification with Jesus, they are also notable for their silences. Unlike, for instance, the stoning of Stephen in Acts 7, in which Stephen gives a speech to his captors in which he uses the texts of the Hebrew Scriptures to explain the church and the works of God that led up to Jesus, the speeches of the martyrs are comparatively thin on references to Scripture. More notably, there is almost nothing about obedience to Jesus's commandments in the martyrs' speeches, favoring instead obedience to Jesus himself. The stories of martyrdom replace obedience to commandments about living in peace with obedience to the Prince of Peace. This is, in part, the product of the rhetorical strategies of those telling the martyrs' stories: if identification with Jesus is the point, then obedience to Jesus's commandments is beside the point. Indeed, obedience to Jesus's command would distract from the immediacy and intimacy of the connection between martyr and Jesus: obedience to the commandments highlights the very space between the one commanding and the one commanded, a space that identification with Jesus overcomes.

The accounts of the martyrs are, moreover, a sign of the changing function of apologetics at the end of third century: the church is now speaking to itself as much as to the surrounding witnesses. The stories are not only buoying up its members during times of hardship and persecution and shaping visions of virtuous behavior in the church, they are also shaping a vision of opposition between church and empire that isn't so much overcome through reaching out to the world as reinforced by pointing to the failings of the world. By the middle of the third century, the church is large enough to be able to preach to itself and diverse enough to be composed of an audience that needs such preaching.

Without losing the significance of the martyr's witness, it warrants attention that identification with Christ to the point of death is only one possible way of bearing witness to one's faith. The narratives of the martyrs could have pointed to the obedience to Scripture and/or Jesus that the martyrs practiced. They could have treated the martyr's deaths as responses to what God was calling the martyrs to do at that point in time

---

[28] Paul Middleton, *Radical Martyrdom and Cosmic Conflict in Early Christianity* (London: T&T Clark, 2006), 83. See also Candida R. Moss, *Ancient Christian Martyrdom: Diverse Practices, Theologies, and Traditions* (New Haven: Yale University Press, 2012) for the ways that martyrs participate in the imitation of Christ.

without linking it to Jesus's life, death, and resurrection and, therein, to a different point in time. Identification with Jesus's life, death, and resurrection in the stories of the martyrs therein constitutes a kind of doubled return. On the one hand, the writers of these stories are inviting readers to remember the times of the martyrs – some of them quite recent and some one hundred or more years earlier. And on the other, they are inviting readers to use the martyrs' stories to connect themselves to the stories of Jesus told in the New Testament. "People only become martyrs because others make them so," write Jan Willem van Henten and Friedrich Avemarie. "The martyrs are model figures for the groups who transmit and read the writings devoted to them [and they] play an important role in the process of the formation of self-identity."[29] In many instances of the stories of martyrs, self-identity is simultaneously immediate identity with a first-century Palestinian.[30]

As such, where the apologists for nonviolence in the second and early third centuries reveal a myth of return by emphasizing their connection with Jesus's commandments as the sense of his immediate return receded, the martyrs for nonviolence of the later third century reveal a myth of return by connecting themselves to the person of Jesus, leaping across hundreds of years in the process. Moreover, as they did so, they released themselves from the stringency of the authority of the texts and the difficulty of the commands in them. It is, after all, far easier to be obedient to the one you believe you are like than to the difficult commandments that he gives, which might, in fact, reveal how far away from him you are.

The stories of the martyrs advanced this immediate connection between times otherwise separated by several hundred years, and had the effect of elevating purity as a virtue central to Christian life. None were so pure, so noble, so sinless as the martyrs. Stories of the martyrs therein shared this emphasis on purity with other explications of the faith. Purity (of faith in opposition to either lapsed Christians or those whose faith seemed syncretistic; of motives over against political calculations; of desires over against the ways of the flesh; of charity over against self-motivated behavior; of Christians over against non-Christians; of martyrs over against everyone else) grew in prominence as both an attainable

---

[29] Jan Willem van Henten and Friedrich Avemarie, *Martyrdom and Noble Death: Selected Texts from Graeco-Roman, Jewish and Christian Antiquity* (London: Routledge, 2002), 7.

[30] The complex relationships between identity, memory, martyrdom, and the stories of martyrs are explored much more richly in Elizabeth A. Castelli, *Martyrdom and Memory: Early Christian Culture Making* (New York: Columbia University Press, 2004).

possibility for those who were supremely obedient and as a basis for explaining Christian behavior to the church and the wider society. In other words, purity increasingly carried greater apologetic weight.

Contrast this with the primary functions of apologetics prior to the middle of the third century. For nearly two hundred years, "Christian apologetics had two main aims: to show that Christianity is a legal religion that is not connected with criminal activities and does not undermine Roman society; further that it is reasonable."[31] Contrast it, also, with Athanasius's apologetics in the fifth century in which "apologetics is transformed into missionary preaching"; and Lactantius's apologetics reveal him to be a "theologian of divine revelation, not of rational research."[32] In neither of these periods does purity carry the apologetic weight it does in the latter half of the third century and beginning of the fourth century.

The reasons for this are not terribly surprising: the church was large enough, old enough, and interconnected enough to see the need to standardize its orthodoxy, which would also mean increased focus on heresies and their problems. The church had become distinct enough, socially prominent enough, and oppressed enough to have to face questions about the apostasy of members and their behavior during periods of prosperity and persecution (and the times immediately after prosperity and persecution). Neoplatonism, Manichaeism, as well as various gnosticisms, mystery religions, and other dualistic spiritual alternatives flooded the religious marketplace, simultaneously influencing Christian theology and drawing condemnation from the church. The Roman Empire's solidification and centralization lent clarity to what it was about "empire" that Christians should be for and against. A growing body of moral wisdom around virtuous behavior had emerged that attended not only to social interactions but to internal dispositions. None of this should be construed to deny the significance of purity as a good worthy of pursuit in the church prior to the latter half of the third century (e.g., 1 Timothy 5:22 calls on believers to keep themselves pure and 1 John 3:3 connects believer's purity to Jesus's purity). My intent is merely to highlight purity's growing prominence during that time period. Where earlier exhortations might have encouraged Christians to be faithful, morally upstanding,

---

[31] Oskar Skarsaune, "Apologetics in the Early Church," in *Religion Past and Present: Encyclopedia of Theology and Religion, vol. 1,* ed. by Hans Dieter Betz et al. (Boston: Brill, 2007), 318.

[32] Oskar Skarsaune, "Apologetics in the Early Church," 319.

modest, patient, and/or wise, the third-century church increasingly asked them to be pure.

This pursuit of purity had several effects. It lent clarity to behavior in terms of knowing which actions to accept and which to rule out, specificity to biblical interpretation in terms of downplaying ambiguity in a text or contradictions between texts, and congruity to the relationship between behavior and belief, calling believers to will one thing in both thought and action. It also invited the use of examples in telling stories about the faith of the faithful – the stories of the martyrs – and encouraged a generalized logic of contrasts in understanding oneself vis-a-vis the rest of the world: "I will define myself by what I am not and reveal what I am for by what I am willing to stand against." This is the motive of martyrdom.

Given the degree to which recourse to violence arises out of contextual fogginess and moral ambiguity, opposing all violence helped believers in their pursuit of purity. Additionally, given the degree to which the Roman Empire resorted to violence and the threat thereof (not to mention linking that violence to the greater good of the empire through the use of theological language), standing over against the empire allowed believers to express their pursuit of purity through a nonviolent witness to the world. That Cyprian would antagonistically write, "[t]he whole world is wet with mutual blood; and murder, which in the case of an individual is admitted to be a crime, is called a virtue when it is committed wholesale"[33] or that Lactantius would write, "[The Romans] think the only path to immortality is that of leading armies, devastating foreign territories, leveling cities, destroying towns and killing free men or subjecting them to slavery… Captivated by the vision of empty glory they call their criminal acts virtue… But if God only were worshipped, there would not be dissensions and wars, since men would know that they are sons of one God"[34] is as revelatory as the explosion in stories of the lives of the martyrs during the latter half of the third century.

It is ironic, then, that the period during which the church increasingly came into its own sense of power, reach, and independent legitimacy was not only the one in which it developed its purifying myths of persecution

---

[33] Cyprian, "To Donatus" in Long, 27.

[34] Lactantius, "The Divine Institutes," in Long, 34. Having cited Lactantius above with regard to his offering an apologetics of "divine revelation, not rational research," I should clarify that Lactantius bridges the pre- and Constantinian period and that "The Divine Institutes" pre-dates Constantine's ascendance to the throne.

and martyrdom but the one in which Christian participation in and understandings of the military were most varied and in which opposition to Christian participation in the military is most vitriolic. The church would carry that sense of power and a developing attention to formalizing polity and theology for an empire-wide religion into its post-Constantinian engagements with Rome, funded not only by recently shaped myths but by longer practices of participation in civil society and the military. Ideas about a sudden "fall" from a purer faith with the ascendency of Constantine manage to be both funded by the myths of persecution and martyrdom and falsified by the historical data about the church's first several centuries of existence.

2 IMPLICATIONS FOR AN ENVIRONMENTAL AGE

Several generalizable implications follow from this examination of the way the pacifist tradition narrates the history of nonviolence during the sixty or so years prior to the ascendance of Constantine, each of which has implications for the way we might think about Christian pacifism moving into the environmental age.

First and most obviously, narratives about events need not arise from the time in which those events occurred. Although the martyrs described in the stories of Christian martyrdom died in the second century (and even the first), the myths about them arose in the latter half of the third century. The distance between event and narrative need not imply inaccuracy, though it can contribute to it. Careful telling over time, especially in oral cultures, can help narratives maintain coherence and correspondence to the facts of the events. However, when narratives arise or become prominent significantly later than the events about which they speak, both their telling and their prominence reveal the existence of motives on the part of those telling them.

As this book moves from assessing the conventional narrative about the movement of Christian pacifism through time to constructing an alternative narrative that might prove more resilient and useful in addressing climate-shaped conflict, one important component will be recovering under-regarded stories from the tradition. St. Francis, for instance, is valorized by both Christian pacifists and Christian environmentalists. It is worth questioning why both groups valorize him and how his attention to both peace and the natural world are part of a single narrative. The Amish, as another example, are famous not only for their pacifism, but also for their rural ways. What is it about their founding theological convictions that leads to such emphases? Christian pacifism in an environmental age may benefit from retelling narratives about St. Francis or giving more attention to the thought of Jakob Amman alongside more renowned radical reformers like Menno Simons and Conrad Grebel.

Second, narratives serve purposes. Though the martyrs portrayed in the stories of martyrdom may have died centuries earlier, the cultic qualities that promoted the myths of the martyrs arose when those myths were useful to the church. There are many reasons to tell stories: to entertain, to enlighten, to persuade, to bind people together, to help people understand the places and people from whence they have come, etc. Where normative weight is being placed on these stories – especially when these stories are offered as history – understanding the purposes the narratives have served is as important as understanding the stories themselves. Sometimes, these purposes trump the narrative. As Candida Moss notes, "[i]t seems that all of the early Christian martyr stories have been altered ... This matters because the reason people are interested in saints is because of what they said and did. The rationale for their veneration is grounded in who they were... It's clear that these stories, while inspirational and heroic, are far from reservoirs of historical truth."[35]

In the instance of re-narrating the tradition of Christian pacifism, one obligation will be to name purposes. As I have already suggested, my primary purpose is to shape a narrative that is more resilient and useful in addressing climate-shaped conflict in an environmental age. As such, I will foreground those stories from the tradition that serve such a purpose. In this instance, for example, reaching back to the apocalyptic stories that arose during a time in which the Parousia of Jesus was imminent will be less likely to bear fruit than stories that arose later, if only because Jesus's imminent return led the early church to downplay a theology of creation in favor of a theology of new creation. The goal of narrating the Christian pacifist tradition for an environmental age isn't (and ought not be) to simply fill in more details of the tradition. It isn't to add more colors to a palette already ablaze with multiple hues, as if more leads inexorably to better. Instead, the goal of such a narrative is to shape meaning for those searching for it in a time of need.

Third, the same narratives need not serve the same purposes. Eusebius (~260–340 C.E.) was one of the foremost tellers of the stories of the martyrs of his time. He also had no interest in telling a story about pacifism – indeed, he is widely regarded as the greatest apologist for

---

[35] Moss, *The Myth of Persecution*, 125.

Constantinian imperialism. Yet the myths of the martyrs would also fund other Christian narratives, including narratives in defense of pacifism in some quarters, and narratives in defense of violence in others. Indeed, some of these myths include acts of violence by martyrs. Sometimes, then, narratives serve different purposes during different times. If nothing else, this confirms their resilience. At other times, though, narratives can serve different purposes during the same time and even when told by the same person. Narratives about history themselves have complex histories: not only can those providing the narratives tell them for a variety of reasons, driven by a range of conscious and unconscious motives, but audiences receive narratives for a variety of reasons and motives.

Though the myths of the martyrs generally served the purposes of reinforcing the third-century church's emphasis on purity and reshaping its theology toward more fully integrating believers into the life of Jesus, neither purity nor such a mode of integration need to be central to the faith. Nor do the actual lives of the martyrs need to be read in order to support such things. The stories of the martyrs might serve quite different purposes in an environmental age. Where the emphasis on purity promoted group solidarity and identity during periods of persecution, such an emphasis may distract from the church's ability to speak intelligibly into a context in which believers are not so much persecuted as ignored and in which the diffusion of agency and culpability that mark engagements with climate change make aspirations toward purity not only unhelpful but distracting. In systems where nobody can appeal to superior holiness as a basis for moral authority, the pursuit of purity manages to be both self-absorbed and self-distorting. Where the emphasis on integrating one's life with that of Jesus helped the faithful connect to one whose life and teachings during his historical existence was becoming less central to the church than was the theological significance of his identity as both human and divine in the fourth and fifth centuries, such an emphasis in an environmental age may undermine the obligation of human beings to explore their connections with the natural world. In systems where all of creation is multiply interlinked and profoundly interdependent, choosing to focus on one's connection to the divine may reveal unjustifiable privilege and insularity.

In the midst of the sixth great extinction, perhaps the stories of martyrs might remind us again that others have always paid extraordinary costs on our behalf. In an age in which the earth's capacity to sustain life is constrained by the limits of its natural resources, perhaps the stories of the martyrs might be better interpreted as attempts to make faithful sacrifices – imperfect though they may be – for the good of a greater world in need of persons willing to give up something precious in order to sustain life for others.

Finally, a fourth general implication might be the recognition that the purposes behind the telling of narratives tend to flatten out the rough and difficult places in those narratives. One of the primary purposes of telling the stories of the martyrs was to reinforce notions about the ideals of the church, especially about its purity and the holiness of its most revered members. Such claims to purity served political purposes. Likewise, these stories of the martyrs promoted a vision of the church as threatened and embattled, a body saved only by the power of God and the faithfulness of its truest members. Yet to the degree that the martyrs' actual lives and deaths were not nearly so pure as the myths describe and the church's history was not nearly as persecuted as the myths promote – which is to say to a substantial degree, indeed – the myths must cover over history. There are political forces at work in the construction of martyrdom narratives and the irony is that these even as these narratives served particular political purposes, they were advancing a vision that, in fact, sits at cross-purposes with politics itself.

In an era in which Christians had limited power in shaping the world around them, this flattening out of narratives for particular ecclesial ends had limited and (mostly) identifiable costs. In the environmental age, though, human beings not only have enormous collective power to reshape the earth, but that power is complexly and unequally distributed. Among other places, that power resides within a world religion (Christianity) that counts almost one out of every three people in the world among its adherents. Narratives that serve a beneficial political purpose in one place may serve a deleterious one in others (as when visions of geoengineering solutions have the potential not only to stimulate the imaginations of leading thinkers but to direct funds toward unviable solutions in the face of more basic needs and approaches). As such, bringing the political forces that shape narratives to light may constrain potentially deleterious consequences. Moreover, in the global context of climate change, any single universal narrative may founder under the weight of its translations across cultures and contexts. Perhaps attention to the political forces that shape narratives toward particular ends may have the effect of revealing the need for multiple and contextually specific meaning-shaping myths, including within the global church. The ordering narratives of the church in Lebanon, Peru, Côte d'Ivoire, and the United States may no more be the same than the approaches each country takes in addressing the climate-shaped conflicts it faces.

What hopefully has become clear in all this is that no Christian tradition can claim the church's stories as uniquely its own. Neither can the pacifist tradition claim that the church existed one way before Constantine and another way after him. The selective recovery of history, the isolation of particular issues (e.g., nonviolence), and the distorting effects that such recovery and isolation engender distorts history and inhibits the power of historical events to help us understand the past, our present, and the possibilities and limits that exist in the future.

Yet this is actually good news. A richer vision of the history of the church prior to Constantine – one in which the church consistently struggled to make sense of its relationship to violence – can help us not only avoid overly simplistic understandings of the church and of history, but it can also model a struggle to make sense of our relationship to violence during a time of significant historical change. A refusal to accept a preoccupation with purity, as if only those who were perfectly nonviolent can provide either models or insights about violence, can help us understand how to gain access to insights about peace from those who are not pacifists. A project of demythologizing the early church – especially with regard to its relationship to nonviolence – can help us return it to history and humanize its members in the first several centuries. Likewise, a refusal to isolate particular issues like nonviolence from their larger historical contexts can help us gain a greater understanding of the complex ways in which a God who desires peace might operate in a world that is larger than any ideology can contain.

Constantine's rise to power did not, then, inaugurate the church's transformation into its imperial form or lead to a sudden acceptance of violence or military participation. That transformation had been underway for well over a century even if it was most immediately shaped by the few decades preceding that rise. Constantine's rise to power did, however, allow the newly legal religion to solidify its new vision and accelerated the changes it had been undergoing at the same time that it reshaped the Roman Empire and, therein, the way the church and the empire would relate to each other. These transformations, some of their impact since then, and the way pacifists have interpreted them are the topics of the next chapter.

PART II

THE CHURCH AND NONVIOLENCE AFTER CONSTANTINE

"The religious sect is almost bound to be either pacifist or crusading, because the sect demands a higher level of Christian deportment than is ever attained by an entire community. If then the Church has coalesced with society so that every citizen is deemed a Christian, and Christians are not distinguishable by their behavior, then the sect must either dissociate itself from the Church and the community – this course will commonly entail pacifism – or else it must seek to impose its code upon the Church and the community – and this course will issue in a crusade."[1]

Roland Bainton

"The peacemaking purpose of past Christians has often been lost because Christians, like most other believers, chose to ignore the violent episodes of their own history. For example, the theological Summa *of Thomas Aquinas is not usually understood as offering a peaceful alternative to the violent methods of the first Inquisition. When read in relation to the Church's struggle with the Cathar heresy, however, its peaceful purpose becomes obvious."*[2]

Roger A. Johnson

---

[1] Roland Bainton, *Christian Attitudes Toward War and Peace*, 120.

[2] Roger A. Johnson, *Peacemaking and Religious Violence: From Thomas Aquinas to Thomas Jefferson* (Eugene, OR: Pickwick Publishing, 2009), 3–4.

4

Christian Pacifism and Constantine

The previous section ended just prior to Constantine's rise to power in the early fourth century. Throughout that section, I was busy dismantling a set of myths about the role of pacifism in the pre-Constantinian church, the most pernicious (because most subtle) being a myth of return: that the earliest church is best, that the same church was nonviolent for ideological/theological reasons, and that Christian faithfulness, especially with regard to questions about violence, demands a return to the vision and actions of that church. Such dismantling is necessary, but it also consisted of a demythologizing project that, time and again, took resources away from or rejected resources of the pacifist tradition. No matter my motives – a desire not to reject pacifism but to historicize and humanize it so that the tradition of nonviolence might be of use to us in the twenty first century as we address climate-shaped conflict – I can imagine that readers, and particularly pacifist readers, may be feeling disoriented, combative, or both. "What," they may want to ask me, "do you have to say about the pacifist tradition that is commendatory or affirming?"

This chapter, I hope, starts to answer that question. In it, I will argue that once we have begun to shear away the myth of return from the Christian tradition of nonviolence, we are not only likely to gain a greater appreciation of what the pacifist voices of the church's history – both old and new – can offer, but also to discover a greater range of useful voices than the tradition tends to recognize or claim. I begin with, perhaps, the most surprising voice of all: Constantine, himself.

I A COMPLEX CONSTANTINE OR A CONSTANTINIAN COMPLEX?

The conventional narrative about Constantine offered by proponents of nonviolence is that he either is the direct cause of, or initiates the fall of the church into its captivity to worldly power:

- "Historians have not failed to notice, and in some cases to deplore, the immense compromise to which the Church was committed by her alliance with [Constantine]."[1]
- "In regard to the question of Christianity and war, the crucial change began under the Emperor Constantine the great. When he converted to Christianity (in 312), Christianity began to turn toward the State for support, and became reconciled to war and the soldier's calling."[2]
- "Then in A.D. 313 a startling thing happened. Constantine, the Roman Emperor, declared himself a Christian and recognized Christianity as a legal religion. From this point on a great change came over the Christian Church. The emperor himself being a Christian soldier, it was natural that soon there would be many Christians in the army. In the course of time the church gave up its nonresistant position and Christianity became the religion of an imperial state."[3]
- "With the accession of Constantine the Church very largely, though not wholly, abandoned pacifism."[4]
- "The accession of Constantine terminated the pacifist period in church history."[5]

As if to summarize all this, Jean-Michel Hornus ends his chapter on Constantine and Eusebius with a quote from Roman Catholic writer E. Laboulay[6] and a condemnation: "[T]he kind of Christianity that Constantine symbolized … is also the kind of Christianity against which Christ himself stands as an uncompromising accuser."[7] Hornus isn't so much wrong in his condemnation as pinched: faced with an imperfect church, Christ the judge stands as accuser against all the

---

[1] C. John Cadoux, *The Early Christian Attitude to War*, 257.

[2] G. J. Heering, *The Fall of Christianity*, 33.

[3] Guy Franklin Hershberger, *War, Peace, and Nonresistance*, 70.

[4] Edgar W. Orr, *Christian Pacifism*, 77.

[5] Roland Bainton, *Christian Attitudes Toward War and Peace*, 85.

[6] "Constantine – murderer of his wife and his son, doubtful Christian, pagan pontiff at the same time as external bishop."

[7] Jean-Michel Hornus, *It Is Not Lawful for Me to Fight*, 212 (including quote from Laboulay).

expressions of Christianity that have ever arisen in history, including those expressions that identify as pacifist. Yet Christ the savior is also the one whose work – first on the cross and through the tomb and then throughout history – also redeems all those expressions of Christianity, including those that identify as pacifist. Pacifism may provide vital resources to the Christian faith as it engages the problems of violence, but those resources differ with regard to form and approach, not quantum levels of purity or righteousness. Pacifism offers great moral insights and practices to the faith but those insights and practices, shaped as they are by human beings, are, nonetheless, ambiguous insights and practices. Closer attention to the dawn of the Constantinian age can help us see why.

There is no doubt that the accession of Constantine augured dramatic changes for the church beginning with Christianity's status as a legal religion and including its access to worldly power, its relation to the state, its explosive growth, and all that these changes would lead to. Those changes, though, do not include the move from pacifism to violence (as shown in the previous chapter), and the pacifist portrayal of Constantine not only gets him wrong but misses the dramatic role that forces internal to the pre-Constantinian church played in its own shift toward a new way of understanding itself vis-a-vis the state and society. A growing body of scholarship on Constantine shows him to be neither the opportunist who uses Christian symbols and the church to consolidate power (à la Burckhardt's argument in his 1880 book, *The Age of Constantine the Great)* nor the Christian convert who suppressed paganism whenever political exigencies allowed (à la Baynes' thesis in his 1972 book, *Constantine the Great and the Christian Church).* Nor, certainly, is he the primary, albeit ham-handed, actor in the project through which the church became connected to worldly power and surrendered its faith in Jesus in favor of faith in the sword. Constantine is – and always has been – more complicated than any such characterization of him admits, which helps explain why he has become such a "controversial historical figure."[8]

---

[8] Fred Ledegang, "Eusebius' View on Constantine and His Policy" in *Violence in Ancient Christianity: Victims and Perpetrators,* ed. by Albert C. Geljon and Riemer Roukema (Leiden: Brill, 2014), 56. Ledegang notes that Constantine has been controversial for centuries and, as such, functions as something of a Rorschach test for scholars: their opinion of him reveals more about their own perspectives than about who he was.

In *Constantine and the Bishops: The Politics of Intolerance*,[9] H. A. Drake builds a case for treating Constantine as a politician of tolerance with a marked concern for the poor. Constantine, Drake argues, continued to be shaped by the vision of the labarum that he had prior to the Battle of Milvian Bridge (October 28, 312) and its perceived connection to Christianity, but he was also was constrained by the various political forces contending for his favor. Constantine both used these political forces (in order to gain political clout and credibility in the empire) and was used by them to advance their own interests, and primary among those who used him were the various bishops of the Christian church.

At the center of Drake's analysis is the need for contemporary scholars to separate theological questions from political ones. So, for instance, explorations into the sincerity and depth of Constantine's conversion are built around theological questions, whereas the effects of that conversion – including his acquisition of and alignment with a new constituency in the empire – the church – are political ones. Religious intolerance is a theological issue; the use of coercive force to either extend or combat religious intolerance is a political one. Whether a monotheist or polytheist vision of the divine is more true is a theological question; whether to promote monotheism within the body politic is a political question. Constantine, Drake argues, was masterful at forging political consensuses among his various constituencies in order to both stabilize his empire and promote tolerance among his subjects. After all, stability and tolerance were both priorities to which Constantine needed to attend. Stability was needed to reinforce his own credibility as a leader, having come into power from the outside through force of arms rather than from within the courts of the emperor. Tolerance was also needed as Christians became increasingly prominent in an empire that was still smarting from the economic and political catastrophe that had been Diocletian's persecutions.

Towards those ends, Constantine negotiated a series of theological and political arrangements with the bishops of the church, many of whom were fiercely – even violently – at odds with each other. He provided the bishops patronage in the form of exemption from public duties, titles, subsidies for their ministries, and even occasions to gather and debate –

---

[9] H. A. Drake, *Constantine and the Bishops: The Politics of Intolerance* (Baltimore: Johns Hopkins University Press, 2000). My dependence on and gratitude for Drake's analysis, though not blind, is deep and is already visible in the preceding paragraph.

again, sometimes even violently – the shape of theological orthodoxy. He entered into their debates and would eventually lend military force to support their agendas. In turn, the bishops helped bring their constituencies – the members of the local churches – into the empire. This was no small matter, as the bishops not only had their own agendas but also had constituencies who themselves could be "peculiarly volatile and anarchistic."[10] Bishops both shaped and directed those tendencies, pointing their members toward groups (especially other Christian groups) unlike them: heretics.

The church (or at least some prominent members of the church, including the bishops and, I would argue, church fathers like Tertullian) had long desired doctrinal clarity and pursued the rejection of heresies. In the rough-and-tumble of a politically tenuous existence surrounded by a wide range of available religious and philosophical alternatives, such a desire had manifest itself not only in debates and accusations but in splintering and political infighting for control of the church's vision. Under such contexts, the use of coercive force by which to "win" such debates was not a readily available alternative and, as we saw in earlier chapters, there were theological reasons to reject such force had it been available. Yet neither the desire for clarity nor the suspicions and antipathies that both shaped and were the products of doctrinal debates went away. Tolerance tended to be in short supply in such debates, and clarity was likely to manifest itself only in morally ambiguous (if not morally abhorrent) language about one's opponents. For at least one hundred years – and really since debates between Peter and Paul – the tension-filled and often overtly antagonistic relations between various Christian groups were as constrained by the limited access to power that a pre-Constantinian church had as by theological commitments toward unity and neighbor-love. Tolerance among church leaders – including among pacifists – was often in short supply. When such leaders perceived alternative teachings as a threat to the church's coherence and, at times, very existence, a willingness to live with those teachings was tantamount to faithlessness.

Of course, the church might have gone in a more tolerant direction. If nothing else, the history of the Christian church has demonstrated that Christians with quite distinct beliefs can nevertheless live around each other in relative harmony. And archaeological and literary evidence demonstrates a willingness on the part of most Christians of the time to live with neighbors – both Christian and non-Christian – with whom they

---

[10] H. A. Drake, *Constantine and the Bishops*, 30.

disagreed theologically. So "Beloved, let us love one another, because love is from God; everyone who loves is born of God and knows God" (1 John 4:7) might have trumped "Beloved, do not believe every spirit, but test the spirits and see whether they are from God; for many false prophets have gone out into the world" (1 John 4:1).

That it didn't is, in part, due to the growing prominence of an ascetic tradition in which one's opponents could be, quite literally, demonized. The burgeoning monastic tradition carried the third century's preoccupation with purity and the lives of saints into a focus on resisting Satan: "In refusing to abjure Christ, the martyrs resisted Satan and the monks were disposed to follow their example in this as in all other things."[11] Contentious church leaders blended their opposition to Satan with their opposition to those who disagreed with them in the church. Heretics weren't supposed to be argued with; rather, they were supposed to be condemned and removed not only from the church, but from positions in which they might influence the church. The dualism inherent in a single-minded pursuit of purity, when manifesting itself in a political form, led not only to lines being drawn but to intolerance toward those on the far side of those lines.

The church of the second through fourth centuries, then, was being shaped by leaders – including prominent pacifists – whose vision of theological clarity meant rejecting heretics and who were motivated by a pursuit of purity that favored dualisms of cosmological dimensions. Yet such a vision – even motivated by such a pursuit of purity – would not necessarily lead the church to accept the coercive use of force in order to mandate adherence to that vision and eliminate those who would offer a different one. That next step, toward the use of violence, requires political structures in which at least some persons would favor using force rather than losing the battle for hearts and souls. Religious intolerance, in itself, does not necessarily lead to the use of force; such use requires political structures that allow for it. That is, in the politically turbulent times at the start of the fourth century, a vision of theological and moral clarity of the sort arising out of the pacifist emphases of the second and third centuries, when combined with a desire for personal and communal purity (also notably sought by the pacifists of the third century), still needs a political form in which the intolerance arising out of vision joined to motive can manifest itself.

---

[11] H. A. Drake, *Constantine and the Bishops*, 415.

The political form that invited intolerance, Drake argues, was neither the result of the church's failure to pursue its own better, peaceful, angels (*contra* the conventional pacifist narrative), nor to the church's emphasis on monotheism (*contra* the scholarly argument that monotheism breeds violence[12]). The church wasn't that peaceful, and there were pagan versions of monotheism operative at the time as well. Instead, according to Drake, it was due to the inevitable way that communities of human beings engage each other: "[I]ntolerance ... is a phenomenon that extends far beyond the particular problem of Christian-pagan relations in antiquity, or the normal boundaries of religion and theology. Intolerance exists, at least in a latent state, in every human group and organization, and in every group there are individuals who are inclined to favor repression and coercion over other methods of social interaction as a means to promote their views."[13] All religious intolerance needs in order to enact its vision coercively is a willingness to use power – not "the power of the sword" or "the power of the state," necessarily, but power nevertheless. Since power flows through all social groups, pools in and around particular persons, and grows as the size of the group grows, Drake argues, wherever such groups are large enough, someone or some small group of persons is inevitably going to use that power coercively.[14] The church in the fourth century had certainly grown large enough for this to happen. It is for this reason that Drake focuses on the bishops. Not only were they the significant political players of the day, often at odds with each other and in need of resources for maintaining order among their restive, growing, and occasionally anarchic political bases, they didn't all think the same way about how to challenge each other on matters of great theological import. On Drake's reading of the times, it isn't Constantine that invites the church to use violence; it is the church leaders doing what they've been doing for centuries, only now with far larger constituencies as their power bases expand as they enjoyed far greater access to the powers of the state – including the sword – in order to pursue their goals.

[12] See, e.g., Regina Schwartz, *The Curse of Cain: The Violent Legacy of Monotheism* (Chicago: Chicago University Press, 1998).

[13] H. A. Drake, *Constantine and the Bishops*, 28.

[14] Drake's realist perspective is most apparent here. Yet there are many kinds of realism, and they don't all think about power in identical ways. One wishes he had spent time reading Reinhold Niebuhr, who at least frames his realism theologically and, in the process, avoids falling into the Machiavellian trap of insisting that power is the most potent force shaping individual and group interactions. For the difference between theological and political realism, see Robin Lovin, *Reinhold Niebuhr and Christian Realism* (New York: Cambridge University Press, 1995).

Drake's reading brings to light three ironies of the age. The first irony is that two of the three forces that led to the church's widespread acceptance of the use of violence – its rejection of heresy and its promotion of purity – sprang out of the heart of its nonviolent tradition and the third – the coercive use of power – was the inevitable product of its success in bringing in new members. Yet this does not entirely answer one of Drake's abiding questions: given that Christianity also preached peace and neighbor-love, why was it that an intolerant version of the church so successfully aligned itself with the state? Even if the church would inevitably gain access to the sword, why would the acceptance of the sword become so indiscriminate?

Toward answering this question, Drake points to two other significant fourth-century events: the destabilizing absorption of large numbers of new members into the newly legal and, a half century later, official religion of the empire, and the anti-Christian agenda of Constantine's nephew, Julian, who ruled from 361 to 365. Julian's reign "rekindled Christian fear of state-sponsored hostilities and created litmus tests that polarized opinion in new and dangerous ways. The effect of these twin changes was to make the militant message more credible"[15] and to entrench the church's sense that it needed to use its newfound coercive power in the face of a hostile world.

Confrontation with heretics and converts in the fourth century had the effect, moreover, of driving the church toward a narrative that was useful in dealing with both sorts of persons. That narrative clarified boundaries between Christians and non-Christians, offered clear patterns for Christian behavior, and expanded the range of social activities that were subject to church oversight. To achieve these ends, the narrative had to provide a history of the church that made the ends coherent. It did this by selectively picking particular persons, events, and ideas from the church's past and emphasizing them to the exclusion of other persons, events, and ideas that also constituted that past. That is, the narratives that gained prominence in the fourth century came out of "a reinvention – and to a certain degree redefinition – of a less complicated past,"[16] thereby yet again perpetuating a myth of return.

The second irony follows from the first: the church narrative that was most able to promote ecclesial coherence in the fourth century was the one associated with a militant version of the faith. This was due, in part, to the

[15] H. A. Drake, *Constantine and the Bishops*, 409.
[16] H. A. Drake, *Constantine and the Bishops*, 423.

church's absorption of large numbers of new members and its need to offer a compelling response to Julian's antagonisms. This narrative had been shaped through its opposition to fuzzy theologies and syncretistic visions of faith and it had been refined through its response to the persecutions of the latter half of the third century. As such, its resources were readily available to deal with the fuzziness and syncretisms of a rapidly expanding faith and the challenges presented by Julian. Moreover, the myth of return implicit in this new narrative repeated and drew from the pattern of such returns to earlier and clearer days that had been put into practice by the theologians of nonviolence. Undoubtedly, Tertullian, Origen, and those who shared the stories of the martyrs would likely have been appalled by the way their approach to narrating the history of the church was used for the purposes of using force against heretics and non-Christians. Equally undoubtedly, however, the patterns they put in place for perpetuating myths of return were the best resources for the intolerant church. It was, after all, precisely those segments of the church that were most likely to demand theological clarity and moral purity that achieved prominence in the third and fourth centuries.

It was also these same segments that were least likely to accept the vagaries of politics, the ambiguities of doing theology and ethics under conditions of sin and finitude, and the ambivalences that come with loving the actual neighbors one has rather than demanding that they conform to one's own vision of what the neighbor should be. That is, the church that came into power after Constantine was the church that was least trained in the reflective and mediated use of power. One wonders what a church in which just war thinking was dominant would have done with its new-found powers after 315 C.E. Perhaps the contrasting example of Augustine, the "father of Christian just war thinking," is instructive here: he, too, was willing to use violence against heretics. To judge from his writings, however, reaching that conclusion took more time and effort on his part than it seemed to have taken many other bishops. He never truly seems comfortable with this decision since he also "argued against the notion that anyone should be 'violently coerced to communion by the force of any secular power'"[17] earlier in his career and felt the need to offer

---

[17] H. A. Drake, *Constantine and the Bishops*, 407. The embedded quotation from Augustine is from *The Retractions*. Indeed, on this interpretation of the history of pacifism, I could argue that Augustine should be read not so much as a vocal advocate for violence as a theologian attempting to restrain a trajectory toward unrestrained violence that had been developing in the church since well before Constantine and for which the pre-Constantinian pacifists bear at least partial responsibility. Rather than promoting

apologies for changing his position on the matter later in his career that were based not on theological so much as political reasons (giving priority to the effectiveness of force in combating heresy rather than the faithfulness of force in doing so).

The third irony in all this is that, on Drake's read, Constantine's was the voice of tolerance within Christianity. Whether this tolerance grew out of Constantine's Christian faith is a theological question that, Drake argues, is beyond the scope of his (or, perhaps, anyone's) ability to determine. At a political level, however, Constantine pursued the development of a broad consensus that emphasized noncoercion and patience with other citizens as a way of stabilizing his empire and his rule. Indeed, even his willingness to use troops to quash heretics was a way of keeping the bishops (and, therefore, their power bases among his constituencies) happy – and this willingness came about only after a significant period of reluctance about using troops in this way. Whatever else he was, Constantine was a politician. That made him more comfortable with vagueness and ambiguity than the clarity-seeking bishops and more willing to make and accept compromises than the purity-seeking bishops.

Yet Constantine was a politician whose ear was attuned to arguments for thoughtful and stabilizing engagements within the empire. Among the most prominent of voices making such arguments in his ear was Lactantius (250–325), his Christian advisor. Lactantius had carefully defended Christianity prior to Constantine's conquest of Rome (and had, in fact, served under Diocletian prior to his conversion to Christianity) and blended his training in Greco-Roman rhetoric with Christian apologetics to argue not only for the credibility of the faith but for the underlying freedom that allows people to make faith meaningful. Part of Lactantius's argument against critics of Christianity was that those critics aligned themselves with those who had been willing to use coercion rather than reason against Christians when it was still an illegal religion, persecuting and martyring those who refused to deny their Christian faith. If Constantine's sense of his own conversion shaped the possibility of Christianity being taken as a meaningful faith, Lactantius's understanding of his own conversion helped shape a vision of conversion as a matter of conscience built on the freedom to choose between faiths. Along the way, he also gave voice to the conviction that a faith worth having must

violence, Augustine attempts to offer a vision in which such violence needs to be constrained, directed, and mitigated because it cannot be abolished. This argument, though, needs further reflection, closer detail, and much greater support than I can give here.

emphasize care for the weaker members of society, particularly orphans and widows: "It is no less a great work of justice to protect the destitute children and widows and to defend those needing help which the divine law so prescribes to all."[18] Constantine would even begin his *Oration to the Saints* by describing the church as "the cherisher of tender and inexperienced age, guardian of truth and gentleness."[19]

None of this is to ignore the way Constantine, Lactantius, and the bishops all relied on rhetoric in order to advance their particular political agendas. Constantine wanted personal legitimacy and social stability, Lactantius wanted to justify his own conversion and undermine the arguments of traditional Romans (especially wealthy ones), and the bishops wanted to maintain their growing power while spreading their particular version(s) of the faith. Certainly, both Constantine and the bishops were willing to wield the political tools at their disposal to achieve their objectives. Yet the bishops represented particular constituencies within the empire and so wielded those political tools to achieve the goals of those constituencies, whereas Constantine was emperor over a range of constituencies and so wielded his political tools to achieve the goal of keeping those constituencies from fighting with each other and therein destabilizing the empire. The bishops lobbied but Constantine ruled, so the political resources and goals of each were different. The bishops pursued discrete and not necessarily commensurable agendas against each other and, eventually, against the wider society even to the point of sacrificing their own well-being, but Constantine's agenda was to keep himself in charge, which meant creating an empire in which many different agendas could coincide.[20]

Toward his own ends, Constantine regularly inserted himself into ecclesial conflicts (most notably, the battle between Arius and Athanasius) with the goal of preventing the most violent outcomes, mediating the most combative approaches, and promoting a vision of religion in the public sphere that was broadly inclusive. As Drake notes, "[t]he

[18] Lactantius, *The Divine Institutes*, quoted in H. A. Drake, *Constantine and the Bishops*, 343.

[19] Constantine, *Oration to the Saints*, quoted in H. A. Drake, *Constantine and the Bishops*, 343.

[20] "The relationship between the bishop and his congregation pertains directly to the growth of Christian coercion. Intolerance may underlie the use of coercion, at least in theory, but the connection is not as easy or as direct as it is usually depicted. Local studies have indicated that the bishops were the critical factor in determining how a community responded to the opportunities to coerce." H. A. Drake, *Constantine and the Bishops*, 400.

type of players Constantine was looking for were those who would advance his agenda for a moderate and inclusive Christianity, who would in turn be part of a coalition of Christians and pagans united behind a policy that provided a religiously neutral public space."[21] As a shrewd politician, he likely did so because he wanted to maintain power and the best way to do so was to keep the most moderate of his subjects placid. Yet to judge from his own speeches and actions, Constantine also sought this kind of Christianity because his own faith led him this way – as it also led him to pursue social programs that offered aid to the poor within his empire.

None of this is to say that Constantine is a wholly admirable figure. He pursued his own ends with Machiavellian clarity, had members of his own family killed when he saw them as threats, and played different constituencies off against each other in order to neutralize them while providing the appearance that he was above the fray. Constantine was a warrior, an emperor, and a politician and he behaved like it. Successfully behaving like a warrior, an emperor, and a politician, however, can also mean behaving like a consensus-builder, a moderate voice, and a tolerant leader whose own vision of the empire is as shaped by resistance to the use of coercion as by the use of force. By way of contrast, one need only note the failure of Diocletian to maintain a successful reign or the intemperate and ideologically driven demands of the bishops to see why good politics, in the long run, aligns with nonviolent means where possible and can limit violent means even when they are seen as necessary. It was toward those ends that Constantine established the Edict of Milan – a document that should be seen not so much as making Christianity legal but because it was "the first official government document in the Western world to recognize the principle of freedom of belief."[22] And freedom of belief not only preserves and promotes tolerance in an often-intolerant world, but has served as the foundation of Christian pacifist thought since at least the Reformation.[23]

---

[21] H. A. Drake, *Constantine and the Bishops*, 271.

[22] H. A. Drake, *Constantine and the Bishops*, 194.

[23] I have relied largely on Drake's book in shaping this vision of pacifism and violence at the beginning of the Constantinian age. The direction Drake has taken in reclaiming Constantine and the church of the fourth century from the arguments of those who treat Constantine's rise to power as the onset of the fall of the true church has been, I have noted, enormously instructive to me. However, Drake is not the only scholar reclaiming Constantine. Among other texts about Constantine and the age that challenge the narrative of a Constantinian fall, see Elizabeth DePalma Digeser, *The Making of a Christian Empire: Lactantius and Rome* (Ithaca: Cornell University Press, 1999), Robert Markus, *The End of Ancient Christianity* (Cambridge: Cambridge University

2 LESSONS OF HISTORY

The advent of Constantinianism is significantly more complicated than both his defenders and his critics suggest. It was neither the profound good that church historians like Eusebius described nor the unmitigated disaster that later pacifists would decry. Likewise, both the visions of church-as-triumphant and church-as-victim that follow from such narratives lack nuance. With its newfound access to power, the church after Constantine perpetrated any number of harmful policies and pursued accommodationist trajectories that have continued to bear bitter fruit ever since. However, its access to power did not initiate the church's pursuit of such policies and trajectories; that pursuit was underway for decades before Constantine, having been nursed within growing and power-conscious ecclesial structures. With the benefits of hindsight and careful research in place, such complexity is unsurprising. There are, though, several other generalizable nuggets of wisdom that can also follow from recognition of this complexity, especially for those who would offer a theologically faithful and historically accurate narrative about the church's movement through time. Repeating the pattern established in earlier chapters and building from the general insights named there, we might now include the following:

First, equating persons with larger and longer-running trends in history not only reduces complex persons to stereotypes (or, worse, scapegoats), it inhibits processes for recognizing and charitably incorporating the wisdom of persons and the subtleties of history into narratives that can help structure normative arguments, including those for compassion, peace, and justice. Perpetuating the anachronism of attributing the church's failings beginning in the latter part of the

Press, 1990), Peter Brown, *The Rise of Western Christendom: Triumph and Diversity, A.D. 200–1000, 10th Anniversary Ed.* (Malden, MA: Wiley-Blackwell, 2013), Oliver Nicholson, "*Civitas Quae Adhuc Sustentat Omnia*: Lactantius and the City of Rome" in *The Limits of Ancient Christianity: Essays on Late Antique Thought and Culture in Honor of R. A. Markus*, ed. by William E. Klingshirn and Mark Vessey (Ann Arbor: University of Michigan Press, 1999): 7–25, Hans A. Pohlsander, *The Emperor Constantine*, 2nd ed. (New York: Routledge, 2004), P. J. Leithart, *Defending Constantine: The Twilight of an Empire and the Dawn of Christendom* (Downer's Grove: IVP Academic, 2010), Paolo Prodi, "Corruption in the Church: An Age of Constantine?" in Regina Ammicht Quinn, Lisa Sowle Cahill, and Luis Carlos Susin, *Corruption* (London: SCM Press, 2014): 69–80, and Edward L. Smither, ed., *Rethinking Constantine: History, Theology, and Legacy* (Eugene, OR: Pickwick Publishing, 2014). Most recently, Noel Lenski has published *Constantine and the Cities: Imperial Authority and Civic Politics* (Philadelphia: University of Pennsylvania Press, 2016), an excellent book that builds significantly on earlier work named above but also came out after my completion of this chapter.

fourth century to Constantine's ascension in the first part of that century gets history wrong in ways that are factual, historiographical, structural, moral, and pedagogical.

Factually, attributing the church's failings at the end of the fourth century to Constantine's ascension near its beginning is simply incorrect. If historians have an obligation to offer the best interpretation they can given the data they have access to, and if theologians, ethicists, and others have the obligation of critically honoring the insights of these historians, then no one ought to repeat claims that they know have been shown to be erroneous.

Historiographically, attributing the failings of the latter part of the fourth century to Constantine reveals itself as a form of the "great man" or "rational actor" theory of history. This idea "presumes that . . . a figure has complete freedom of action to achieve goals that he or she has articulated through a careful process of rational analysis involving full and objective study of all pertinent information and alternatives . . . [and who is] so fully in control of the apparatus of government that a decision once made is as good as implemented."[24] Yet freedom, rational analysis, and control are always constrained by physical, psychological, and social forces that impinge on any actor's ability to understand, let alone shape, his or her actions. Worse, having placed undue stock in the power of a great man or woman to shape history, the rational actor theory of history motivates those still living to either seek after or make leaders whose presence and actions change the course of history, elevating "leaders" whose inevitable limits and failings ultimately tend to cause misery and disillusionment.

Structurally, perpetuating the anachronism of attributing the failings of the latter part of the fourth century to Constantine misidentifies the causes of those failings (intolerance, persecution, the illegitimate use of force). It also disables us not only from seeing the actual causes and their complex origins but from recognizing them when we pursue similar patterns of behavior. Blaming Constantine becomes an efficient way to avoid looking at the forces that motivated the church long before it gained the power to cause the harms that it did. If those who forget the past are condemned to repeat it, those who misremember the past in such a way as to avoid complicity with the failings they find there not only repeat it, they cause and/or exacerbate the suffering caused by that repetition.

---

[24] H. A. Drake, *Constantine and the Bishops*, 24.

Morally, perpetuating the anachronism leaves us vulnerable to the indictment of the Golden Rule as it is applied to history. None of us want to be blamed by future generations for failings that are not ours; our own failings, we imagine, are more than sufficient. Why, then, would we be willing to blame those in our own past for failings that were not theirs?

And, pedagogically, perpetuating the anachronism of attributing the failings of the late fourth-century church to Constantine – and therein dismissing him as someone from whom we might learn something – only reduces our conversation partners and ignores the peculiar wisdom that Eusebius, in spite of his overstatements and valorization of Constantine, may have gotten theologically right: God can speak through whomever God wishes and God can act through whomever God wishes. Constantine the emperor promoted social stability through religious tolerance, established programs that provided care for the weaker members of his empire over against a history of ignoring or exacerbating their suffering, and resisted (not, in the end, successfully) calls from the church to persecute heretics. To the degree that tolerance, compassion, and the pursuit of alternatives to violence are virtues central to the pacifist tradition, Constantine becomes a far more interesting conversation partner for (and even participant in) that tradition.[25]

As Bryan Litfin notes, "Emperor Constantine is one of the most frequently drawn caricatures from the historical past ... The judicious use of an eraser – correcting a flaw here, an embellishment there – helps us imagine the first Christian emperor in a more accurate way."[26] Constantine need not be the bugaboo of pacifist history any more than early church fathers like Tertullian need be its exemplars. Better that he – and they – be human, that his – and their – thought be insightful but imperfect, and that he – and they – find charity in our interpretations of

---

[25] Several essays in *Rethinking Constantine: History, Theology, and Legacy* take up this matter, including Brian Shelton's chapter on the impact of Lactantius's thought on "an imperial religious policy in the wake of the Milvian Bridge that was far more tolerant and liberal than might first be imagined" (147). Paul Hartog's chapter on the way the free church, including those communions who have been so critical of the Constantinian turn, continues to rely on and favor worship patterns – including Sabbath worship – that arose from Constantine's engagement with longer traditions of Christian worship, and Edward Smither's chapter on the continued significance of Christian mission work after the rise of the Constantinian church. See Edward L. Smither, ed., *Rethinking Constantine: History, Theology, and Legacy* (Eugene, OR: Pickwick Publishing, 2014).

[26] Bryan M. Litfin, "Epilogue," in Edward L. Smither, *Rethinking Constantine*, 146.

them rather than either condemnation or valorization so that we, too, might be treated as human: insightful but imperfect and with charity.

3 THE ADVENTS OF THE CONSTANTINIAN AGE AND THE ANTHROPOCENE

The history of modern environmental catastrophe, and particularly those catastrophes associated with anthropogenic climate change, is full of unintended and unanticipated consequences, idealistic visions dashed by their confrontations with the baser instincts of human beings, and hypocrisies large and small. So, too, is the history of war. Where environmental change is reshaping conflict, simplified narratives (especially those with the purpose of weighing out blame or claiming distinctly righteous behavior) will not only almost certainly be based on lies; they will conceal some important resources and potentially valuable conversation partners. Richer narratives will be more complicated to use, but on matters as complex as climate-shaped conflict, complicated and even ironic narratives – including, for instance, those that attend to significant expenditures on renewable energy research and production by major petroleum companies and the military pursuit of morally problematic weapons with low environmental costs like drones – may be important to hear.

Structuring arguments and insights in binary terms risks misunderstanding the movement of power through social systems. Over the past several decades, attention to power – the way it pools in some places and streams through others; its multiple forms and the way one form is used to engage another form; the way it simultaneously shapes goals and is used to achieve them; the sometimes surprising limits within its forms that have been determined by biology, psychology, sociology, and language – has become a growing preoccupation within academic guilds, including those associated with philosophy, theology, and history. Whether one relies on classical power theorists like Michel Foucault or Antonio Gramsci, historians like Michel-Rolph Trouillot, psychologists like Alfred Adler, political theorists like Bonnie Honig or John Mearsheimer, feminists like Iris Marion Young or Virginia Held, or others, the study of power has become so important within the social sciences and the humanities that ignoring it is tantamount to academic malpractice.

In most instances, power theorists reject binaries (e.g., strong/weak; rich/poor; oppressor/oppressed) in favor of attention to the way that different persons and groups use distinct sources of power to achieve their particular goals. This is not to say that all forms or pools of power are equivalent. Obviously, some people and groups are stronger than others; some are richer than others; some are oppressive and others are oppressed. However, it can be said that in the complex social systems described by historians – including those systems associated with the Roman Empire and the church during the fourth century – attributing power to one person or group over against another ignores the ways that all groups use the powers at their disposal to achieve particular kinds of goods and ends.

The strength of Drake's work on Constantine lies in the way he attends to Constantine's use of power and its limits, shaped as they are by the powers of other forces including the bishops of the church and the citizens of the empire. Drake also focuses on the bishops' use of power and its limits in engaging Constantine, each other, and their local constituencies. Not only are these just some of the powers at work in the first half of the fourth century, they don't yet begin to address the complex interplays of persons and powers throughout the century nor the way power dynamics can change dramatically. So, for instance, Drake begins with the bishop Athanasius beseeching the Emperor Constantine for support in 335 C.E. and ends with the bishop Ambrose asserting the authority of the church over the emperor Theodosius in 390 C.E. Within a lifetime, power relations between church and state had changed dramatically and, more importantly, they had done so through a series of processes so convoluted and shaped by the vagaries of historical actions and accidents that nobody could have possibly accounted for them, much less deliberately set them in motion. The church was neither static nor monolithic; nor was the empire. Various forms of power were used intentionally, unintentionally, and sometimes, seemingly, in ways that defy assessment according to intentionality.

While the New Testament repeatedly references the limits of human and demonic power in the face of divine power and the limits of the power of the masses in the face of the power of a church that worshipped a Lord whose "power is made perfect in weakness" (2 Corinthians 12:9), it is simply unhelpful to ignore the way the church has always had access to and then used various forms of power for imperfect purposes. So, for instance, David L. Dungan notes that

We look in vain for any record that any bishop or theologian ever objected that Constantine – who was not baptized, had never joined a church, knew little theology, and was not ordained – had no right or authority to do any of [the things he did]. After decades, indeed centuries of resisting imperial harassment and sporadic persecution, why did the church authorities all acquiesce in Constantine's extension of imperial power now, when he suddenly began to ingratiate himself to them? The reason appears plain: to a man, they welcomed the emperor's interventions because they were convinced that he had been given authority to do all these things by their God.[27]

If Dungan is correct that the church welcomed Constantine and his efforts, then either the church had changed so dramatically and suddenly at the ascension of Constantine that it could no longer discern God at work in the world or the church continued to discern and behave in the complex ways – including with regard to the use of force – in which it had always behaved. A narrative that heaps blame on a church outsider like Constantine in order to maintain a vision of the (nonviolent) "true" church misses both the significance of the interactions between emperor and church and the role the church had as a driver in shaping religious intolerance and advocating the use of violence to promote its intolerant positions. Accepting binary relations allows one to build an opponent of straw to knock down, but it also means constructing heroes of straw that cannot support the praise heaped upon them. That is, attention to power in its complexity helps resist both binarity and building with straw.[28]

Power analyses are likely to be especially important and complex in an environmental age. On the one side, power sources will not only become more varied but the fungibility of various forms of power will become more complicated within the context of climate-shaped conflicts. After hundreds of years of thinking of war as primarily fought for political purposes, the return of resource wars, the weaponizing of environmental goods, the

---

[27] David L. Dungan, *Constantine's Bible: Politics and the Making of the New Testament* (Minneapolis: Fortress Press, 2007), 95.

[28] Hans A. Pohlsander's work on Constantine is representative of a more measured assessment. He writes:

> Unlike Nero and Domitian on the one hand and Antoninus Pius and Marcus Aurelius on the other, Constantine cannot simply be assigned to the list of the "bad" emperors or to that of the "good" emperors. Any such attempt would not do justice to the complexity of the record... Some scholars have spoken of a "Constantinian revolution," while others have avoided that term. Why is that so? It is true that in the course of his career Constantine made two epochal decisions: to support Christianity, and to establish a new capital in the East. These decisions, however, did not cause a break with the past in many aspects of the life of the empire. Constantine fostered a new upper class of salaried imperial officials, both civil and military, whose appointment and advancement were based on merit. But there was no radical reordering of society; neither the emperor nor the church seems to have aimed at such.

> Hans A. Pohlsander, *The Emperor Constantine*, 2nd ed. (New York: Routledge, 2004), 90–91.

destabilizing effect of climate refugees, and the reshaping of mutually beneficial alliances (not to mention what will count as mutual benefit), among other things, will lead to a rethinking of the causes, types, exacerbating factors, and understandings of war in a warming world. To the degree that the Christian pacifist tradition will offer its resources toward preventing, reducing, mitigating, and recovering from war, it will need to do so not only on the basis of its own integrity but in light of a growing capacity to apply its own power analyses to conflicts. The good news is that over the past several decades, growing numbers of pacifists have been developing this very capacity, doing so through re-examinations of biblical texts and history. The bad news is that they've not yet done so with an eye to climate-shaped conflict; as such, they will face steep learning curves.

Moreover, to the degree that such power analyses do grow in importance and complexity, they will have to address the real and indirect costs borne by people around the world in light of climate change and the way those costs both motivate and disable wise response. Moreover, even as powers diffuse and diversify, making analysis difficult, power analysts will face growing numbers and types of victims of climate-shaped conflict who behave in morally ambiguous – if not flatly immoral – ways. Already, for instance, the world has seen Somali fishermen who, as their livelihoods have disappeared due to overfishing and climate change, first turned to piracy and then found themselves among the victims of the warlords and other radicals who arose in the face of the political instability that the turn to piracy engendered.[29] More and more people are likely to become victims as a result of the way power flows through climate-shaped conflicts, but they are also likely to become morally ambiguous victims whose own actions reshape or exacerbate power disparities and create new victims of political conflicts and environmental catastrophes.

If "history is a set of stories we tell in order to understand better who we are and the world we're now in,"[30] then the more resources from history we have at our disposal, the richer the stories we tell and, therein, the better we understand who we are and the world in which we now live. Constantine will never be known for the gracefulness of his political

---

[29] See, e.g., Christine Parthemore with Will Rogers, "Sustaining Security: Now Natural Resources Influence National Security" (The Center for a New American Security, June, 2010), 19ff. Available at https://s3.amazonaws.com/files.cnas.org/documents/CNAS_Su staining-Security_Parthemore-Rogers.pdf?mtime=20160906082030. Accessed on June 21, 2016.

[30] Rowan Williams, *Why Study the Past? The Quest for the Historical Church* (Grand Rapids: Eerdmans Publishing Company, 2005), 1.

writings or the insights of his theological ones. Nor will any careful reading of his own sometimes violent history suggest that he ought to be beatified (as he has been). Nevertheless, his actions in working to accommodate the church into the empire, promote tolerance, and care for the least well-off signal his capabilities as a politician and, more importantly, offer insights into processes for avoiding, minimizing, and/or mitigating the causes and sources of violence. Imagine, then, the story that could be told of Constantine as someone who invited the church to engage the empire constructively rather than seduced it to work toward profane ends; as someone who promoted tolerance as an alternative to violence; as someone who put systems in place that centered around the practices of Christian charity rather than the pursuit of purity. Or, more properly, imagine the story that ought to be told of Constantine who invited the church into constructive engagement and who used the church for his own purposes; who promoted tolerance and provided martial resources to the intolerant; and who established systems of care for the poor and of patronage that helped some rise in power, prominence, and wealth. The grace of accepting the resources of history where we find them and as they are provided by persons with whom we would not align ourselves does not so much reveal wishy-washiness or weak convictions as humility, confidence, and wisdom.

In his book, *On Liberty*, John Stuart Mill suggested four reasons we ought to listen to the opinions of those with whom we disagree. First, none of us is infallible and so all of us need to treat others' opinions as at least potentially true. Second, the opinions of others, even if erroneous in the whole, may still contain portions of truth that we need to hear. Third, even if our own opinions turn out to be true, if we don't allow them to enter the fray of discourse with other opinions, we cannot distinguish our opinions from prejudice. And, fourth, the alternative to vital engagement with others is deadening dogmatism.[31] Perhaps the theological equivalent to Mill's arguments is that proposed by the Swiss theologian Karl Barth, who wrote that God could speak through a flute concerto or a dead dog.[32] If God can speak through a dead dog, then surely God can speak through a conversation partner – no matter how long dead, how presumably antagonistic, or how cumbersome and flawed – with whom we disagree. We are enriched in our own lives and our own understandings of the

---

[31] John Stuart Mill, *On Liberty* (Buffalo, NY: Prometheus Books, 1986), 60–61.
[32] Karl Barth, *Church Dogmatics*, vol. I, part 1 (Edinburgh: T&T Clark, 2nd edition, 1975), 55.

world when we listen charitably to others. The Quaker theologian George Fox meant something like this when he called on persons to "walk cheerfully over the world, answering that of God in all persons."[33]

The way Lactantius is treated in the literature is an interesting case study in this regard. Early in his career, Lactantius had written powerfully of the mandate for pacifism:

For when God forbids us to kill, He not only prohibits us from open violence, which is not even allowed by the public laws, but He warns us against the commission of those things which are esteemed lawful among men. Thus it will be neither for a just man to engage in warfare, since his warfare is justice itself, nor to accuse any one of a capital charge, because it makes no difference whether you put a man to death by word, or rather by the sword, since it is the act of putting to death itself which is prohibited. Therefore, with regard to this precept of God, there ought to be no exception at all; but that it is always unlawful to put to death a man, whom God willed to be a sacred animal.[34]

Yet later in his life, Lactantius's opinion on the matter had shifted. After Constantine, Lactantius could defend killing in defense of some goods. How, then, to account for the shift? Some modern pacifist historians (e.g., Bainton, Heering, Hershberger, Orr) ignore the shift, picking up only on the statements that Lactantius made prior to Constantine's reign. Others (Cadoux) emphasize Lactantius's pacifist writings while noting in passing that later in his career, Lactantius had eulogized Constantine as a warrior and emperor without attending to the shift that writings from the two periods suggests. And still others (Hornus) attend to the shift but describe it as evidence of the church's fall from its true form into something Augustinian.

That the shift occurred is hard to dispute. The nature and degree of that shift, though, are harder factors to discern. Some of the notes that Lactantius struck in *The Divine Institutes* – for instance, those concerning the need for freedom in choosing a faith – continue into his later writings such as *De Mortibus Prosecutorum*. And others – the strict opposition to taking life – have fallen away. Recognizing the limited number of resources available to us in making sense of the shift, it is difficult to offer a compelling case one way or another on what motivated the shift and how dramatic it was. Certainly, though, Lactantius was a voice in

---

[33] George Fox, *Works*, vol. 1. 1831 edition, p. 288, cited in G. Amoss, "George Fox: An Exhortation to Friends in the Ministry," accessed on September 29, 2015, http://www.qis.net/~daruma/exhortation.html

[34] Lactantius, *The Divine Institutes*, quoted in Michael G. Long, *Christian Peace and Nonviolence*, 36–37.

Constantine's ear, whispering of the importance of freedom from having religion imposed by force and the need for tolerance within an empire where many religions were practiced.[35]

Into the question of the church's transition, though, it is a sign worth interpreting that of the many writings that come from the church during the period between Constantine's conquest of Rome and his death in 337, none of them reject Constantine's rise or his methods. And even later in that century, the texts tend not so much to prohibit taking life as to favor living peaceably (with the possible exception of Paulinus of Nola [352–431]). It is highly doubtful that such writings were ignored and even more doubtful that they were suppressed. And while the church was certainly aware of the dramatic changes going on within the empire, the absence of attention to this presumed change with regard to violence suggests either that the church had become far more comfortable with violence than the pacifist narrative allows, that the writers of the time saw themselves in continuity with their pre-Constantinian forebears, and/or that violence wasn't so pressing an issue for the church once it wasn't being aimed at the church. Lactantius is, perhaps, helpful here; his writings suggest a sense of theological and moral continuity in the midst of dramatic social and political change.

More generally, they suggest that resources don't divide nearly so neatly into "favoring" and "opposing" as the conventional pacifist narrative suggests – all of which returns to the larger argument here: the more resources from history we have at our disposal, the richer the stories we tell and, therein, the better we understand who we are and the world we're now in. And we're likely to have more resources at our disposal – including surprising ones – if we don't assess them as either with us or against us but instead treat them as resources offered by human beings from one age to other human beings in another. As resources of human beings, they are imperfect: coming from a different time and place, they don't entirely fit our own time and place. Since they sit within a tradition that has shaped us, though, it is better to have them to learn from than not. As Charles Mathewes notes, "A tradition is an ongoing act of forgiveness. We inherit our ability to reflect from our elders, and we come to see that their tools only imperfectly fit the problems we face; hence, unless we wish to totally jettison our minds, we find ourselves compelled to work through that

---

[35] For an excellent book on Lactantius, see Elizabeth DePalma Digeser, *The Making of a Christian Empire: Lactantius and Rome* (Ithaca: Cornell University Press, 1999).

inheritance, accepting its imperfections, and this acceptance involves, indeed just *is* in part, forgiveness."[36]

Such forgiveness is especially important across social imaginaries for at least two related reasons. First, the project of interpreting the thoughts and practices from one social imaginary while situated within another is difficult in ways that are both obvious (social priorities may differ) and subtle (the meanings of the same words may differ). As a result, trying to understand how and why others thought and acted as they did in order to understand those thoughts, actions, and persons mandates a self-conscious – if temporary – suspension of judgment on the part of interpreters. Empathy, though perhaps not much discussed in the literature of historiography, is a fundamental virtue of careful historians simply because they wish to understand those in other times and places. They need not agree with those in other times and places. Critical engagement is another virtue of careful historians, if only because they have resources at their disposal for understanding those other times and places that the people they study do not and their obligation includes using those resources to better locate the ideas, practices, and technologies in wider historical scope. Also, where empathy and critical engagement join, forgiveness (joining, as it does, judgments against another and a refusal to condemn another on the basis of those judgments) is likely to follow. That those in the Christian pacifist traditions have given inadequate attention to the natural world in their theologies of peace and violence is a kind of judgment. That those in the Christian pacifist traditions failed to give adequate attention to the natural world in their theologies because they were focused on making sense of other genuine goods and pursuing other legitimate projects is an expression of empathy. Pursuing resources within the Christian pacifist traditions that will help pacifists attend to the natural world in more faithful and helpful ways is a form of forgiveness.

A second reason to emphasize forgiveness across social imaginaries turns on the self-consciously reflexive recognition that, much as we make judgments about those who came before us, we will be judged by those who follow us. Just as we seek to evaluate past imaginaries, they may be using resources, criteria, and values that may be quite different from our own. We are no more likely to be beyond reproach than those who came before us are likely to avoid reproach from us. As a way of shaping the virtues carried into the future and admitting to our interests in

---

[36] Charles Mathewes, *Evil and the Augustinian Tradition* (New York: Cambridge University Press, 2001), 69.

the qualities of our own legacies, then, it is in our own interests that we display forgiveness in our assessments of persons from earlier social imaginaries. When exploring matters as morally troubling as the systematic use of violence to achieve political ends and as theologically discordant as the significance of creation in Christian thought, nobody is likely to come out "smelling like roses." To paraphrase from Jesus's Sermon on the Mount, if you forgive others their trespasses, those who come after you will also forgive you; but if you do not forgive others, neither will those who come after you forgive your trespasses.[37]

A final general insight that might conclude this chapter is this: history is marked by both slow continuous and rapid discontinuous change. The causes and natures of these changes, though, are complex and often the product of unintended events and unforeseeable consequences. As such, simple explanations and immoderate judgments about such changes are generally deceptive and unhelpful. One component of the larger project of which this book is a part is the attempt to offer a theologically interesting and evidentially compelling account of how traditions move through time. In this attempt, I have argued for the need to attend to both continuous and slow change over time and also rapid and discontinuous change. Certainly, with Constantine's rise to power, the church went through a period of rapid change within only a few decades. From the perspective of the pacifist tradition, that period was also so discontinuous and troubling as to amount to a fall from its original vision and purpose. This perspective not only ignores the continuities of thought and action as they were expressed by the church during these transitions, but the complexities of the subject matter and the absence of scholarly consensus. As Hans A. Pohlsander notes, "[T]here is no consensus of scholarly opinion on important aspects of Constantine's person and reign. Not surprisingly, it is especially in the religious sphere that we note this lack of consensus."[38]

Constantine, Lactantius, Julian, and the bishops weren't the only actors of the age any more than Justin Martyr, Tertullian, and Origen were the only theologians of the pre-Constantinian centuries. The Battle at Milvian Bridge, the Edict of Milan, the Council of Nicaea, and the

---

[37] Matthew 6:14: "For if you forgive others their trespasses, your heavenly Father will also forgive you; but if you do not forgive others, neither will your Father forgive your trespasses." (NRSV)

[38] Hans A. Pohlsander, *The Emperor Constantine*, 90. See, also, the Pohlsander quote from footnote 30 above.

Theodosian Decrees weren't the only events of church history during the fourth century any more than the spread of Christianity into Europe and northern Africa and the martyrdoms of Diocletian were the only events prior to Constantine. The rise of ecumenical councils and growth of the monastic tradition were not the only ecumenical movements in the fourth century any more than the expanding forms of apologetics and the rise of heretical communities were the only movements of the second and third centuries. And certainly the notion that the church's history can be divided into a short period of a few hundred years at its beginning and a long period stretching from 313 to the twentieth century can't stand up to the sheer volume of changes that the church has undergone since Constantine died. Arguments to the contrary (and, for that matter, arguments premised on that division of history) serve particular rhetorical purposes for describing the state of the contemporary church, not formal purposes for describing the long existence of the historic church. As Paolo Prodi notes,

[t]he historian's idea or paradigm of the "Age of Constantine" as a long time span in the history of the Church from the fourth century up to today was conceived during the first half of the twentieth century by theologians (from Karl Barth onwards) to call for church reform and a return to a "primitive state." ... I have always thought this call ... was an evasion of the Church's responsibility as a body and of the need for a deeper theological inquiry into the meaning of its presence in the history of salvation. It has become a device to avoid the problem of the historicity of church institutions and their development, which somehow manages to relegate outside the body of the Church responsibility for the undeniable power system which the Church itself developed over the centuries.[39]

This isn't to say that such rhetorical purposes don't have their place in contemporary arguments. Concerns about "Constantinianism" having to do with the multiple and sometimes problematic interrelationships between church, state, and society in western culture certainly warrant attention. There is a place for what philosopher Richard Rorty called "strong misreadings" of ideas and history.[40] It is, though, to say that such purposes ought to be noted as such rather than treated as foundational claims about the shape of the history of the church that can't bear the weight of such ecclesial importance. The present, like history, is complicated; explaining it, like telling history, should be so as well.

---

[39] Paolo Prodi, "Corruption in the Church: An Age of Constantine?", 69–70.

[40] See Richard Rorty, *Contingency, Irony, and Solidarity* (New York: Cambridge University Press, 1989).

The complications of telling history involve recognizing the way actors, events, and movements not only all interact with each other but the way each has been shaped by social forces that extend far back in time. So, for example, the church's growing acceptance of the use of force is only possible because the church had, over time, been shaping itself toward that end. Or, for another example, the first ecumenical council in Nicaea could only have come about because the church had slowly been establishing centers of authority (i.e., bishops) scattered throughout the cities of the empire and because the bishops didn't all agree with each other on various theological matters even while they shared a common commitment to the growing Christian faith. Even Constantine's willingness to interpret his vision of the *labarum* prior to the Battle of Milvian Bridge as a sign from the Christian God was the product of many forces and persons (apologetic defenses of the rationality of Christianity against pagan philosophers, the impact of Lactantius's teaching within his court, the rapid spread of Christianity throughout the empire, the failings of Diocletian rule and persecutions, etc.) that preceded the vision by decades and centuries.

Abrupt and discontinuous change, then, is the product of the social forces actively shaping steady and continuous change. Perhaps these forces achieve new levels of success that clear the way for discontinuous change by displacing or mitigating the impact of countervailing social forces. Perhaps these forces come into opposition with each other and the conflict between them leads to rapid change when neither triumphs. Perhaps the failings of established social forces become apparent as new ideas, technologies, and concerns arise. The point is that discontinuous change shouldn't be understood as the consequence of a single actor, event, or movement.

Nowhere is this more likely to be the case than in the transition into the Anthropocene. Up to this point in human history, we have largely been able to ignore the impact of social forces shaping planetary change simply because those forces did not have the capacity to affect such change. That is not only no longer the case, but the ways that myriad social forces do shape discontinuous change across cultures and nature are far more complex than anything human beings have yet encountered in their projects of making sense of the world. Climatologists are showing us that causes can be multiplied, consequences unanticipated, effects delayed, feedback loops unknown, and the power to bring about change diffused at levels previously unimaginable. Indeed, one way of interpreting the almost wholly misplaced debates about the existence of anthropogenic climate change is seeing them as arising from our failures to imagine the previously unimaginable.

The preceding paragraphs may comfort historians who call us to attend to the complexity of our movement through time. They are less likely to satisfy theologians who still ask a nagging question: what has God to do with all this? After all, the first great Christian historian, Eusebius, treated Constantine's rise to power as evidence of a divine plan through which Christianity would triumph. Not only does Eusebius's narrative unduly simplify history, it ignores the mysterious ways of God that are always discerned and never obvious. Indeed, it is ironic that Eusebius is so clearly a "bad guy" not only to historians (Burckhardt called him "the first thoroughly dishonest historian of antiquity"[41]) but to pacifist theologians who condemn him for celebrating Constantine and supporting the use of violence, since the conventional pacifist narrative condemns Constantine and the fourth-century church's use of violence through a method that Eusebius employs; namely, theologically interpreting God's work in history in ways that are too simple.

How, then, might we theologically interpret God's actions in history? Toward addressing that question, we turn to the long stretch of the history of Christian pacifism between the fourth and the nineteenth centuries. Throughout that history, particular individuals and, especially, communities asking that question regularly addressed it through a series of appeals to Scripture and the God described therein.

---

[41] Jacob Burckhardt, *The Age of Constantine the Great* (New York: Pantheon Books, 1949), 283.

5

Pacifist Interpretations of 1500 Years of Faith, Community, and Nonviolence

According to the conventional narrative of Christian pacifism, once Theodosius declared Christianity the official religion of the Roman Empire in 380 C.E., fidelity to the nonviolent ethic of Jesus would express itself almost exclusively in a few remarkable individuals (e.g., Paulinus of Nola [352–431], Francis of Assisi [1182–1226], Erasmus [1469–1536], and radical reformers such as Conrad Grebel, Menno Simons, Michael Sattler, and Jakob Hutter) or in relatively small and scattered groups (e.g., the Benedictines [c. 529], the Cathars [twelfth century], the Lollards [late fourteenth century], and the churches of the Radical Reformation [Brethren, Mennonites, Quakers, and their offshoots]). Even the few exceptions to this narrative in which the imperial church behaved in nonviolent ways (e.g., the Peace of God in the late tenth century and the Truce of God in the eleventh century) are understood as limiting, rather than prohibiting, violence and understood as operating in the breach more than as being observed.

For instance, among the major historians of Christian nonviolence,[1] Cadoux concludes his work with a few comments about Ambrose and Augustine, and Hornus with Martin of Tours (356); both therein reinforcing the idea that the earliest church got it right and things fell apart after Constantine. In their defense, both describe their books as exploring

---

[1] Here, just by way of reminder, it's important to note that I'm excluding the work of John Howard Yoder (which I will take up in a separate chapter) and Michael G. Long's edited book *Christian Peace and Nonviolence*. I exclude the former because Yoder is an especially interesting, provocative, and important historian to take up and the latter because Long's book is a collection of primary sources and doesn't offer an (explicit) narrative of the history of pacifism and nonviolence.

112

early Christian attitudes toward war and so might be let off the hook for not going further forward in time; after all, why condemn people for failing to complete projects other than the one they intended? Yet such a defense still needs to attend to the facts that:

a) The choice of when to end their respective studies is not arbitrary; they've prioritized that which they thought was most important.

b) Their texts are used by other historians of pacifism to justify a particular telling of history in which the early church got it right and things fell apart after Constantine; and,

c) Both write their texts as a way of addressing Christian attitudes toward war generally, not just in the first several centuries C.E. That is, they both write to resolve endemic (and contemporary) problems by recourse to only the first few centuries.

Beyond Cadoux and Hornus, other historians of pacifism include longer histories. Orr writes that "Pre-Reformation and Reformation sects can for the most part be dealt with briefly"[2] and then does so, working his way through the Cathars, Waldenses, and Lollards in less than half a page before arriving at the Anabaptists,[3] who get five pages before Orr reaches the twentieth century in a short chapter entitled "Revivals of the Ancient Testimony." Hershberger is slightly more generous, providing almost an entire page (though with few details) for the time between Augustine and the Reformation and then another two pages on Lutherans and Calvinists before beginning his documentation of the peace churches' histories. Those churches – especially the Mennonites – get about twenty pages of treatment to encompass the length and breadth of their witness between their start in the sixteenth century and the American Civil War.

---

[2] Edgar W. Orr, *Christian Pacifism*, 86.

[3] "Anabaptist" is something of a derogatory term as it means "baptizing over again" or re-baptizing, which communions who identify themselves with the Radical Reformation don't recognize themselves as doing, arguing instead that baptism is for believers and so any prior baptisms given to infants or children simply shouldn't be understood as baptisms. The term was originally used pejoratively by those who persecuted such communions and is seldom used by members of such communions. Of course "radical reformers" isn't necessarily value-neutral either, leaving open questions about what makes a reformer "radical." As a rule, I will refer to "peace churches" or "historic peace churches," (recognizing that there are examples of communions that are part of the radical reformation that are not peace churches such as the Münsterites and the Batenburgers) and use the term "Anabaptist" only when explicating a position held by someone else who uses the term.

Roland Bainton offers a more complex treatment of pacifism after Augustine, blending its history into the larger history of Christian engagements with violence, including Just War and Crusade approaches to such matters. Braiding the histories of these three strands of Christian thought (pacifism, just war, crusade) through sixteen centuries, 120 pages, and seven chapters, Bainton covers major and minor figures and movements without losing the thread of his larger argument about Christian attitudes toward war and peace. That thread consists of his conviction that from among the three traditions, only pacifism is both faithful and coherent: having weighed both crusade and just war thinking and found them wanting, he is left to argue that "[i]f the crusade and the just war are rejected as Christian positions, pacifism alone remains. The writer takes this view."[4]

Toward reaffirming that view, Bainton's summary and analysis of the history of Christian attitudes towards war and peace follows a pattern in which pacifism is best (Christian humanists, Anabaptists, and Enlightenment thinkers sound remarkably similar to each other, collectively driven by their intellectual and moral aversion to violence) and non-pacifist traditions are, at best, faltering echoes of pacifist convictions.[5] According to Bainton, the non-pacifist traditions pursued reasoning based in natural law, displacing the unique wisdom of the gospels, thereby reinforcing the peculiar binarity between pacifism and all alternatives at epistemological levels. The Peace of God and the Truce of God in the eleventh century and Christian humanism in the sixteenth collapse into just war; just war blurs, almost inevitably, into crusade; nominally pacifist and avowedly heretical communions revert to violence when pressed; the intermingled powers of the state and powers of the church bring out the worst in both. On Bainton's telling of history, there is pacifism and everything else that is not pacifism.

Bainton's genius consists of his ability to offer an outline of the history of war and peace in Christian thought without losing his consistent emphasis on the priority of pacifism or the soft (and occasionally not-so-soft) prejudices of a scholar who thought that things had gone horribly wrong after Constantine. The church's entrance into the Middle Ages thus

---

[4] Roland Bainton, *Christian Attitudes Toward War and Peace*, 248.

[5] "The Church [in the thought of Thomas Aquinas] sought thus to repristinate and by adaptation to conserve the just-war theory as a restraint upon war. But better far would it be if there was no war, and valiant efforts were made for its eradication." Roland Bainton, *Christian Attitudes Toward War and Peace*, 109.

is seen to proceed from the barbarian invasions and theological divisions of the early fifth century and into a period that "began in chaos, with pacifism in recession and the code of the just war violated in practice and strained in theory. The Church struggled to subdue the warlike propensities of the Northern peoples and to allay their feuds through a great peace movement, which curiously was turned into a crusade when a plea for peace at home ended in a summons to war against the infidel abroad."[6] This is the approach that allows him to treat pacifism as the fundamental ethic of the church and just war and crusade as either corrupted versions of that ethic or non-Christian alternatives to it in spite of the facts that pacifism wasn't nearly so clearly the fundamental ethics of the church that Bainton describes, that Christian just war thinking, if not principles, predates Constantine by a century at least, and that such thinking finds grounds in Scripture as well as natural law.

Among the problems that result from such a reading is the blurring together of centuries of history as Bainton jumps around between episodes and arguments on his way to making his case. So, for example, Chapter 7, "From the Just War to the Crusade and Sectarian Pacifism," vertiginously treats "Medieval" as an unchanging state of affairs that lasted a thousand years rather than a long stretch of history in which things changed. Toward making such a case, Bainton, as a modern pacifist, judges much that comes after Constantine in quasi-anachronistic ways (as, for instance, when he argues that an ill-defined "theory of universals presents a threat to individualism"[7]). On one page, we read that "[t]he churches of the Reformation, with the exception of the Anabaptist, all endorsed a theory of the just war as basic"[8] only to be told a page later that "the Reformed Churches moved in the direction of the crusade, partly because they became involved in wars of religion and partly because of their theocratic concept of the Church ... in a sense in the succession of Thomas Muentzer,"[9] therein suggesting an incoherence in their political ecclesiology without much support and connecting them to a figure who had rejected Lutheran and Reformed perspectives on the way to advancing his own vision of theology. We're left in the peculiar position of reading a great church historian who sees the bulk of the history of the church (sixteen of its twenty centuries) as a vast dark expanse disrupted by brief

---

[6] Roland Bainton, *Christian Attitudes Toward War and Peace*, 102.
[7] Roland Bainton, *Christian Attitudes Toward War and Peace*, 107.
[8] Roland Bainton, *Christian Attitudes Toward War and Peace*, 142.
[9] Roland Bainton, *Christian Attitudes Toward War and Peace*, 143.

points of illumination, regardless of the profound ideas, moving testimonies, and world-bettering activities that took place over that time.[10]

Put more directly, Bainton's entirely appropriate focus on war and peace in Christian thought, once combined with his prioritization of pacifism as central to Christian ethics, leaves his telling of this history untethered from much of the rest of the history of the church in the west. Given that Bainton published nearly forty monographs on a wide range of topics (the reformations, heretics and their heresies, particularly prominent theologians, ideas, and art, and a variety of issues with which the church contends), sixty-odd chapters in anthologies, and over 150 articles, it is hard to imagine any other context in which so prominent a historian – especially one best known for his work on the Reformation – gives such short shrift to the goods of history in so prominent a text. Contrast his treatment of war and peace, for instance, with his more evenhanded, if shorter, treatment of sex, love, and marriage, which receive more charitable and broadly equivalent treatment throughout the history of the church and without the emphasis on a return to the pre-Constantinian church.[11]

I RECONSIDERING REFORMATIONS AND THE MYTH OF RETURN

This brief rehearsal of the treatment of the history of pacifism on the part of the major historians of pacifism brings to the fore at least two important questions: Why is so little attention given to the Reformation? Additionally, why does this treatment give such a uniformly negative view of so much of history?

An answer to those questions begins in the recognition that, at least methodologically and historiographically, very little actually changes during the Reformation from the perspective of the pacifist historians. The peace churches of the Reformation don't constitute a new way of

---

[10] A further bit of evidence worth interpreting on how Bainton relates pacifism to Christian thought: he scatters repeated sections on various expressions of pacifism throughout his book, giving three pages to medieval pacifism (Francis, the Hussites), eight pages to humanist pacifism (Montaigne, Erasmus), fourteen pages to the historic peace churches (of which Quakers absorb ten of those pages), and eleven pages to enlightenment thinkers (Voltaire, Rousseau). By contrast, Thomas gets about a page, Luther gets six pages, the Reformed churches get five, and Cromwell and the Puritans five (and Henry VIII gets a vague sentence and Anglicanism begins with the American Revolutionary War).

[11] See Roland Bainton, *What Christianity Says about Sex, Love, and Marriage* (New York: Association Press, 1957).

being pacifists or being churches in the world so much as yet another expression of the way a few discrete groups and enlightened individuals within the Christian tradition have always found pacifism and engaged the world. Like earlier communities and individuals, the peace churches "rediscovered" the original moral vision of Jesus Christ and the early church as they read the New Testament and tried to live into that moral vision.[12] In this, these churches were, paradoxically, claiming a central insight of the Reformation (that Scripture is uniquely authoritative and broadly sufficient as the basis for shaping ecclesiology and ethics) in order to downplay the significance of their own location as interpreters of texts and shapers of ecclesiology and ethics. The peace churches of the Reformation were attempting to pattern their way of life on that of the church during its first few centuries, not to shape a new ethic for the sixteenth.

[12] Unsurprisingly, the Sermon on the Mount from Matthew was especially prominent among the New Testament texts to which these small, embattled, and faithful communities turned in order to find themselves and shape their ethic. So, e.g., in his commentary on Matthew 1–7, Ulrich Luz mixes descriptive and normative claims when he writes,

The most fruitful thought is that the Matthean theology can be understood frankly as a classical example of "sect theology," i.e., as a theological draft of a minority group which was led by Jesus to *its* life-principle of obedience and love. Matthean theology is basically perfectionistic... The examples from the history of interpretation which will be given with the comments on the individual texts will show that it was again and again such small groups for which the Sermon on the Mount was central and which came very close to its meaning. Examples are the early church in the time before Constantine, early monasticism and church fathers close to it such as John Chrysostom, medieval marginal groups of the Reformation period, particularly the Anabaptists, also the Quakers and early Methodists. They all advocate a "perfectionist" type of interpretation. For all of them the command of God was a basic and immovable element in their piety and their life. It is astonishing in what measure one can find in these groups analogies to the Matthean design. In comparison to this, it is amazing how distant the main churches are from the Sermon on the Mount.

(Ulrich Luz, *Matthew 1–7: A Continental Commentary*, trans. by Wilhelm C. Linss [Minneapolis: Fortress Press, 1989], 219.) That marginal Christian groups find themselves in the Sermon on the Mount is unsurprising; that it should be read in perfectionist ways and that "main churches" are distant from it, though, is a different question. Contrast Luz's claims in this paragraph with two volumes on the reception history of the Sermon on the Mount (Clarence Bauman, *The Sermon on the Mount: The Modern Quest for Its Meaning* [Macon, GA: Mercer University Press, 1985] and Jeffrey P. Greenman, Timothy Larsen, and Stephen R. Spencer [eds.], *The Sermon on the Mount Through the Centuries: From the Early Church to John Paul II* [Grand Rapids: Brazos Press, 2007]), which reveal not only that the text has been interpreted in a variety of ways but that it has never been too far removed from the thoughts of Christians throughout history.

Likewise, the pacifist historians of the twentieth century were attempting to emphasize a first-century Jesus ethic, not a sixteenth-century peace church one. For such historians, darkness is pervasive in history except where light shines from the early church of the first centuries C.E. The language of Mennonite political theologian James Reimer is representative and breathtakingly broad here:

Already in the fourth century, the monastic movement (anchorites and cenobites), in their retreat from the centers of power and culture into the desert to live out the teaching of Jesus as expressed in the Sermon on the Mount, were implicitly if not explicitly protesting the Constantinian synthesis of Christ and culture, the Christian church and state. Some early Christian groups that were anathematized as heretics by those who were able to define the nature of "orthodoxy" – groups such as the Donatists and Pelagians for instance – might be considered part of this anti-Constantinian tradition in their call for a purer, uncompromising church. In the Middle Ages, various sectaries like the twelfth-century followers of Peter Waldo in Italy (the Waldensians), Wycliffe and his fourteenth-century followers in England, the fifteenth-century Hussites in Czechoslovakia, and others denounced the Constantinian church, calling for a restitution of the early New Testament church. In the modern period, those dissenting groups have found themselves within the so-called Free Church tradition, beginning in the sixteenth century with the Anabaptists and Mennonites, and continuing with dissenting groups from within the Church of England (Brownists, late sixteenth century; Baptists, early seventeenth century; Quakers; mid-seventeenth century; Methodists, eighteenth century) and the later Church of the Brethren and Brethren in Christ (nineteenth century), Pentecostals and numerous evangelical groups (twentieth century). All would to a greater or lesser degree reject the Constantinian shift in favor of a return to pre-Constantinian, "primitive" Christianity.[13]

Why model your community and its ethic on one from the fourth, twelfth, sixteenth, or any other century when that community was, itself, attempting to model itself and its ethic on one from the first and second centuries? If you feel that you are a part of a small and embattled community surrounded by a great "foreign" empire – a small and embattled community that is, nevertheless, founded upon a vision in which God's way of working in the world aligns with your own and God's way of working is ultimately triumphant – what better model can there be than

---

[13] A. James Reimer, *Toward an Anabaptist Political Theology: Law, Order, and Civil Society*, ed. by Paul G. Doerksen (Eugene, OR: Cascade Books, 2014), 57–58. Reimer is especially interesting in this regard as he is critical of the emphasis on a "Constantinian fall" that is so representative of modern pacifist thought even as he repeats the myth of return within that thought.

the small and embattled New Testament church that was surrounded by the Roman Empire and so intimately connected to Jesus?

On the one hand, this mimetic project has clear advantages. It offers a comparatively clear ethic and a means through which to identify oneself and one's community with the founding church: morality and ecclesiology, surely among the most important components of a viable and practicable Christian community, are emphasized. It gives prominence to the authority of Scripture, providing a means of adjudicating potential conflicts and a brake on appeals to more arbitrary sources of authority. It clarifies the church's locations vis-a-vis surrounding cultures that recognize the distinctive shape of Christian community without downplaying the importance of and need for God's continuing work in transforming church and world. It locates its theological center in the life and work of Jesus, therein providing a particular vision of the divine upon which to build a meaningful doctrine of God that can be manifested in worship.

Yet there are also problems with the project. The ethic, though clear, is perfectionist in shape and thereby not only sits in tension with confessional awareness and empirical evidence of the imperfections of the lives of individuals and groups, but initiates ecumenical relations from a position of moral disapprobation. The ecclesiology glosses over complex questions about how two communities existing in different places and times are, necessarily, also going to be different and ignores the implications of those differences. It emphasizes some Scriptures over others without offering reason for such emphases that, themselves, are grounded in the authority of Scripture, thereby opening itself to arbitrary uses of the authority of Scripture. It downplays the degree to which Christians never exist in one community but are always participants in many communities, only one of which is the particular manifestation of "church" to which they link themselves. It has tended to emphasize a particular version of Christology over against a more fully Trinitarian vision of God. The mimetic project's strengths are also the sites of its weaknesses.

This, in itself, is neither surprising nor distinctly problematic. Any community's (and any ethic's) weaknesses tend to be expressions of the shadow side of its strengths. Yet there are other concerns having to do with how such communities locate themselves in history that come with the mimetic move so characteristic of Christian pacifism. The mimetic move tends to downplay other resources in history – especially those that arose after Constantine – and to ignore the failings of the resources that came prior to Constantine. It promotes a vision of pacifist communities as isolated from each other in space and time. It treats instances of a community "discovering" the teachings of Jesus as novel events. It lends itself toward treating most of the history of the church as something to be overcome, not only ignoring the trajectories of thought and action that have shaped those communities but also tacitly advancing a doctrine of God in which God doesn't seem to be doing much beyond fighting rearguard actions between the time of the New Testament church and the eschatological consummation of all things. Lacking such trajectories, it struggles to imagine a future in which gradual change and further improvement – imperfect though those changes and improvements be – are not only good but meaningful.

These are historiographic problems that arise out of a myth of return. Having shaped so discontinuous a vision of history, conventional narratives of the history of Christian pacifism leave themselves, ironically, isolated from history and shorn of a wide range of resources by which they can make sense of the world around them and God's work in it. Where discontinuity dominates such narratives, the threads of continuity through which Christian communities weave coherent narratives of their existence are weakened.

Is there a way, though, to honor the energy that motivates the conventional narratives of the history of Christian pacifism without succumbing to the historiographic problems that arise out of the myth of return? Likewise, is there a way to recognize that no viable Christian narrative of the movement of the church (or God) through time can treat history as a clear and continuous unfolding of divine plans and ever-improving human action? To admit that discontinuity must be part of such Christian narratives? To confess to the failings of the church and individual Christians to live up to their own best visions of their life and work in the world – failings that have heaped enormous amounts of suffering upon that world? To join attention paid to the obligations of fidelity to the Christian God with attention to the work of that God in all of history?

Perhaps the problem isn't with the existence of discontinuity in the conventional narrative of the history of Christian pacifism but with the theological vision that undergirds the structure of that discontinuity. In the conventional narrative, discontinuities arise out of the vagaries of history and the failings of the post-Constantinian church and are driven by the justifiable sense that the Jesus ethic as described, especially, in the Sermon on the Mount doesn't align with the behavior of the church. In that narrative, a myth of return is all but mandated not only for moral and ecclesial reasons but for existential ones as well: there simply is no other location in time and place from which to draw so coherent and stable a vision of life in the world. As a result, anything short of or different from pacifist engagement must be understood as an expression of the church's failure to live into its pacifist essence: just war thinking and any other Christian defense of the use of violence are expressions of imperfection and inadequate regard for the core values of the church rather than expressions of how Christians might act on the basis of standards that also make claims to be core values of the church.

One of the problems with this narrative is that it elides two questions: "What does it mean to be faithful to the Jesus of the New Testament?" and "What does it mean to be faithful to the God described in the New Testament?" The New Testament is, after all, rich not only in stories about Jesus but in descriptions of him and his work – and those descriptions don't all align with each other.[14] Indeed, the early history of the church consists, necessarily, of a series of debates about how to understand the person and work of Jesus that may begin for the church in New Testament texts but hardly end there. For instance, the New Testament is not univocal about how Jesus of Nazareth relates to the God described in the Old Testament – let alone to the Holy Spirit or the Holy Spirit's relationship to the God described in the Old Testament. Nor is it univocal about the relationship between the "fully human" and "fully divine" sides of Jesus or about how to understand the relationships between Jesus's incarnation, life, teachings, works, death, and resurrection. Nor, for that matter, is it univocal about how those things impact the lives of individual believers and the church. The very variety of answers within these debates drives each particular expression of the church to look beyond a particular subset of texts as the basis for its ethic, to engage other perspectives, and to recognize any single perspective as participating in a longer, wider, and larger set of conversations that stretch through the history of the church catholic.

Answering the former question – about fidelity to the Jesus of the New Testament – is already more complicated than some pacifist approaches admit. Which Jesus in which texts and why that Jesus?

---

[14] See, for instance, David Bartlett, *What's Good about This News? Preaching from the Gospels and Galatians* (Louisville, KY: Westminster-John Knox Press, 2003) for the way five different New Testament writers describe the person and work of Jesus, each of which carries distinct theological and moral claims with their descriptions, and that only explores the writings of five of the many authors of books in the New Testament.

Yet even if such a question admitted of a fairly complete answer, that answer still would fall short of an answer to the second question concerning fidelity to the God described there. Moreover, there simply are not resources available in the New Testament alone to answer the latter question. Those hoping to address such a question will inevitably be drawn into the Old Testament and into church debates that go on for several hundred years after the New Testament canon is formed. In other words, the latter question mandates attention to stretches of time that go much further back and much further forward than the period described in the New Testament. Additionally, attention to sources that come before and after the New Testament bring in voices and perspectives about values central to a Christian ethic and the actions that follow from them that are far more expansive than the conventional narrative about the history of pacifism, with its myth of return, will allow. In those sources, one finds defenses and criticisms of violence, defenses and criticisms of the works and commands of God, and defenses and criticisms of the communities that have aligned themselves to that God.

Having dislocated conversations about fidelity to God from an exclusive focus on the New Testament or a particular vision of Jesus described there, the impetus that stimulates the myth of return is diffused, if not dissipated entirely. The New Testament and the early church may still play central roles in shaping an ethic for the church, but they cannot play the only roles in such an ethic, nor can non-New Testament sources be regarded as simply derivative of New Testament texts or as lacking any authority. Not only have these other sources helped shape traditions of thought within pacifism that lend them coherence but they have also functioned as sources through which to make sense of the New Testament. Or, to state all this differently, once the myth of return has been demythologized, the New Testament and early church actually gain their places in a history that is far longer and richer than an exclusive focus on them allows.

Admittedly, then, teasing apart questions about fidelity to the God to whom the New Testament bears witness from questions about fidelity to Jesus as described in those texts raises important theological and moral questions for the church: How is Scripture to be understood as authoritative for those who see it as such? What is the relation between the second person of the Trinity and the person of Jesus of Nazareth who is described in the gospels? How, theologically, do Jesus's two natures (fully human and fully divine) express themselves and what are the implications of such expressions for how Christians understand their relationship(s) to Jesus and the obligations that flow out of those relationships? What "rules" for scriptural interpretation follow from the exegetical, hermeneutical, and theological questions above? How does one adjudicate between or prioritize particular texts and how does attention to larger theological perspectives about the Trinity, Jesus's two natures, and the authority of Scripture shape the way people and communities pursue such adjudication/prioritization? How do Christians make sense of texts that, within their own confessional traditions, are both recognizably human artifacts and the inspired Word of God?

While this cannot be the place to adjudicate all such questions,[15] it is at least worth pointing to a few of the benefits that come with this particular approach. Among these benefits, at least three are worth noting here. First, separating out the "fidelity" questions helps expand the ways of thinking about how to be faithful beyond a tacit preoccupation with an *imitatio Christi* ethic. There is, after all, a tendency to link Jesus's teachings on nonviolence to Jesus's generally nonviolent actions and then assume that the way to obey the teachings is to imitate the teacher. Imitation may play an important role in thinking about faithful Christian actions, but it is not the only way to think about faithful activity. There is surprisingly little in the New Testament that actually recommends imitation of Jesus as the center of moral life, and a focus on imitation tends to gloss over the difficult problem of how to imitate one who is both fully human and fully divine. Second, treating questions about fidelity to Jesus as he is described in the New Testament as a subset of questions about fidelity to the triune God to which the New Testament bears witness mandates giving attention to larger theological concerns about scriptural interpretation that can inhibit temptations toward proof-texting and the arbitrary favoring of some passages over others. Third, the former question all but mandates attention to the project of locating texts and interpreters in history: What are the contexts of the story described in the text, of the author of the text and his location, of the original and succeeding audiences of the text, and of the current interpreter? How do all those different contexts figure into interpretation and fidelity to God?

---

[15] For thoughtful treatments of some of these questions, especially from a variety of perspectives within Christian ethics, see, among other sources, Wayne G. Boulton, Thomas D. Kennedy, and Allen Verhey, *From Christ to the World: Introductory Readings in Christian Ethics* (Grand Rapids: Eerdmans, 1994), esp. pp. 15–58.

The second problem with a conventional pacifist narrative that locates discontinuity in the vagaries of history is that such a narrative is not itself theologically rendered in a way that is consistent with the larger claims of that narrative about the work of God and the hope that springs from that work. The conventional narrative tacitly assumes that discontinuity is due to the repeated failings of the church after Constantine to conform itself to its intended pattern and the infrequency with which some subset of that church rediscovers its intended pattern. On such infrequent occasions, the implications of the Sermon on the Mount, other teachings of Jesus, crucifixion and resurrection, and the life of the early church must, like the wheel, be repeatedly reinvented because the time between the first centuries C.E. and the present moment will not offer much by way of insight or resource. Within such a framework, a theological rendering of history lacks sufficient teleological momentum to escape the archaeological gravitational pull of the first few centuries of the church's existence. As a result, reflections on how God relates to and acts in time, how the eternal relates to and might envelop the temporal, and how to discern teleological purposefulness within the continued flow of events through vast swaths of history are bent toward the past at the expense of present and future. The conventional pacifist narrative allows its "myth of return" reading of history to trump its eschatological view of theology.

What if the discontinuities of history might be interpreted not so much as the products of a Constantinian fall but as the complex manifestations of a God who trades in crucifixion and resurrection? Things do (and even must) die; new things can (and do) come into existence. From within complex confessional frameworks of thought, one self-consistent God insistently brings about new things. The Christian vision is not of a faithful past and a perfected future separated by a great stretch of infidelity and imperfection. Nor, though, is it a vision of perpetual, continuous, and gradual improvement. Instead, it is a vision of creation, death, rebirth, and the eschatological consummation of all things. This eschatological consummation is already underway, and is one that may not be grasped but can be glimpsed, albeit out of the corners of one's eyes and probably not with sufficient permanence to continue to register on one's spiritual retinas in ways that relieve doubts or perfect faith.

In such a vision, the ironies and disjunctions of history aren't manifestations of the limitation of God's ability or willingness to work in time so much as signs that point to the mysterious qualities of the ways in which God works. Discontinuity is not illusory (things are lost and we grieve; things that are gained can seem to come from nowhere and even our rejoicing in them is tempered by their imperfections and our fears of their passing). However, neither is discontinuity disconnected from the deeper continuity that bears witness to the continued work of the Triune God and the way that eternity envelops time.[16]

The theological/historiographical failing of the conventional pacifist narrative of pacifism after Constantine, then, is that it has prioritized a (perceived) fall at the expense of giving coherent witness to the continued grace of God. Ironically, it sins in its own preoccupation with sin rather than focusing on an unfolding awareness of grace. Small wonder that from within the conventional myth-of-return narrative, the world is dark and violent (rather than the site of divine activity), the church is small and embattled (rather than the first expression of a grace that shapes an outwardly focused community), and ethics are shaped by obligation and the pursuit of perfection (rather than gratitude, forgiveness, and hope). The conventional narrative may recognize that sin infects all things but it loses sight of the way sin is always parasitic on a deeper and further reaching divine love. It may recognize that imperfections still haunt us, but fails to note that the very fact that these imperfections haunt us also hints at our eventual perfectibility. It registers the way threats of violence should still drive it toward the pursuit of more peaceful ways of living but without giving due note to the way even those threats can be enveloped by a faith in which nothing can separate one from "the love of God in Christ Jesus our Lord" (Romans 8:39).

2 LESSONS FOR NEW NARRATIVES: FIDELITY AND ITS QUESTIONS

What lessons, then, can we learn about how to tell the histories of the way traditions move through time and how can these lessons be helpful to those who would apply the resources of Christian pacifism to climate-shaped conflict? There are at least three lessons, each with its own implications.

First, history is full of ironies – but not all of them work against you. One of the arguments animating this project is the recognition that the large plans and projects of history seldom work out the way they were intended, and that recognition of this fact should shape how we understand the movements of traditions through history. In many, if not most instances, the ironies of history manifest themselves as failures to reach

---

[16] See Emmanuel Levinas, *Totality and Infinity: An Essay on Exteriority*, trans. by Alphonso Lingis (Pittsburgh, PA: Duquesne University Press, 1969).

hoped-for goals or disruptions to settled plans. Thus, for instance, Reinhold Niebuhr wrote *The Irony of American History* to describe the way that American ascendance as a global power had the effect of constraining the country's ability to act freely in the world during the cold war. He argued that American pretensions of innocence restricted the political tools it was willing to use to engage the world, that growing prosperity restricted American understandings of the very virtues that motivate its desire to help others, etc.[17] The irony of history, as a trope, is generally used to express ways that unanticipated outcomes and unfortunate effects inhibit the coherence of any narrative about the flow of history that can move us into the future.

Yet since the conventional narrative of pacifism is so colored by the incoherence of the past and the inability of most of the church throughout most of history to live up to its calling, the great irony of the conventional narrative of pacifism is that things aren't nearly so bad as the narrative suggests and that the movement of the pacifist tradition through history is more coherent and substantial than that narrative suggests. To see why and how this might be the case, it helps to begin by naming the fundamental set of questions that stimulate the tradition.

The fundamental set of questions that drive Christian pacifism (and that should also prod all those who are not pacifists) are those of fidelity: "Who is the God to whom we are faithful?" "How are we to be faithful to the God whom we worship?" "How should this fidelity shape our engagements in the world?" "What does fidelity demand of us?" In the face of so many other significant questions about what God is like, what people are like, how and whether to measure the efficacy of our actions, and how the church relates to the larger world, questions of fidelity serve as constant reminders of our relationship to God and our obligation to link that relationship to all our other relationships. Pacifists throughout history and the conventional narrative about the history of pacifism highlight fidelity and therein bring into relief any ethic that would hope to attain the adjective "Christian." As Christian pacifist traditions move into the future, answers to these questions may be reviewed and revised but the questions, themselves, won't go away. They define the tradition and remind those outside of the tradition of the obligations that come with faith-shaped relationships.

---

[17] See Reinhold Niebuhr, *The Irony of American History* (Chicago: University of Chicago Press, 2008).

Yet within the conventional narrative of the history of Christian pacifism, these questions are unduly constricted. The narrative constricts the God with whom Christians relate in faith to the Jesus (or a version of the Jesus) described in the New Testament. As a result, the narrative also constricts understandings of fidelity: faithfulness to Jesus means being obedient to his commands as given in the gospels; faithful activity means conforming our actions to match his. Undoubtedly, Christian faithfulness includes obedience and conformity. After all, Jesus's greatest act of faithfulness – his giving of his own life on the cross – came out of his willingness to be obedient: "not my will but yours be done" (Luke 22:42). Being faithful and being obedient, however, are not the same thing.

The meaning of faith takes on the aura of the larger cultural context in which the term is used. Where human beings are autonomous actors, "faith" appears as an object from which one can be separated as Carl Henry would suggest. In a market society, it takes on the properties of a commodity, the value of which is fungible with other goods like reason and efficiency and might be expressed as a kind of Sheilaism (as described in Bellah's *Habits of the Heart*[18]). Where relational stability is emphasized, it takes on a patina of trust (see, for example, the work of John Calvin). Where existentialist approaches predominate, a la Paul Tillich, faith is a universal quality of human existence, expressing itself as the most fundamental concern – the "ultimate concern" – of each individual. And where communal order and sacrifice are emphasized, faith glistens with a sheen of obedience.

Obedience has a binary structure: one either obeys or does not obey a particular command; one either is or is not obedient. Whereas some meanings of faith can be expressed along continuums (one's trust can grow; one's ultimate concern can grow deeper), the linkage between faith and obedience doesn't lean in such directions; nor do the qualities of moral engagement when they are driven by an equation that binds fidelity to obedience. We either express our faith through a prescribed set of actions or we are not faithful. We either are or are not pacifists. We either are or are not nonviolent. Attempts to make arguments favoring some forms of peace and rejecting others, or to balance peace with other goods like justice, even where they are productively raised, begin wrongfooted as a result. Pursuing ways to be less violent, comparing forms of

---

[18] See Robert Bellah et al., *Habits of the Heart: Individualism and Commitment in American Life* (Oakland, CA: University of California Press, 2007).

violence, or struggling with justifications for some forms of violence get downplayed, lost, or rejected.[19]

Unsurprisingly, where obedience shapes definitions of fidelity, the range of possible faithful predecessors and conversation partners shrinks. Very few people, morally ambiguous as they are and living in complex times as they do, achieve the kind of purity to which an obedience ethic aspires. With that shrinkage, occasions of faithful behavior are likely to be viewed in more episodic, isolated ways and consistent patterns of behavior more linked to liminal communities. That the conventional narrative of the history of pacifism plays up occasionality and marginality – that it emphasizes discontinuity, silence, and inconsistency – follows from the way the historians of pacifism have engaged the question of fidelity.

Surely the most remarkable things about the various recitations of the history of pacifism between the fourth and nineteenth centuries as they have been offered by the significant historians of pacifism are their silences and incoherencies. Cadoux and Hornus end their narratives only a few centuries into the history of the church and then treat those narratives as having offered a sufficient trajectory for pacifist thought that they need not attend to the time between the early church and the modern one. Heering, Hershberger, and Orr offer rather cursory summaries of the time between the fourth and sixteenth centuries and then narrow their focus to the free churches of the Radical Reformation. And the best known of the historians, Roland Bainton, struggles to construct a coherent narrative through the middle chapters of his book, jumping back and forth in time, flattening out distinctions between various pacifist movements and building walls between pacifists and those non-pacifists who, nonetheless, offer thoughtful insights on the importance of peace in Christian thought at other times.

Such an approach to history, especially under conditions of modern historiography, has the perverse effect of isolating the historians of pacifism from the wider traditions of thought and action through which the

---

[19] The historians who have advanced the conventional narrative about the history of pacifism have repeatedly argued that one of the causes of the Constantinian downfall and the rise of just war thinking was the church's adoption of natural law thinking: Having strayed from its attention to Jesus's commands, it focused on the commands revealed in nature (as revealed by readings from outside the Christian corpus). The irony here is that while pacifists and natural lawyers may argue about the *authorities* to which we should turn in making moral judgments, they have nevertheless aligned themselves with regard to the *processes* involved in making moral judgments: Discern what you are being commanded to do by a law that is greater than you and then do that thing.

church has made sense of its place in time and pursued peace. Where does one fit in history when the history one sees is a series of starts and stops, of moments of faithfulness separated by long periods of failure, of liminal communities surrounded by apostasy, of a period of gospel fidelity that disappeared after only a few centuries? And how does one assess the coherence, credibility, and fidelity of past actions and actors to the demands of the gospel when those demands are so universal and fundamental as to be atemporal? A kind of anachronistic error follows from such isolation and assessment.

In the instance of conventional narratives of the history of pacifism, not only do contemporary assessments of earlier approaches to questions of fidelity gloss over the ways that understandings of "fidelity" change over time (fidelity to whom or what? expressed through what kinds of actions? towards what ends? according to what standards? in contrast to what other goods/values that were being emphasized at any given time?) but they have linked fidelity-as-obedience to imitation in a way that has not yet, itself, been justified. Thus, though an *imitatio Christi* ethic has been a staple of Christian ethics for centuries (one thinks of Augustine, St. Francis, Thomas à Kempis, John Calvin, and Charles Sheldon as all advocating such an approach), the nature of *imitatio* and the *Christi* being imitated have both been subject to so varied a range of perspectives as to turn "*imitatio Christi*" into a moral Rorschach test, revealing more about the values and perspectives of the one advocating such an approach than the power of imitation and the nature of the one being imitated. In the case of twentieth- and twenty-first-century historians of pacifism, the tendency is to locate the Christ being imitated in the character(s) Jesus of Nazareth, who was obedient and nonviolent even to the point of death.

Three ironies have followed from this. First, the conventional narrative of the history of pacifism glosses over a wide range of resources (scholars, communities, and movements) with whom pacifists might find common cause or from whom they might glean insights. For instance, Bainton fails to mention the penitential books of Celtic Christianity (indeed, fails to mention the whole of Celtic Christianity) in spite of their recognition of the need for anyone who takes a life to do significant and sometimes severe penance. Peter Damian, who wrote letters to religious and secular leaders of his day appealing to the ways of nonviolence, is ignored, as is Nicholas of Cusa, who wrote *De pace fidei*. Also strong if not univocal proponents of peace (St. Francis, Thomas Aquinas, Wycliffe and the Lollards, Peter Chelciky and the Hussites) are regarded as having failed to live up to the proper standards of pacifism, ignoring the degree to which they expressed radically peace-oriented views in their own times. Without an exploration of how contemporary pacifists' own locations in time and space might allow them to promote a purer vision of pacifism than would have been possible for those in earlier times and places,[20] such judgments are not only unduly severe but fail to note the fact that they can be made now because of the influence of earlier, less "pure" thinkers.

The second irony that follows from this is that the emphasis on discontinuity that is manifest in the conventional narrative's myth of return ignores the source of continuity that has driven peace-emphasizing and peacemaking convictions throughout the history of the church: the questions of what faith in the Triune God looks like when it is expressed in the practices of Christian community. Having located fidelity in a particular answer (obedience to Jesus of Nazareth expressed through imitation of his nonviolent ways), the pacifist church finds much of church history to be unfaithful, unenlightening, and unhelpful.

It isn't the answers to the questions of fidelity that abide, though; it is the questions. Answers will change depending on their historical contexts as each of those contexts is shaped by a particular set of values, virtues, visions, social structures, habits, and technologies. Those answers – as all answers – can be interrogated and admired, rejected, adapted, or adopted. And eventually all those answers – as all answers – will fall short partly because they were imperfect to begin with and partly because over time they will fit new contexts less and less comfortably. The questions, though, not only animate the pacifist tradition(s); they reside within the heart of the Christian faith, thereby revealing not only their significance but their centrality as questions that all Christians must take up. At the dawn of the shift into the social imaginary named the Anthropocene, the questions may be understood differently due to changing understandings of faith, action, and the Triune God, but some version of them will continue into that age even if some of the settled answers to those

---

[20] John Mueller has argued that war is an idea and that, as an idea, it has been increasingly and successfully challenged by those who have advanced a case for peace rather than war since the mid-nineteenth century. On Mueller's read, the arguments for peace have become increasingly compelling and influential since the end of the American Civil War. If Mueller is right, then pacifism as an idea has gained the very kind of currency it needs in order for contemporary pacifists to envision and then justify the levels of stringency and purity that would have been inaccessible to earlier generations. See John Mueller, *Retreat from Doomsday: The Obsolescence of Major War* (New York: Basic Books, 1989) and *The Remnants of War* (Ithaca: Cornell University Press, 2004).

questions – including those provided by a myth of return – no longer function in the way they once did.

The third irony that follows from all this is that the conventional narrative of the history of pacifism has rendered itself in overly ironic terms. Driven by a myth of return, it hasn't appreciated the way that the same God who was at work in the gospels and the early church has continued to work in history, making a return to the past unnecessary. Assuming the episodic and/or marginal qualities of the persons and communities that constitute its history, it has ignored a range of witnesses and conversation partners that not only have enriched it but have helped to shape it over time. Shaped by its emphasis on discontinuity, it hasn't recognized that the very questions that so characterize it have expressed themselves continuously through time, motivating patterns of behavior that may have changed over time and stimulating answers that may not align with each other but that have consistently exerted a kind of conceptual gravity that has drawn Christians throughout history to attempt to be faithful to the Prince of Peace. The irony of the conventional narrative of the history of pacifism is that the tradition is longer, richer, and deeper than it has given itself credit for.

Prognostication is, obviously, difficult; predictions about how things will be in the future necessarily remain shrouded in the mysteries of "not yet." That said, Christian pacifists in an environmental age will have the privilege of living after modernity. Not only has modernity been awash in careful and critical scholarship (benefits of its Enlightenment origins) that has found stable purchase and some permanence of thought in literate societies, but the environmental emergencies and the emerging social imaginary that they have given rise to are, in the words of James Howard Kunstler, "long emergencies."[21] That is, they are no less catastrophic than more temporally acute events (indeed, they are among the most catastrophic events in human history), but they are slow-moving catastrophes: sea level rise doesn't happen overnight, desertification and ocean acidification slowly lead to the loss of foodstuffs, species extinction can be met with projects of DNA preservation. As we face long emergencies, twenty-first-century human beings, with our capacity to see what is

---

[21] James Howard Kunstler, *The Long Emergency: Surviving the End of Oil, Climate Change, and Other Converging Catastrophes of the Twenty-First Century* (New York: Grove Press, 2006). Given the controversies that have surrounded this book, I suppose I should hasten to note that referencing Kunstler's title isn't the same as agreeing with his outlook. Indeed, I find myself both more pessimistic and more optimistic than Kunstler.

coming and act to either mitigate the more deleterious effects of war in a warming world or preserve knowledge through which to imagine new ways of understanding and living in the Anthropocene, are better situated than at any point in the past in the project of bringing the wisdom of one age into another.

As such, not only will the pacifists of the Anthropocene have an enormous range of resources from within their traditions at their disposal as they reconceive those traditions; they'll have the capacity to look back and see how those traditions have actually moved through time and learn from their look backward in the process (this book being just one part of that project). One aspect of this capacity will involve thinking through the existential meanings and theological forms that shape and motivate questions of fidelity. In this regard, Christian pacifists may learn not only from their own ancestors in the tradition, but from the wide range of Christians and non-Christians for whom questions of fidelity have been central to their lives and work. The breadth of resources in the history of Christian pacifism and range of conversation partners exploring the shape and power of fidelity that are accessible to Christian pacifists in a new social imaginary will almost certainly produce a stunning array of new ironies and disjunctions. Yet perhaps this is not a wholly bad thing: sometimes, ironies can work for you.

3 HISTORY, THEOLOGY, AND RICHER NARRATIVES

The second general implication that can follow from this chapter's analysis of the way historians of pacifism have misconstrued that history is the recognition that in the absence of access to an objective rendering of history, any theological rendering of history ought to reflexively subject itself to its own best theological instincts. No historian can stand outside of the flow of time in order to understand and evaluate the movements of traditions through it. Historians of pacifism have shown no interest in even trying to do so. Quite the contrary, in fact, as these historians have often offered not only narrative structures through which to make sense of the tradition but apologetics for the tradition's significance (and even superiority) during times when violence is causing enormous suffering in the world. Untimely claims to objectivity and dispassionate assessment seem not only analytically unfounded but morally troubling. We *ought* to care about the things that pacifists care about and should read their lack of objectivity not as a sign of their failure to be responsible historians but as evidence of their attempts to be responsible human beings.

At least from a theological perspective, modern appeals to and attempts at objective renderings of history fail on multiple fronts. For one thing, history cannot be observed from the outside. All historians are shaped by their own contexts, and those contexts themselves are the precipitates of the movement of ideas and technologies through time. Historians exist in history and are shaped by their own locations in time. For another, historians are necessarily invested in their work. The motives that propel historians into their studies are not simply expressions of the precipitates of historical data. Instead, those motives are signs pointing to basic human desires to encounter, to understand, and to create. They suggest an anthropology at work, hinting at a vision of human beings as encounterers, as problem-solvers, and as meaning-seekers, one manifestation of which is to inquire into, shape, and tell histories. Shorn of this anthropology and absent these motivating forces, history fades into the dull confusions of endless and pointless background chatter. Moreover, these investments carry implicit normative judgments about what the histories we tell should mean to us and how they should motivate us. We tell histories as a way of making arguments and providing appeals, advancing certain ideas and rejecting others, suggesting ways forward and paths to avoid, and we do this to offer resources through which we and others can live better. One way that at least some historians account for the non-objective character of their work is to connect that work to a larger theological vision of God, the world, and time.

Seeing history through theologically tinted lenses complicates the project of telling history, but not necessarily more than having seen it through any other set of lenses (e.g., Marxist, sociobiological, right Hegelian, etc.). It does, though, complicate those projects in distinct ways. On the one hand, attempts to integrate the mysteries of the divine into the complexities of history – to discern patterns that are larger than whatever material forces are apparently at work – not only raise barriers between historians and readers who do not share their convictions but mandate a degree of tentativeness on the part of such historians in their approaches. In this, approaching history theologically is akin to approaching the divine: a bit of caution is in order when faced with something that is, at least in part, intransigently mysterious and far bigger than we are. Such tentativeness can be experientially unsettling to readers who have sought after ideas that are complete or wholly adequate. The quest for our own completion – to know ourselves and the world around us with certainty by knowing precisely where and when we are – can send us to history in the first place. We want to understand; to be told that our understandings will be incomplete and transient is deeply unsatisfying.

On the other hand, to offer explicitly theologically framed tellings of history brings to the surface particular sets of values and visions that can be assessed by readers. Readers need not agree with the theological convictions that shape theological historiographies in order to recognize them as theological and even understand their broad sources and basic meanings. Perhaps a historian may be writing in light of a profoundly personal revelatory moment, but once that historian touches pen to paper or fingers to keyboard, that revelatory moment enters into a social world full of people who have not had such a moment. The very use of words through which to express ideas and visions (which is a quintessentially public act, given the social origins and purposes of language) presupposes possibilities for recognition and understanding.[22] Better to have those theological convictions at the surface and available for review than submerged, leaving readers guessing after questions of perspective and motive.

The historians of pacifism I have been describing in this chapter have provided excellent examples of how to tell theologically tinted history in a way that avoids the conceptual cul-de-sacs of quests for objectivity and advance explicit moral claims about why such history should matter. Cadoux ends his text with a call to promote the history of pacifism for the good of those who suffer from violence: "It is for [those who have seen the church's failure to live up to its calling] to pass on to the world in its confusion and to the Church in her perplexity the knowledge that the true remedy for the most crying and scandalous evil of our time – an evil beneath which the whole human race is groaning and suffering – lies in a new and closer application to thought and life of the teaching of the Prince of Peace."[23] Hornus ends his book with an invitation to deeper faith: "At long last, however, the Church is becoming aware, at least in Europe, that the Constantinian age is finished – and for good. This is a momentous reversal, which implies a severe judgment on the illusions of the past. But it is also an opportunity to rediscover the ancient and authentic hope of the faithful."[24] Hershberger quotes Menno Simons

---

[22] For further reflections on revelation and language from a Christian theological perspective, see my *Confessing Christ in the Twenty-first Century* (Lanham, MD: Rowman and Littlefield, 2005), Ch. 3.

[23] C. John Cadoux, *The Early Christian Attitude to War*, 265.

[24] Jean-Michel Hornus, *It Is Not Lawful for Me to Fight*, 226.

not to convey information about what Simons said in the sixteenth century but to suggest that Simons offers "the combination of factors which will enable the Mennonite Church of our day to go onward showing for the way of true Christian discipleship in the home and family, in the neighborhood and community, in economic and business relationships, in relationships between races and classes, between employers and employees, between nations and states."[25] Bainton concludes his book with two full chapters advocating pacifism as the sole coherent Christian position for the church to take with regard to state violence and as the means through which to address the conflicts of his own day, including those associated with the threat of nuclear war.

One way of reading such concluding sentences would be to treat them as special dispensations offered by benevolent readers, as our own acts of charity to the writers for their work in informing us about the tradition. Having learned from them, we will now give them permission to say something personal about their own confessional commitments. Such a reading, though, not only ignores the facts that the writers wrote their books because of those commitments and that those commitments pervade their texts, but fails to take seriously the fact that we, too, have worked through their texts because we have our own commitments and purposes, among which are to encounter the thoughts and visions of others through their own narrations of history, often in hopes that our own perspectives will be affirmed, deepened, and challenged. These final words from the historians of pacifism are not simply expressions of their own opinions but evidences of the reasons we came to read their books in the first place.

If, then, we neither can have nor would want access to an objective telling of history – and particularly a theologically framed telling of history – then by what standards might we assess the qualities of such tellings? While answering that question would warrant its own book-length response (and any number of books have been written on the subject), at least one part of an answer involves assessing the reflexive ability of the telling to be congruent with its own larger theological visions of God and the world while maintaining fidelity to the data of history. In other words, does the theology implicit in the historiographic methods operative in the text fit with the theological vision advanced by the texts' authors as well as events themselves?

---

[25] Guy F. Hershberger, *War, Peace, and Nonresistance*, 283.

The answer to that latter question is mixed – as all such answers are likely to be. On the one hand, ideas about purity of thought and action, imitation and obedience, and the distinctiveness of the church from the world as described and advocated by the historians of pacifism are broadly consistent with much of the history of pacifism. These ideas are all present, for instance, in writings from Tertullian to the Schleitheim Confession (1527) and beyond. In this regard, the historians fit the history of Christian pacifism into their own narratives. And where there may be differences at particular points (e.g., what it means to be separate from the world even as one writes books to be read by that world; whether arguments about the efficacy of pacifism should play any role in its advocacy, etc.), these are differences in detail rather than over essential claims of the pacifist church.

On the other hand, those same writings do advance a vision of a Triune God, made most clearly (but not exclusively) manifest in Jesus of Nazareth, who continues to work in history and will continue to do so until the consummation of all things. Thus, for instance, the Schleitheim Confession begins,

May joy, peace, mercy from our Father, through the atonement of the blood of Christ Jesus, together with the gift of the Spirit – who is sent by the Father to all believers to [give] strength and consolation and constance [sic] in all tribulation until the end, Amen, be with all who love God and all children of light, who are scattered everywhere, wherever they might have been placed by God our Father, wherever they might be gathered in unity of spirit in one God and Father of us all; grace and peace of heart be with you all. Amen.[26]

Recognizing that this introduction advances neither the complex anthropology of *simul iustus et peccator* of Lutheran thought nor the strong claims about divine sovereignty within Calvinist thought, it nevertheless recognizes a Triune God who continues to work in history, offering consolation and uniting Christians with each other until the end (Amen). That theological vision of history not only warrants greater attention generally but suggests further theological reflection on the possibilities and limits of human activity in the world – including giving attention to the work of the Holy Spirit inside and outside the church, the purposes and roles of the state and its relation to the church, and the complex interactions within and between cultures – than the conventional pacifist narrative suggests. The gap between the explicit theological

---

[26] Schleitheim Confession, trans. by John Howard Yoder. Accessed on November 5, 2015 at www.anabaptistwiki.org/mediawiki/index.php/Schleitheim_Confession_(source).

history that the historians of pacifism have developed and the implicit one that they haven't suggests that there is further work to do.

Over the last few decades, contemporary theologians from within the Christian pacifist traditions have been filling this very gap. To name just a few: Martin Luther King, Jr., Dorothy Day, and John Howard Yoder (the three of whom will be the focus of the next chapter), James Reimer, Stanley Hauerwas (and a wide range of those who have studied with Hauerwas including William Cavanaugh, Jonathan Tran, and others), Ellen Ott Marshall, Marcia Riggs, Robert Brimlow, Paul Ricoeur, John Paul Lederach, John Milbank, etc. Indeed, as the next chapter will high-light, the last century and the half of western theology is marked by a profusion of pacifist theological perspectives, many offering thoughtful advancements of pacifist narratives that are moving beyond the conventional one. A few of these have also been exploring and re-narrating that history.

There is also an important insight tucked within the congruence between the theological values espoused by the historians of pacifism and the theology of the subjects and communities whose history they are narrating. Such congruence suggests that the vision of history that drives the conventional narrative of the pacifist tradition is not nearly so episodic as that narrative suggests. The historians of pacifism reveal, in their own theological convictions, a level of continuity of thought and action that their telling of the history of Christian pacifism doesn't recognize. Resources for responding to the historiographical failings of the myth of return that drives the conventional pacifist narrative also reside within that narrative.

This insight adds further credibility to the idea that, at least in tradi-tions with any staying power (i.e., traditions that have continued through long periods of time and across multiple social imaginaries), traditions carry within themselves resources for their own repair. It also highlights the degree to which traditions are richer (the voices more diverse, the visions more stimulating, the practices more pliant to new meanings) than most narratives about those traditions recognize. Indeed, one reason this book approaches the history of Christian pacifism as it does – criticizing the way that tradition has been conventionally nar-rated – is that the range of resources that these traditions offers as we enter into the new social imaginary of the environmental age is extensive and the utility of such resources awaits further exploration. These will include attention to the theologies of creation and their implications for the natural world, as those theologies have been advanced by scholars from within the traditions of the peace churches.

4 QUESTIONS, ANSWERS, AND THE MOVEMENTS OF TRADITIONS THROUGH TIME

The third general implication of this assessment of the conventional narrative of Christian pacifism between 380 and 1865 is that it begins to reveal a more coherent way of describing the movement of traditions through time. Rather than treating traditions as accumulations of wisdom or arguments extended through time (both of which emphasize continuity at the expense of real discontinuities) or as unhelpful projects to be dismantled or dismissed as exerting illegitimate authority over the present (emphasizing discontinuity at the expense of recognizable continuities), we might see that the questions at the heart of a tradition exert a kind of centripetal force on the tradition whereas the answers to those questions exert a centrifugal force. Traditions both exist in and are interpretations of the movement of persons, ideas, and technologies through time. Because they are contingent and susceptible to forces that cause change over time, traditions change. Because they connect persons, ideas, and technologies through time, they offer stability and durability in the face of change. Traditions, put simply, both manifest and absorb change.

These abilities to manifest and absorb change shape a tension that all traditions must account for within their narratives; namely, the ability to offer thick enough descriptions of themselves to account for both continuity and discontinuity over time. The means by which they do so, however, vary. Some traditions re-describe their own changes in such a way as to suggest that what they now think and do is actually what they've always thought and done. For example, official Roman Catholic moral philosophy continues to rely on its Thomist bases even as the Magisterium addresses new issues brought on in light of contemporary findings in science and modern political philosophy. Some traditions incorporate change into their own self-descriptions (one thinks of Continental philosophy and the impact of its Hegelian origins in shaping terms like "postmodern" and "deconstruction"). Some traditions treat change as a corrective on the way to an already-determined *telos* that is unchanging.

The conventional Christian pacifist tradition has addressed this tension by developing its myth of return. Emphasizing discontinuity in its thought, it nevertheless links all its discrete and discontinuous moments in history to the church of the first few centuries, and these connections provide an anchor to the pacifist narrative. The tradition, it claims, does not so much change over time as rediscover its essential self in new times and places. So a myth of return that at first blush emphasizes the discontinuous qualities of the pacifist tradition turns out to reveal continuity: Christian pacifists through the ages consistently repeat the refrain that the church ought to return to those practices of its first few centuries of existence, arguing that Christians at that time got the answers to the questions of fidelity right. By emphasizing the discontinuous character of the church's faithful witness through the centuries, the historians of Christian pacifism have, paradoxically, revealed a kind of continuity at work in the tradition.

The paradox of this emphasis on continuously expressed discontinuity is a sign that warrants further interpretation. Is there something unique about the tradition of pacifism that leads to this paradox or does the pacifist tradition bring into clearer relief a paradox that recurs through many traditions? What sustains the paradox in the face of narratives that would submerge or eliminate it? How does the paradox sustain and/or undermine the tradition? Are there other ways to address tension between continuity and discontinuity? If so, how good are these other ways to address the tension at retaining the qualities that sustain the tradition while addressing and resolving the qualities that undermine it?

A starting point for thinking about the paradox of continuously expressed discontinuity would be to recognize that traditions are never mono-vocal; persons with diverse voices, perspectives, and habits inhabit all traditions. While one way to deal with this multi-vocality would be to deny it, such an approach inhibits the sustainability of tradition. When narrators of traditions seek to minimize or paper over this diversity, they inflict multiple harms. If they have to ignore or deny significant portions of their own history, then their telling of history invariably becomes professionally shoddy. Choosing which voices they will listen to, their treatment of minority voices and positions is morally deplorable. Failing to recognize that traditions are sustained by diversity, their approach is intellectually short-sighted. Ignoring or denying diversity isn't a tenable way forward. Instead, the diversity of voices, perspectives, and habits within a tradition needs to be recognized. Yet recognizing this diversity both troubles and sustains the tradition.

Recognizing diversity troubles traditions because it makes their tellings of history more complicated. How does one weigh the various voices, perspectives, and habits against each other? How do we tease coherence out of what can, at first blush, sound cacophonous? How stable or static are the centers and margins of traditions over time? How does one discern where those centers are, how many margins are there, and whether there are outer limits to these margins beyond which one would simply say, "This voice/perspective/habit is not part of the tradition"? Where does one tradition end and another begin? How do new voices/perspectives/habits enter into traditions and how do others exit? The task of telling the history of a tradition is complicated yet, in the face of nostalgia and other expressions of amnesia, it is also vital.

Recognizing diversity also sustains traditions. Over time, the settled answers to the very questions that traditions are meant to answer become less viable or coherent as the historical contexts through which traditions flow change and the traditions' answers become less adequate as a means of addressing new problems and reconstructing old ones. Where diversity within traditions has been honored in their telling, the possibility that minority voices, perspectives, and habits might offer new insights for new contexts grows. In the case of the pacifist narrative, for instance, the rise of the monastic traditions – some of them, like the Benedictines, fundamentally pacifist – gave Christians one way of engaging the wider societies in which they lived while also honoring commitments to peace that they found within Scripture. And over time, these monastic traditions became more diverse. The Dominican order produced Thomas Aquinas, who thought about the importance of peace in one way, and St. Francis, who founded the Order of the Friars Minor and gave voice to a different way of thinking about peace. The capacity of the church to inculcate and sustain particular communities of faith would, in turn, shape the rise of groups like the Waldensians and the Lollards as well as the peace churches of the Reformation, each of which gave voice to their own distinctive visions of nonviolence. Yet the tradition also would reject other pacifist communities, including the Montanists and the Cathars, revealing that diversity within Christian pacifist communities has its limits. Just as the development of distinct Christian communities reveals something about diversity within the pacifist tradition, so the reasons for being pacifist (e.g., obedience to a command to behave in nonviolent ways, rejection of state-related idolatry, the experience of the horrors of war, convictions about the superior efficacy of pacifist responses to violence, etc.) reveal its diversity.

Yet as I have insistently maintained, the myth of return also inhibits the Christian pacifist tradition, especially during times of dramatic change.

It provides an anchor when the tradition needs a rudder and a map instead. So rather than treating the first two centuries as offering the answers to all the questions that emerge over time, perhaps it would be worth exploring how the central questions of the tradition may offer a way of recognizing continuity over time. It is, after all, only a slight generalization to state that the questions of fidelity at the heart of the pacifist tradition recur consistently and insistently throughout its history, pulling the discrete faith communities within the tradition toward unity and continuity.

The answers to those questions, though they may overlap in places, do not exert such a unifying force. Each age and each community understands and answers those questions in a way that reveals how it has been shaped by its own sense of its place in history and in light of its own larger context. Benedictines, Franciscans, Lollards, Christian humanists, and Mennonites all seek to answer in their lives the questions of fidelity. Yet each of those communities expresses its distinctiveness through the way it answers the questions of fidelity, particularly as those answers reveal particular and discrete perspectives with regard to how a community understands the God to whom it is obedient, the Jesus it imitates, the shape of obedience and its role in community-formation, the place of its community vis-à-vis the wider society, and the nature of its obligations to the state. Overlapping but distinct theological visions, perspectives, and habits shape the tradition's discontinuity even as the tradition's central questions fund its continued existence. Particular persons and communities use those overlapping but distinct theological visions, perspectives, and habits to answer the questions of fidelity (and justify their answers to the question), but they do not answer them in the same way. The result is a range of answers, with each answer challenging, reaffirming, querying, and/or ignoring other answers from within that range.

Said differently, questions exert centripetal forces within the Christian pacifist tradition, linking communities separated in time to each other. Answers to those questions, on the other hand, exert centrifugal forces on the various communities within the Christian pacifist tradition, pushing them to attend to the specificity of their respective contexts. The questions pull toward a common center; the various answers push toward distinctiveness. As in physics, centripetal questions and centrifugal answers act in tension with each other, giving energy to the connection between continuity and discontinuity. It is this tension between centripetal and centrifugal forces that underlies the complex relations between continuity and discontinuity that structure the movement of the Christian pacifist tradition through time.

Attending to this tension between centripetal questions and centrifugal answers allows the Christian pacifist tradition to escape the limitations of the myth of return without surrendering either the significance of the tradition's role in the history of Christian thought and action or its resources for addressing contemporary occasions of potential and actual violence.

Said differently, as it exposes the failings of the myth of return, this idea of a tension between centripetal questions and centrifugal answers serves to demythologize conventional narratives of the Christian pacifist tradition. Just as importantly, though, it does so in a way that sustains – and even reinforces – the tradition. As long as the myth of return served as the center and source of continuity within the Christian pacifist tradition, that tradition made an anchor of the first centuries C.E. The tradition wouldn't be left adrift, unmoored in the seas of history and vulnerable to the winds (and whims) of historical context. Yet neither would it be able to travel to new lands nor deal with the changing seas of time. Having cast off from that myth, it may lack its earlier anchor but, with centripetal questions functioning as that center and source of continuity within the tradition and centrifugal answers shaping the capacities for diversity within the tradition (and, therein, innovation, novelty, and resilience), the tradition discovers rudder, map, and compass. It can know where it has been without looking only backwards and it can also move forward towards exploring the uncharted seas of the future.

Approaching questions as centripetal and the answers to those questions as centrifugal helps shape a new ecocentric narrative about the movement of the Christian pacifist tradition through time in a distinctly helpful way for an additional reason: it helps to account for the way that natural forces and climatic change over the past two millennia have had an impact on political systems (and the recurrent resort to violence in those systems) and reveals the degree to which pacifism has been a choice, a response to the violence that arose, in part, due to natural forces. So, for instance, historical climatologists have linked the decline of the Roman Empire between 250 and 550 C.E. to increased climatic variability, making the prerequisite stability Rome offered to its empire less possible, giving leverage to forces both inside and outside the empire that sought its change or destruction. The beginning of that period also marked significant growth in the myths of Christian pacifism as one set of answers to the question of who or what to trust when the very empire that has been shaping the terms through which trust and faith are understood is struggling. The Medieval Warm Period (in the tenth to thirteenth centuries) led to fertile fields and social stability; perhaps not coincidentally, the period is also marked by little movement within the history of Christian pacifism. Then, roughly between 1250 and 1300 C.E., the Little Ice Age begins in Europe, which would have its own impact on economic and political systems there, and would also happen concurrent with another period in the resurgence of Christian pacifism. Two hundred years later – roughly during the rise of the radical reformers – the Little Ice Age would reach its greatest strength in Europe, leading to a series of natural disasters (including significant famines at the end of the seventeenth century throughout northern and western Europe).[27]

The point here is not that natural catastrophes (volcanic eruptions, famines, plagues, etc.) – especially as they are related to changes in climate – have *caused* transitions in pacifist thought. Not only is the range of causes for such transitions far greater than those related to events in the natural world, but events in the natural world do not, themselves, lead to changes in social and political systems. Instead, the point here is to begin to attend to the interlinking of changes in the natural world, changes in social and political systems, and developments within the history of Christian pacifist thought. Changes in climate have and will shape conditions that promote political instability. Political instability can manifest in threats of and occasions for violence. Pacifism is one response to those threats and occasions. Rather than being centered on efficacy or social stability, Christian pacifism has been centered around questions of fidelity to the God described in Scripture and whose work is witnessed in the world. The Christian pacifist tradition is a living record of the way those questions have been variously answered throughout history.

Where causal factors are vague and varied but change is observable, taking note not only of those changes but possible factors contributing to those changes is important in order to tell a coherent story that can address both gradual and disruptive changes to traditions. The tension between centripetal questions and centrifugal answers offers one way to think about human engagement with the complex of natural and social

---

[27] Brian Fagan, among others, has done extensive work exploring the relation of climate change to civilizational change. See, among others, his books, *The Little Ice Age: How Climate Made History 1300–1850* (New York: Basic Books, 2001), *The Long Summer: How Climate Changed Civilization* (New York: Basic Books, 2004), and *The Great Warming: Climate Change and the Rise and Fall of Civilizations* (New York: Bloomsbury, 2009).

forces that shape the movements of traditions through time without recourse to the myth of return that drives the conventional Christian pacifist narrative.

This same tension between centripetal questions and centrifugal answers, incidentally, also manifests itself in the Christian just war tradition. Responding to violence with violence – much like the Christian pacifist tradition offers a response to violence with nonviolence – is a choice, albeit a choice in which all the natural and social factors at play rarely if ever reach consciousness. Attending to this tension will help demythologize the myths particular to those traditions and reshape them as they move into the Anthropocene, clarifying the way they address both their continuity and discontinuity over time. Traditions, after all, continue to exert the pull of their wisdom only where the answers they provide prove useful in new times and places but maintain coherence as traditions only where they maintain connection to the past. In an age in which the causes, weapons, exacerbating features, types, and understandings of war are changing, coherent but pliant traditions like Christian pacifism might serve important roles in preventing and/or mitigating the kinds of suffering that wars produce.

6

Pacifisms Since 1865

In his book, *The Remnants of War*, John Mueller provocatively claims that "[i]ndividual voices, some of them very eloquent, have long been raised against war. However, as a significant political cause, the notion that war is a bad idea and ought to be abolished is not much more than a century old."[1] Up until the early decades of the twentieth century, war was, according to the majority of western thinkers, natural, necessary, and even, in a social Darwinist world, progressive. World War I changed such thinking in the West: "[T]he appeal of war, both as a desirable exercise in itself and as a sensible method for resolving international disagreements, diminished markedly on that once war-racked continent. In an area in which war had been accepted as a standard and permanent fixture, the idea suddenly gained substantial currency that war there was no longer an inevitable or necessary fact of life and that major efforts should be made to abandon it."[2] Like slavery, war ceased to be treated as a natural condition of human existence in the West. After World War I (and with the peculiar exception of World War II, which Mueller discusses in some detail), if one wanted to promote war, one had to fight an uphill rather than downhill battle.

Having traced through a number of possible reasons for this shift in perspective (e.g., World War I's destructiveness, the growth of anti-war literature coming out of World War I, changing economic forces at the time), Mueller argues that among the most significant reasons for this dramatic change was the growing power and size of an anti-war

---

[1] John Mueller, *The Remnants of War* (Ithaca: Cornell University Press, 2004), 32.
[2] John Mueller, *The Remnants of War*, 39.

145

movement that had grown in the last decades of the nineteenth century. Especially in Britain and the United States, the movement, shaped as it was during a progressive era in modern human history, captured popular imaginations and visions such that even World War I would be fought as a "war to end all wars." War became an idea and, as an idea, could be rejected as well as accepted:

The decline of war, it seems to me, stems chiefly from the way attitudes toward the value and efficacy of war have changed, particularly during the last century. The key lies in the machinations of idea entrepreneurs, not in wider-ranging social, economic, or technological developments or in the fabrication of institutions, trade, or patterns of interdependence, which often seem to be more nearly a consequence of peace and of rising war aversion than their cause. War, in this view, is merely an idea, an institution, like dueling or slavery, that has been grafted onto human existence. It is not a trick of fate, a thunderbolt from hell, a natural calamity, or a desperate plot contrivance dreamed up by some sadistic puppeteer on high.[3]

And this idea came, as much as from anyone or any group, from Christian pacifists.

There are reasons to argue with Mueller's thesis. He focuses on Western countries yet he generalizes "war" as a global phenomenon. He treats the types of wars that arose after the Reformation during the rise of the modern nation-states as representative of war throughout a much longer history rather than noting that wars have been understood and fought for a wide variety of reasons. Only wars over the past four centuries look so clearly like the von Clausewitzian "war as the continuation of politics by other means" understandings that dominated modern conceptions of war.[4] Even when he nods toward Christian pacifist groups like the Quakers, he under-regards the sources of their thought, the degree to which those sources were shared with other non-pacifist Christian traditions, the continuity of their thought – and that of Christian pacifism more generally – with the longer history of Christianity, and the impact of their thought on the broader public.

Moreover, Mueller's idealist perspective on the causes for the decline of war ignores the way the same ideas that led to its decline also shaped "wider-ranging social, economic, [and] technological developments," not to mention "the fabrication of institutions, trade, [and] patterns of interdependence." Mueller addresses these criticisms, in part, by noting that

---

[3] John Mueller, *The Remnants of War*, 2.
[4] For a wider-ranging (and bleaker) vision of war as a human phenomenon, see Azar Gat, *War in Human Civilization* (New York: Oxford University Press, 2005).

war in the twenty-first century has changed; that conventional war may have disappeared, but it has been replaced by civil wars and policing wars, all of which are being promoted and fought by "criminals – robbers, brigands, freebooters, highwaymen, hooligans, thugs, bandits, pirates, gangsters, outlaws."[5] In this response, Mueller does not resolve all the criticisms but does mitigate some of them.

Criticisms notwithstanding, the central thesis of Mueller's work carries weight: that "[u]nlike breathing, eating, or sex, war is not something that is somehow required by the human condition or by the forces of history,"[6] especially because his thesis not only helps to explain the historically remarkable decline in broad support for war but because it also displays the power of modern anti-war movements. It is as if modern Western civilization was starting to catch up to a church that has simultaneously held pacifist and just war traditions for most of its existence: after 1918, war *might* be necessary but it was always horrible, normally immoral, and generally futile.

Why, though, did anti-war ideas gain traction in the late nineteenth century? Possible answers are legion. Some new technologies had made war more horrible and its costs on human beings more far-reaching and obvious. Other new technologies drove a sense of optimism about a peaceful future and connected persons and states in a way they had not previously experienced. After the chaotic rise of modern nation-states, war had come under political control and, even if war was "the continuation of politics by other means," it wasn't the only way to continue politics by other means.[7] Europe had experienced a near-absence of war for two extended periods (1815–1854 and 1871–1914), providing evidence for the benefits of peace. The expansion of human rights language (and the application of human rights to increasing numbers of people) drove a new appreciation for the value of human beings. Peace societies were formed throughout Western Europe and in the United States. Victorian England and nineteenth-century America were both religious hotbeds in which theological arguments had gained footing in public discourse. Modern capitalism and international commerce were ascendant and new classes of western citizens were becoming wealthy and thinking about war

---

[5] Mueller, *Remnants*, 17.

[6] Mueller, *Remnants*, 4.

[7] Charles Tilly has done a great deal of important work in this area. See, e.g., Charles Tilly, *Coercion, Capital, and European States, A.D. 990–1990* (Cambridge, MA: Basil Blackwood, 1990).

differently for both economic and moral reasons (so, e.g., Andrew Carnegie funded the Endowment for International Peace in New York and Alfred Nobel started giving out Peace Prizes in Oslo). Descriptions of the horrors of war and the benefits of peace were reaching wider audiences (one thinks of the works by Stephen Crane, Leo Tolstoy, Bertha von Suttner, and Norman Angell, for instance). Increased social mobility allowed people not only to achieve fame and fortune away from the battlefield but to treat the attractions of war with bemusement or contempt: war was for those who couldn't succeed in other arenas (so, e.g., Oscar Wilde would quip that, "as long as war is regarded as wicked, it will always have its fascination. When it is looked upon as vulgar, it will cease to be popular"[8]). Undoubtedly, all these answers to questions about the causes for the growth of anti-war movements at the end of the nineteenth and beginning of the twentieth century carry some truth to them.

Into the midst of these answers, though, it is hard to ignore the way Christian pacifism expanded beyond the historic peace churches during that same period. Likewise, it is hard to deny the impact of Christian pacifism on the wider public. William Lloyd Garrison, Fredrick Douglass, and Sojourner Truth all argued against war until the demands of their abolitionism led them to call others to join the Union Army during the American Civil War. Alexander Campbell (of the Stone-Campbell movement), Charles Spurgeon, and Dwight Moody all linked their evangelical impulses to a pacifist "biblical ethic." Lucretia Mott, Jane Addams, and Howard Thurman all linked their pacifism to the liberation of the oppressed. Harry Emerson Fosdick and, for a while, Reinhold Niebuhr advocated pacifism within the context of progressive Christianity. The range of reasons to be a pacifist and the theological bases upon which to build and sustain pacifist commitments grew ever wider. By the end of World War I, the tradition of Christian pacifism was widespread, publicly engaged, and plural. And while the tradition has waxed and waned over the century since the close of that war, it has never constricted to only the historic peace churches and it has continued to grow more and more diverse in vision, approach, and purpose.

I YODER, DAY, KING, AND PACIFISMS

To bear witness to this diversity, John Howard Yoder describes seventeen major types of pacifism in his 1971 book, *Nevertheless: Varieties of*

---

[8] Oscar Wilde, quoted in John Mueller, *The Remnants of War*, 34.

Religious Pacifism (to which he would add four more in the second edition – and he lists eight other types of pacifism that, apparently, didn't rise to the level of "major," in both editions). All told, then, by 1976, Yoder had described twenty-nine varieties of *religious* pacifism alone, and there are any number of secular variations of pacifism as well. Though Yoder's varieties start to overlap and blur into each other – a fact that he treats as virtuous, as the overlaps are meant to be mutually reinforcing – the very fact that he thought a book describing the varieties of pacifism was worth writing says something not only about the real diversity within the recent pacifist traditions but about the value of diversity and Yoder's willingness to build a theological ethic around nonviolence generally rather than a particular vision of nonviolence. This peculiar kind of ecumenicity – a shared moral vision based on distinct and not necessarily compatible theologies – reveals not only something about Yoder (who did, after all, teach at a Roman Catholic school as a Mennonite), but also about the degree to which moral concerns had, during the past century, displaced theological ones as matters of central importance for Christian faith and engagement in the world.[9]

Indeed, Yoder serves as one interesting example and model for thinking about twentieth-century pacifism within the context of the long tradition of Christian pacifism. He shaped burgeoning scholarly attention to and appreciation for the priority of Christian practices over the purity of Christian belief (which is not to say that he ignored purity, belief, or theological concerns. One need only read his incisive criticisms of an earlier generation of theologians like Karl Barth and the Niebuhr brothers to know that his was a first-rate theological mind). He was well versed in

[9] As I enter into explication of Yoder's work on pacifism, it is important to pause and recognize that Yoder's legacy has been severely tarnished by posthumous recognition of his patterns of sexual misconduct. It has become an open question as to whether – and how – to attend to his insights on pacifism given the coercive force he brought to bear on a number of his relationships with women. This is not simply a matter of attempting to segregate his written reflections on nonviolence from his sexual misconduct; it is a matter of whether the habits and patterns of thought that led to that misconduct infect his written reflections on nonviolence. As I hope to demonstrate in this chapter, even as I think that we can still learn from his written reflections on nonviolence, I also think that those writings are, themselves, deeply flawed in ways that make his sexual misconduct unsurprising. We can learn from him but not in ways that suggest we should emulate him. For more on dealing with Yoder, see David Cramer et al., "Theology and Misconduct: The Case of John Howard Yoder," *The Christian Century* 131.17 (August 20, 2014): 20–23 and Karen V. Guth, "Doing Justice to the Complex Legacy of John Howard Yoder: Restorative Justice Resources in Witness and Feminist Ethics," *Journal of the Society of Christian Ethics* 35.2 (Fall/Winter, 2015): 119–139.

the history of the wider church as well as the history of his own Mennonite communion. He was committed to public engagement, defying whatever quietist labels might be associated with the peace churches. He influenced scholars both inside and far beyond his own theological tradition.[10] As Craig A. Carter notes in his introduction to Yoder's thought, "Yoder's impact can be seen in the influence that his thought has had on the increasingly vocal left wing of North American evangelicalism and on mainline Protestants who have grown weary of liberalism and are developing various nonfundamentalist ways of being postliberal."[11]

Yoder, though, was hardly the only prominent Christian pacifist of the twentieth century. During the Great Depression, Dorothy Day, along with Peter Maurin, shaped the Catholic Worker Movement, a collection of Catholic communities oriented toward offering radical hospitality to those who live on margins of society. The Catholic Worker Movement centered its practices around communal living, Catholic personalism, and the promotion of nonviolence. Trained as a writer/journalist and attracted to communism during her youth, Day turned her writing toward advocacy and the promotion of protests against unjust social structures, particularly economic ones. As she did so, her nascent Roman Catholicism grew to become such a prominent part of her vision of the world that her life would increasingly be "shaped by the fact that Jesus Christ – whom she believed to be God incarnate and the founder of her Church – lived in poverty... [which] signaled that Jesus' followers should refuse the world's standards of success."[12] This theological conviction would undergird and sustain her activism throughout her life.

---

[10] One need only note the number and variety of books written about him and his thought (sadly, almost entirely since his death) to see his impact. These would include Stanley Hauerwas et al., (eds.), *The Wisdom of the Cross: Essays in Honor of John Howard Yoder* (Grand Rapids: Eerdmans, 1999); Craig A. Carter, *The Politics of the Cross: The Theology and Social Ethics of John Howard Yoder* (Grand Rapids: Brazos, 2001); Ben C. Ollenburger and Gayle Gerber Koontz (eds.), *A Mind Patient and Untamed: Assessing John Howard Yoder's Contributions to Theology, Ethics, and Peacemaking* (Telford, PA: Cascadia Publishing House, 2004); Mark Thiessen Nation, *John Howard Yoder: Mennonite Patience, Evangelical Witness, Catholic Convictions* (Grand Rapids: Eerdmans, 2006); Peter Dula and Chris K. Huebner (eds.), *The New Yoder* (Eugene, OR: Cascade Books, 2010); and J. Denny Weaver (ed.), *John Howard Yoder: Radical Theologian* (Eugene, OR: Cascade Books, 2014) as well as articles from a variety of disciplines and too numerous to list here.

[11] Craig A. Carter, *The Politics of the Cross*, 15.

[12] Kevin O'Brien, *The Violence of Climate Change: Lessons of Resistance from Nonviolent Activists* (Washington D.C.: Georgetown University Press, 2017), 123.

Living among the victims of economic brutality, Day argued forcefully for the priority and sufficiency of nonviolence to combat cycles of violence at all levels: personal, national, and international. She wrote that "as long as men trust to the use of force – only a superior, a more savage force will overcome the enemy,"[13] in *The Catholic Worker*, turning an organic trope about complex cycles of action and reaction into a mechanical one. Her insistence on breaking cycles of violence through advocacy and protest continued throughout her life and became one of the hallmarks not only of her own perspective but of Christian (and non-Christian) pacifist projects in the twentieth century. That violence should be understood cyclically, linked to power, and embedded in social systems – including those that are not overtly violent – marks not only Day's vision of Christian pacifism but those of a wide number of pacifists since. And while her insistence on this vision of pacifism made her controversial, especially during World War II, evidence supporting her connections between cycles of violence, power, and social systems has only grown since she wrote.

Day's pacifism was unyielding. Recognizing that her form of living involved sacrifice on behalf of those that were not only treated as unlovable by society but could behave in unlovable ways, she nevertheless insisted that radical neighbor love – which included nonviolence – was a commandment that Christians must obey. As she moved further into her Catholic faith, this commitment to nonviolence manifested itself in a growing refusal to accept violent revolution as a way of achieving economic justice. What we need, she wrote, is "a Christian revolution of our own, without the use of force."[14] That revolution regularly felt impractical: she was a poor steward of money (because Christians are called to give abundantly rather than wisely) and a disengaged citizen who never voted in elections. As O'Brien notes, "To those who criticized her impracticalities, Day clarified: 'We are *not* here to prove that our technique of working with the poor is useful, or to prove that we are able to be effective humanitarians.' She dismissed 'usefulness' and 'effectiveness' as ideals of industrial society, which treated people as statistics rather than beloved children of God."[15] Day's pacifism was not only unstrategic; it was suspicious of modes of (pacifist) engagement with even the hint of an odor of strategic orientation.

---

[13] Dorothy Day, quoted in O'Brien, *The Violence of Climate Change*, 124.
[14] Dorothy Day, quoted in O'Brien, *The Violence of Climate Change*, 126.
[15] O'Brien, *The Violence of Climate Change*, 127.

This suspicion becomes more explicable once one recognizes both its source and its focus. Day converted to Christianity having already lived as a social radical; the conversion may have changed the ground for her convictions but it never disrupted the radicality with which she pursued those convictions. The Christian faith and, in particular, its Scriptures and some of the Roman Catholic Church's more progressive social teachings, fed that radicality. Already disposed toward radicality, Day's Christian commitments fed that disposition, and radicals like Day are often far more shaped by their vision of what can be than by the exigencies of day-in, day-out living. Strategies are far too likely to be grounded in or oriented toward compromises than Day was willing to accept. Rather, Christians should live out their lives trusting in God rather than such strategic wisdom.

Further, Day's focus was on the deleterious effects of early twentieth-century economic systems. The power of capitalism was to seduce all those who acceded to its hegemonic might, inviting citizens into complicity with the causes of economic suffering. This stands in significant contrast to, say, military actions, which are taken on by a subgroup of society and carry within themselves obvious choices about performing actions under conditions of a bracketed morality that accepts otherwise unacceptable forms of violence. One might be able to get away from fighting a war; one would find it much more difficult to get away from participating in the economy. Therefore, people needed to stay on their guard by living a life of simplicity and radicality. Unyielding pacifist activism isn't simply a matter of psychology; it is a matter of will and context as well.

This demonstrates itself also in the life of the most prominent Christian pacifist of the twentieth century: Martin Luther King, Jr. His role in shaping and leading the Civil Rights movement as it worked to overturn segregation in the Jim Crow south, as well as his continued and related efforts to pursue economic justice and his speaking out against the Vietnam War, were neither the product of his denominational upbringing (unlike Yoder) nor a radical conversion (unlike Day). Instead, King's pacifism grew out of his continued development as a Christian thinker and religious activist in contexts where violence not only begat violence but where the ones most likely to come out on the bottom of violent actions were the very people fighting alongside King and those for whom he fought. That King is better known as a practitioner of nonviolent direct action than as a practitioner of pacifism (even if those two terms substantially overlap) hints at the degree to which pacifism was, for King, both a strategic and moral force through which to bring about change.

King was raised as the child and grandchild of clergymen and undertook both seminary and doctoral training with the intent of following after them in the pulpit. And, like many African-American ministers of his time, King's preaching mingled a deep sense of piety with a set of strong convictions about the pursuit of justice: he preached not only to convert persons but to seek the transformation of social systems that hurt and oppressed others, especially those who were most vulnerable. Circumstances and his own brilliance meant that no pulpit could contain him, however. Shortly after King took a church in Montgomery, Alabama, Rosa Parks refused to give up her bus seat and the Montgomery Bus Boycott began with the young minister at its forefront. Success there led not only to national fame but to desegregation campaigns throughout the south and, later, around the United States. When he was assassinated on April 4, 1968, King was still challenging oppressive institutional powers, offering visions of a kingdom in which "the sons of former slaves and the sons of former slave-owners will be able to sit together at the table of brotherhood,"[16] and advocating for nonviolent direct action as a means not only of overcoming injustice but of bearing transformational witness to the power of God in the world.

King's advocacy of nonviolence cannot be separated from the influence that Mohandas (Mahatma) Gandhi had on his thought. Gandhi, the Indian Hindu lawyer and activist who had worked to overcome both apartheid in South Africa and English colonial rule in India, advocated the way of *satyagraha*, or insistence on truth. *Satyagraha* combined Hinduism's emphasis on *ahimsa*, or nonviolence, with self-realization and love for others (including the non-human natural world); it manifested as "soul force," which saw oppressors as in need of purification, not destruction: nonviolent opposition and passive resistance were the means through which love would conquer hate. As such, nonviolent direct resistance of the sort advocated by both Gandhi and King was simultaneously a principled action and a strategic one: not only is it efficacious, it is faithful to their overlapping and deep visions of the world as both filled with goodness and marred by violence.

To say that King borrowed from and then Christianized Gandhi's thoughts would do injustice to both the expansive quality of Gandhi's vision and the imaginative power of King's insights. Gandhi was familiar with Christian thought and King was an original and provocative thinker. Moreover, there are differences – subtle, perhaps, but nevertheless

[16] Martin Luther King, Jr., "I Have a Dream" (speech, Washington D.C., August 28, 1963).

apparent – between the two of them. King's work in nonviolent direct resistance carried a kind of urgency to it: unlike Gandhi's writings, King's writings carry an aura not only of frustration at the power of injustice but exasperation that injustice has been able to achieve the purchase in the world that it has. And Gandhi's writings, unlike King's, treat the pacifism of *satyagraha* as a force that could at least imagine limited and constrained violence if the alternative was obviously much worse. If nothing else, King's advocacy of nonviolent direct resistance following Gandhi reveals the wisdom within the fact that something can be both borrowed and new: one can be both synthetic and novel. King's use of nonviolent direct resistance, especially when done *en masse* by persons trained in nonviolence, reveals the power of pacifism to bring about large-scale social change.[17]

Though all three of these figures – Yoder, Day, and King – each deserve far more space than I give here and though these three figures only begin to scratch the surface of important twentieth-century pacifists in the United States alone, they start to exemplify the range of pacifisms that arose after the late nineteenth century. Day, the unyielding and ideologically committed Roman Catholic activist, pursued the practices of pacifism because they aligned with her vision of an economically equitable world and the intrinsic value of even the least well-off or well-liked. King, the Baptist preacher and movement leader, pursued the practices of pacifism not only as an expression of faith but as a way of converting oppressors into friends. Yoder, the Mennonite scholar and intellectual forebear of a generation of new pacifist scholars, made pacifism intellectually inviting and theologically profound.

In the context of this project, one of the things that makes Day, King, and Yoder especially interesting is that their works address many of the

---

[17] This is not to say that the Civil Rights Movement was quite as pacifist as it is sometimes described. There were those in the movement who quietly admitted to the possibility of pursuing violent actions if things got bad enough – though in the face of bus burnings, beatings, disappearances, fire hoses, dogs, and packed jails, one wonders just what such a line could be. See, for example, Curtis J. Austin, "On Violence and Nonviolence: The Civil Rights Movement in Mississippi," *Mississippi History Now* (February, 2002), available at www.mshistorynow.mdah.ms.gov/articles/62/the-civil-rights-move ment-in-mississippi-on-violence-and-nonviolence, accessed on June 4, 2018 for oral histories on civil rights workers in the 1960s maintaining armed guards around churches and homes used as meeting places or Timothy B. Tyson, *Blood Done Sign My Name* (New York: Broadway Books, 2005), 212ff for an anecdote about how, by 1970, members of the Civil Rights Movement simultaneously affirmed nonviolence and were prepared to act violently.

criticisms I and others have made of the conventional narrative of the Christian pacifist tradition. Yoder's approach added sufficient theological and historical complexity to that narrative to evade those criticisms. King's work added evidence of the success of pacifist practices, thereby revealing its efficacy as well as its fidelity. Day's commitments toward loving the unlovable reveal that pacifism need neither begin nor end in idealism or illusion. So, for instance:

- I (and others) have argued that the conventional Christian pacifist narrative does not give adequate attention to the receding viability of any messianic ethic that is built around the historical Jesus's impending return. Such an approach doesn't give adequate attention to the problems that come with building a politics around a New Testament vision of the coming Kingdom of God, particularly one that treats the gospel's stories of Jesus primarily as historical rather than theological documents. Yet as the very title of his most famous book, *The Politics of Jesus,* strongly implies, Yoder built a political ethic around Jesus as he is described in the gospels (particularly Luke), arguing for the viability of a "Messianic Ethic" even after the early church's naive anticipation of an immediate eschaton had long since faded.[18] As Douglas Harink's book, *Paul Among the Postliberals,* reveals, Yoder's reading of Jesus is mediated through his reading of the Pauline corpus, which complicates any attempt to link that messianic ethic to a historical person, Jesus of Nazareth, without first recognizing the theological lenses through which the writers of the New Testament viewed Jesus.[19]
- I (and others) have argued that obedience to Jesus's commands in the New Testament ignores the contexts in which those texts were written and their distance from our current contexts. Such an approach frames obedience as the straightforward and theologically flat-footed application of commands given in one context and according to one vision of Jesus's teachings to dramatically different contexts and without adequate attention to the theological suppositions that undergirded those teachings. Yet King's commitment to nonviolent direct action is simultaneously deeply faithful to those teachings and expansive enough to

---

[18] See P. Travis Kroeker, "Is a Messianic Political Ethic Possible? Recent Work by and about John Howard Yoder," in *Journal of Religious Ethics* 33.1 (2005): 141–174 for a critical engagement with Yoder's vision of messianic ethics.

[19] Douglas Harink, *Paul Among the Postliberals: Pauline Theology Beyond Christendom and Modernity* (Grand Rapids, MI: Brazos Press, 2003), 105–149.

incorporate Hindu insights via Gandhi, the best of U.S. Constitutional vision, and attention to contemporary socio-political systems, including those that sustained racial injustices after the U.S. Civil War. King never stopped being a Baptist minister but, as a Baptist minister, he found himself reaching out not only toward his foes but toward the insights of figures and ideas that are peripheral to the Christian faith.

- I have argued that the conventional Christian pacifist narrative has unduly elevated the pre-Constantinian church as morally exemplary without giving attention to the anti-Jewish animus that motivated many of the early church's strongest advocates for pacifism. It isn't simply that the writings of Tertullian, Origen, and other early church fathers display both commitments to pacifism and also anti-Jewish screeds; it is that the commitments and the screeds are linked.[20] As such, the early church's pacifism ought to be treated as morally troubling even as it has been treated as politically and exegetically problematic. Yet Day gave almost no attention to this history in her commitment to a radical Roman Catholicism and her social setting, alone, meant that she constantly rubbed shoulders with and valued connections with Jews and Judaism.[21]

- I (and other theologians) have argued that Constantine's ascendance wasn't nearly so deleterious to the church as the conventional Christian pacifist narrative suggests. The conditions that enabled the so-called Constantinian model of church–state relations were in place long before Constantine. Constantine, himself, served as a mediating rather than motivating voice in that new model. And church–state relations

[20] One way Yoder attempts to escape from snares of connecting pacifism to Tertullian and Origen is to distance them from his vision of Christian pacifism: without naming the historians, Yoder notes that "[h]istorians of Christian pacifism have long noted with some embarrassment that although both Origen and Tertullian, in the late second century, retained their pacifism on the level of Christian personal ethics, they had come to affirm without much thought the legitimacy of Rome's governing world" (John Howard Yoder, *The Jewish-Christian Schism Revisited*, 88–9, n. 16). I'm left unclear as to which historians Yoder refers, how much he thinks Tertullian and Origen's positions changed to affirm Roman legitimacy, or the basis upon which he claims such changes happened, though.

[21] See, for instance, her review of Jacques Maritain's *A Christian Looks at the Jewish Question* in *The Catholic Worker* (November, 1939): 7, where she affirms Maritain's statement that "Spiritually, we are Semites" or her unpublished manuscript, "Our Brothers, the Jews," written in 1933 and based in her growing concern about Nazism, especially as it manifested in soft ways in her own New York City. See "Our Brothers, the Jews: A Lost Manuscript, a Continued Call for Solidarity," available at www.americamagazine.org/issue/714/article/our-brothers-jews. Accessed on March 7, 2018.

after Constantine were far more varied – and often more beneficent – than a single disparagingly applied adjective could hope to capture. Certainly, Yoder loudly opposed Constantinian Christianity;[22] indeed, Peter Dula has suggested that "[w]hile there are many forms of ecclesial failure, leading Mennonite theologian John Howard Yoder was most preoccupied with 'constantinianism,' the collusion of church and state which occurred with the fourth century Emperor and which continues in various guises."[23] Yet Yoder also noted that "by the label *Constantinian* we refer less to the man Constantine than to the period, although the man did more than any other person to consummate the change. He was not the only architect of the change; it had begun before him and was not complete until a century after him."[24] For Yoder, the focus ought not be on the man so much as the heresy named for him. As Craig Carter notes, "Constantinianism is not, for Yoder, a complete description of any single church, movement, or figure in history. Nor was it embraced fully and absolutely by any particular part of the church. Nor has it ever characterized the entire church of any age. Rather, Yoder means by Constantinianism a heretical eschatology … [that] proceeds as if the life, death, resurrection, and ascension of the Messiah had never occurred."[25]

- I (and other theologians) have argued that the conventional Christian pacifist narrative has used the term "Constantinian" as a pejorative that refers to any form of church–state relationship in which the two institutions are not categorically distinguished. The conventional narrative claims that links between the two institutions have meant that the goods pursued by both institutions and the means by which they are pursued blur troublingly into each other. Churches and states, we have argued, are both constituted by human beings, vulnerable to the failings of human projects, and in need of redemption. The two institutions

---

[22] See, e.g., John Howard Yoder, *The Royal Priesthood: Essays Ecclesiastical and Ecumenical* (Grand Rapids, MI: Eerdman's Press, 1994), especially "The Otherness of the Church" (53–64) and "Peace without Eschatology" (143–167, particularly 152ff.); John Howard Yoder, *Christian Attitudes to War, Peace, and Revolution*, Theodore J. Koontz and Andy Alexis-Baker, eds. (Grand Rapids, MI: Brazos Press, 2009), esp. Ch. 4; Craig A. Carter, *The Politics of the Cross*, Ch. 6, for just a few examples of the prominence of Constantine and Constantinianism in Yoder's thought.

[23] Peter Dula, "The 'Disavowal of Constantine' in the Age of Global Capital" in Fernando Enns, Scott Holland, and Ann Riggs (eds.), *Seeking Cultures of Peace: A Peace Church Conversation* (Telford, PA: Cascadia Publishing House, 2004), 62.

[24] John Howard Yoder, *Christian Attitudes to War, Peace, and Revolution*, 57.

[25] Craig A. Carter, *The Politics of the Cross*, 155–156.

may differ in awareness of these facts but, theologically, they can't be neatly distinguished by kind: church and state are both analogues of the Kingdom of God.[26] Moreover, we have argued, the terms "church" and "state" encapsulate such a wide range of forms for institutions pursuing such a wide range of projects through such a wide range of processes and in such a wide range of relations to the other as to make the criticism of "Constantinianism" meaningless. Therein, the term confuses phenomenological and theological criticisms. Yet King's work expresses a Christian vision of nonviolence that is not only uninterested in keeping church and state apart, but it links the best insights of American civil religion, particularly expressed in his admiration of Constitutional vision, with a Baptist confidence in the power of God to bring about change in a world made good at the beginning and able to be made good again.

- I (and other theologians) have argued that the conventional Christian pacifist narrative is built around a myth of return, the effects of which are to undermine a telling of history in which God has continued to act in history and to overemphasize the discontinuous qualities of the movement of traditions through time. This myth of return ignores pacifist undercurrents that run throughout the history of the church and treats visions of peace as arising episodically – and rarely – rather than consistently shaping the church's witness, albeit in a wide variety of not necessarily coherent ways, throughout its history. Dorothy Day, however, isn't committed to turning Catholic Worker Houses into contemporary expressions of the early church so much as she is committed to making them places where the continued best wisdom of the Roman Catholic Church can manifest itself in the pursuit of economic equality under conditions of capitalism.

- I (and other theologians) have argued that the conventional Christian pacifist narrative has tended to emphasize purity as an expression of the link between right thinking (orthodoxy) and right action (orthopraxis). Those whose faiths actually are manifest in their actions will display theological and moral purity in a way that sets them apart from both heretics and apostates. The problems with such an emphasis have been not only to reinforce both perfectionism and quietism (where the former would seemingly ignore the grace-based claims of the gospel and

---

[26] The term "analog" in reference to the way the church and the state relate to the Kingdom of God is Karl Barth's. See Karl Barth, *Church and State* (Macon, GA: Smyth and Helwys, 2012).

the latter the Christian mandate to share that gospel), but to shape relations with those in the surrounding cultures as oppositional in a way that does not account for the persistent interactions of those cultures. Yoder, though, never seemed to be happier than when he was engaging others – either as sparring partners or as comrades in the battles against the forces of "Constantinianism."[27] It is worth noting, for instance, that in his essay, "The Nonresistant Church: The Theological Ethics of John Howard Yoder," Stanley Hauerwas locates the primary dualism in Yoder's approach not between perfection and imperfection but between a church that, though imperfect, recognizes its mandate to a form of discipleship that engages surrounding cultures by revealing that war and violence cannot be normative, on the one side, and a world in which war and violence are inevitably viewed as necessary, on the other. This, Hauerwas claims, allows Yoder to escape many of the criticisms (perfectionism, quietism, confusing justice with theology, etc.) directed at pacifism.[28] It is further worth noting that Jeffery Stout, in challenging the "new traditionalists" (MacIntyre, Hauerwas, and Milbank) that cause him such concern over their tendency to quarantine themselves/the church from the larger world, takes up the very essay in which Hauerwas makes that claim to challenge Hauerwas's interpretation of Yoder as *still* being more sectarian than Hauerwas claims: "For purposes of argument, I am not going to dispute Hauerwas' interpretation of Yoder. But Scott Davis has persuaded me that Yoder probably had a more subtle position on justice than Hauerwas thought he did."[29] If anything, Yoder emphasized coherence, not purity, in linking orthodoxy and orthopraxis. In my view, this is the basis for Yoder's distinction between military and policing actions: "We may thus conclude that the state never has a blanket authorization to use violence. The use of force must be limited to the police function, i.e., guided by fair judicial processes, subject to recognized legislative regulation, and safeguarded in practice against its

[27] Among the more provocative conversation partners for Yoder in this regard has been Oliver O'Donovan, with whom he shares strong Christological claims while differing on how that Christology manifests itself politically. See, for instance, Dorothea H. Bertschamann, *Bowing Before Christ – Nodding to the State? Reading Paul Politically with Oliver O'Donovan and John Howard Yoder* (London: Bloomsbury, 2014).

[28] Stanley Hauerwas, *Vision and Virtue* (Notre Dame: University of Notre Dame Press, 1981), 197–221.

[29] Jeffrey Stout, *Democracy and Tradition* (Princeton, NJ: Princeton University Press, 2004), 321, n. 7.

running away with the situation."[30] Policing is an expression of the minimum amount of force necessary to maintain order in a state, and order, Yoder recognized, is a fundamentally good thing.[31]

Day, King, and Yoder remind critics of the dangers of simplifying the pacifist tradition, undermining the conclusions that can come with such simplifications. And yet . . .

Yoder, King, and Day's complex theological visions of pacifism and their significant arguments in its defense nevertheless manifest new expressions of the very problems that they attempt to escape.[32] So, for instance:

- While Yoder escapes the conventional Christian pacifist narrative's failing of a messianic ethic that ignores the way that early ethic was premised on Jesus's immediate return through recourse to Pauline theology, Yoder's messianic ethic is premised on a primary distinction between a church that recognizes Jesus's current and messianic reign and a world in which that reign is hidden rather than in Paul's primary distinction between an old creation (in which the church continues to participate) and a new creation (in which the world also participates).[33]
- While King escapes the conventional Christian pacifist narrative's failing of a simplified Christology around which to shape the obligations of obedience through an *imitatio Christi*, his expansive vision of the power of religious faith to bring about social change can be so encompassing that it is difficult to see what makes his arguments distinctly theological (or, more accurately, an expression of a distinct theology among a range of theologies). King is a theological *bricoleur*, drawing

---

[30] John Howard Yoder, *The Christian Witness to the State* (Scottsdale, PA: Herald Press, 2002), 36–7.

[31] One wonders what to do with Yoder in light of Mueller's arguments that conventional war is passing away (which, itself, can be read in quite eschatological ways) and the remnants of war, who are more interested in self or ideology than politics, need to be policed, albeit through military means.

[32] Each of the criticisms that follow warrants far more attention than I can give here. Fortunately, such attention has been given by others. The point of this paragraph is to connect three of the most prominent pacifist theologians of the twentieth century to the assessments of the conventional narrative of Christian pacifism that I have described in this and the previous chapters in a way that reveals further hints at doing theological historiography.

[33] For a much more detailed exploration of this, see P. Travis Kroeker, "Is a Messianic Political Ethic Possible?", esp. 157ff, in which Kroeker notes that Yoder's criticisms of Augustine and a (Platonic) Augustinian eschatology are caricatures of Augustine's actual account of the City of God and the City of Man.

from parts of his black Baptist heritage, his own doctoral work in theology (including attention to Howard Thurman and its streak of Boston University personalism), American civil religion, and even conceptually differentiated religious traditions like Hinduism. In prioritizing morality and the moral overlap between these various sources as he made his arguments against racism, economic injustice, and war, he leaves himself vulnerable to criticisms about the underexamined theological differences between these traditions, the theological anchor point of his own piety, and a Christology that shows little regard for the abiding theological significance of, e.g., the great Christological debates of the second through sixth centuries.

- While Day escapes the supersessionist tendencies that have troubled the conventional Christian pacifist narrative by attending to contemporary anti-Semitism and reveling in her personal connections to Jewish friends, her activist temperament that shaped her responses to poverty and oppression, combined with a theological mysticism that led her to believe that all people would be made one in Jesus Christ, left her peculiarly silent in addressing some of the more pressing interreligious concerns that separated Jews and Christians. Among these questions were those pertaining to the establishment and defense of the modern state of Israel (which is peculiar, given the attention that, as of the mid-1930s, *The Catholic Worker* paid to the plight of Jews in Europe and the marginalization of Jews in America), Jewish understandings of Judaism as a religion, and the problems of linking Judaism and Christianity via the person and work of Jesus. Claiming that all people – including Jews – will ultimately be reconciled in Jesus Christ may not be anti-Semitic in any immediate political sense (she does recognize the Jewishness of the person of Jesus), but it still displays a kind of eschatological supersessionism by thinking about the significance of Jesus for Jews in distinctly Christian ways.[34]

---

[34] See, e.g., Myles Werntz, "Many Roots, One Tree: Dorothy Day on the Mystical Body of Christ, Judaism, and War," *Journal of Scriptural Reasoning* 14.1 (June, 2015), available at https://jsr.shanti.virginia.edu/back-issues/vol-14-number-1-june-2015-politics-scrip turc-and-war/many-roots-one-tree-dorothy-day-on-the-mystical-body-of-christ-juda ism-and-war/, accessed on June 4, 2018, for the way Day's efforts at combatting anti-Semitism and supporting Jewish colleagues still drain Judaism of its distinctive theological character and separate her colleagues' identities from their religious faith. It is also worth noting that Yoder, too, imports a distinct and methodological form of supersessionism when, from a Christian perspective, he treats pacifist threads from exilic and Rabbinic Judaism as normative for and central to Jewish thought and builds his reconciliatory strategies from those threads in spite of the fact that his Jewish interlocutors didn't

- While King escapes that portion of the myth of return that denies the continuous witness to peace in the church after Constantine, he also reinforces the structures that support that myth by consistently returning to and equating a particular reading of the New Testament as the best way to read the New Testament. This leads him to blur a theological problem about violence with a historical one about the way the early church related to the Roman Empire. The twentieth-century American church – including the black church within which he worked – simply did not look like the first-century church, and the empire that America had become by the middle of that century did not look like the Roman Empire. The differences are the products of thousands of years of unfolding history, most of which King ignored in his work. King was a prophet, theologian, and activist of the first order; he was not, though, a political historian.

- While Yoder escapes the tendency to collapse a wide range of church-state relations into a single derogatory term, "Constantinianism," he also reinforces the idea that the power with which the state should be most closely identified is that of the threat and use of violence – an idea that *may* refer to the modern nation-state but isn't as generalizable as Yoder suggests. The idea that a state is defined largely by its monopoly on the legitimate use of force is a peculiarly modern idea, but hardly the only modern definition of the state.

- While all three escape the perfectionist and quietist character that inheres in the conventional narrative of Christian pacifism, the way Day and Yoder, especially, focus on the church/world division sometimes has the effect of contrasting an idealized community (the church) and a deprecated society (the world), a contrast that allows them to offer unduly stinging criticisms of many of their

recognize those same threads as carrying the weight Yoder placed on them. See, e.g., Peter Ochs, "Commentary," in John Howard Yoder, *The Jewish-Christian Schism Revisited*, 38–40, Michael G. Cartwright, "Afterword: 'If Abraham Is Our Father ...' The Problem of Christian Supersessionism *after* Yoder" in John Howard Yoder, *The Jewish-Christian Schism Revisited*, 205–226, P. Travis Kroeker, "Is a Messianic Political Ethic Possible?" esp. 160ff, and Peter Ochs, *Another Reformation: Postliberal Christianity and the Jews* (Grand Rapids: Baker Academic, 2011) for much greater detail on Yoder's supersessionism, including Ochs's claim that "Without explicitly naming it as such, Yoder offers his theology as an equivalent of what I call Christian postliberalism, and he associates that postliberalism with non-supersessionism. In practice, however, his arguments about Judaism include some clearly supersessionist claims" (Peter Ochs, *Another Reformation*, 3).

interlocutors.[35] This is, perhaps, the rhetorical risk of prophetic pacifism: no system, when viewed through lenses of social analysis that are colored by realism and suspicion, will look good in comparison to an idealized version of another system.

Sitting behind all these affirmations and criticisms are background conditions that implicitly preoccupied all three of them but about which they said relatively little. These are the conditions of modernity, including the distinct ways modern thought has shaped how we think about history and tradition, the state, biblical interpretation, the church, ethics, the self, peace, and the relation of theology to morality.[36] So, for instance, the power behind Day's thought was that she was able to bring her interpretations of Catholicism and communism to bear on social crises in twentieth-century America that were being driven by an ascending form of capitalism; her willingness to pursue alternative ways of living helped give her the critical distance needed to see the economic problems of the day and to render them into a theological framework. Yet the irony of her thought is that this very distance may have inhibited her ability to recognize nearby conversation partners like Howard Thurman and exacerbated her tendency to romanticize events that were farther away like the Cuban revolution: modernity shapes a particular way of understanding and treating the "other." The power behind King's thought was connected to his ability to link a set of nonviolent practices to a range of traditions such that Protestant Christianity, American civil religion, and Gandhian Hinduism all shaped the way forward for the Civil Rights Movement. Yet the irony of his thought is that he never grounded these practices in the history of those traditions in order to reap the benefits of the centuries of wisdom associated with each of them: modernity treats historical traditions with suspicion. The power behind Yoder's thought is that he was able to see the forces to

---

[35] So, for instance, See P. Travis Kroeker, "Is a Messianic Political Ethic Possible?" Paul Doerksen, "Share the House: Yoder and Hauerwas Among the Nations" in Ben C. Ollenburger and Gayle Gerber Koontz, eds., *A Mind Patient and Untamed*, 187–204, Romand Coles, "The Wild Patience of John Howard Yoder: 'Outsider' and the 'Otherness of the Church'" in Peter Dula and Chris K. Huebner, *The New Yoder*, 216–252, Grady Scott Davis, "Tradition and Truth in Christian Ethics: John Yoder and the Bases of Biblical Realism" in Stanley Hauerwas et al., eds., *The Wisdom of the Cross*, 278–305, and just about anything that James Gustafson wrote about Yoder, including *Ethics from a Theocentric Perspective* (Chicago: University of Chicago Press, 1981).

[36] A far more detailed exploration of modernity and its impact on how we tell the narratives of the various Christian traditions shaped to deal with violence will occur in the next volume in this series, in the section on Just War thinking. For now, these few sentences will have to operate as placeholder in anticipation of that book.

which modernity gave rise as forces that could be contested; his recourse to a biblical realist vision of God's divine sovereignty expressed in Jesus Christ as Lord offered Yoder a remarkably stable location for criticisms and affirmations of those forces. And the irony of Yoder's thought is that he located the point of historical crisis for the church some fifteen centuries prior to the modern age; in doing so, he gained some historical traction (by attending to those intervening centuries) but lost some of the power that could have driven his more immanent criticisms of contemporary political structures: modernity offers a self capable of choosing between the forces that drive it.[37]

The frustrations with the wisdom of Day, King, and Yoder that follow such ironies is that the tools they used in contesting violence were themselves shaped by modernity; as such, their ideas retained aspects of the very forces they were trying to undermine. The wisdom in their thought is that their continued beholdenness to the conditions of modernity neither invalidates nor neuters the power of their arguments. The theological insight that makes possible this wisdom – an insight upon which they all implicitly relied – is that the reality of divine sovereignty and grace expressed most fully in the new creation will trump every fading manifestation of the old one.

2 LEARNING BEYOND WHAT THEY TAUGHT: SHAPING STRATEGIC PACIFISM

One particularly troubling manifestation of their beholdenness to modernity, though, is their lack of attention to the natural world. In this, we might take Yoder as a prototypical example, if only because the breadth of his writings was greater than that of Day or King and so if any of them would have been likely to include such attention, it would be him. It is as if Yoder's preoccupation with the politics of the Kingdom of God hid from him the abundance of a new creation that enveloped that Kingdom. One searches his work in vain for any sustained attention to ecology, the environment, nature, or creation. None among the twenty-odd forms of pacifism in *Nevertheless* connect to either origins in or responsibility for the natural world. And this absence is made all the more peculiar by the facts that Yoder always identified himself as Mennonite (a tradition that

---

[37] That Yoder referred to the age of the Enlightenment with the ungainly term "neo-neo-Constantinianism" should have signaled the need to address such an irony. See Craig A. Carter, *The Politics of the Cross*, 169.

has long had a close connection to the land), that pacifists throughout history have extended their commitment to pacifism to include peace with creatures great and small (one thinks, for instance, of St. Francis), and that one of Yoder's first essays was on farming for the Mennonite Encyclopedia.[38] Perhaps his lack of attention to the natural world was a product of his studies with and use of Karl Barth, whose concerns about natural theology are mirrored by Yoder's opposition to starting theology from anywhere other than within the confessing church as it is ordered by the Lordship of Jesus.[39] Perhaps Yoder's lack of attention to the natural world was informed by his susceptibility to a myth of return, which consistently oriented him around a particular reading and prioritization of the New Testament and its apocalyptic insights as authoritative. Such an approach might focus more on the new creation than creation. Or perhaps his lack of attention to the natural world was the product of all of these and even other forces. Regardless, as Yoder's insights into pacifism move forward into the environmental age, they will need to be reshaped to attend to the natural world as part of the world of peace to which Yoder so consistently and insistently pointed. So, too, will the pacifisms of Day and King.

The conventional narrative of the Christian pacifist tradition in which Day, King, and Yoder play prominent roles disregards the natural world. In spite of the biblical connection between peace and both the created order[40] and the peace of a new creation (in which, through Christ, "God was pleased to reconcile himself to all things, whether on earth or in heaven" [Colossians 1:20] and which, Revelation 22:1–3 notes, has at its center a garden), the conventional narrative ignores creation in its root text, the Bible. In spite of examples like St. Francis of Assisi who was both pacifist and lover of the whole of creation, and the long history of farming

---

[38] John Howard Yoder, "Farming among Mennonites in France," in *The Mennonite Encyclopedia*, vol. 2 (Hillsboro, KS: Mennonite Brethren Publishing House, 1956): 306–7.

[39] See Craig A. Carter, *The Politics of the Cross*, Ch. 2, "Yoder and the Theology of Karl Barth," for a systematic overview and appraisal of the connections between Yoder and Barth, including the claim that the only significant site of disagreement between the two had to do with Barth's use of a *grenzfall* case in the context of war.

[40] See, e.g., Genesis 1:30 for a vision of Eden so complete that all creatures are vegetarians; Leviticus 26:6 for God's promise to grant the kind of peace to the Israelites in which "no one shall make you afraid [for] I will remove dangerous animals from the land, and no sword shall go through your hand" or Isaiah 11's vision of a peaceful kingdom in which wolves live with lambs, leopards lie down with kids, and nursing children play with snakes, for "the earth will be full of the knowledge of the Lord as the waters cover the sea."

in the peace churches,[41] the conventional narrative ignores premodern figures who linked their pacifism to creation-care.[42] In spite of examples like David Dodge, whose concerns with war in the nineteenth century included its destruction of the natural world, the conventional narrative has largely ignored the cost of war on the environment.[43] And in spite of the connections between pacifism and earth-care emphasized by figures in the environmental movement like Arne Naess, Rachel Carson, and the Evangelical Environmental Network,[44] the conventional narrative ignores provocative outside voices.

Perhaps, though, there are at least two other insights to pick up from Day, King, and Yoder. First, there are many people with whom to talk and from whom pacifists might learn. After all, their willingness to engage such a wide variety of conversation partners – from both the past and the present and from both pacifist and non-pacifist perspectives – revealed the very type of capacious spirit that can motivate and shape an environmentally attuned pacifism. Second, questions about how to be

---

[41] Though see Walter Klaassen, "Pacifism, Nonviolence, and the Peaceful Reign of God," in Calvin Redekop, ed., *Creation and Environment: An Anabaptist Perspective on a Sustainable World* (Baltimore: Johns Hopkins University Press, 2000), 139–153 for the argument that the agrarian practices of the peace churches were driven by necessity and their tendency to separate themselves from other groups of people more than love for creation.

[42] The paucity of systematic attention to creation in, e.g., Mennonite and Anabaptist theology is striking. So, for instance, Thomas N. Finger does not touch on creation in his 600-page *A Contemporary Anabaptist Theology* (Downers Grove, IL: Intervarsity Press, 2004) and A. James Reimer does not include a section on creation in his even longer (650-page) *Mennonites and Classical Theology: Dogmatic Foundations for Christian Ethics* (Kitchener, ON: Pandora Press, 2001) – though he does touch, incidentally and on few occasions, on the idea of "environment." Gordon Kaufman, who is Mennonite, does write on creation but not in a way that reveals his connections to the Radical Reformation.

[43] See David Dodge, "War Inconsistent with the Religion of Jesus Christ," in Long, *Christian Peace and Nonviolence*, 111.

[44] Naess is best known as the philosopher who coined the term (and was an advocate for) "deep ecology." He regularly relied on Gandhi in his work. Rachel Carson, the author of *Silent Spring*, also wrote, "Until we have courage to recognize cruelty for what it is – whether its victim is human or animal – we cannot expect things to be much better in the world. There can be no double standard. We cannot have peace among men whose hearts find delight in killing any living creature." (Rachel Carson, quoted in Andrew Fiala, "Introduction: Violence and Nonviolence in the Environmental Movement," *Value Inquiry Book Series*, vol. 282 (2015): 15). The Evangelical Environmental Network's "On the Care of Creation: An Evangelical Declaration on the Care of Creation" repeatedly connects peace and creation care. See "On the Care of Creation: An Evangelical Declaration on the Care of Creation," in Long, *Christian Peace and Nonviolence*, 275–277.

faithful are far more important to pacifism than questions about how to be effective. So, for instance, Day's mature criticisms of capitalism and violence and her commitment to establishing Catholic Worker Houses are based in her conviction that alternative ways of living are possible and worth modeling even if they never become widespread because such ways of living conform to the will of a God who will draw all people together – making them truly catholic – through Jesus: mystical oneness will trump present divisions. King's notion that nonviolent resistance could reshape American culture by reshaping American hearts would be naïve were it based simply on social analysis; it became coherent and viable because sitting behind it was his conviction that "the universe is on the side of justice."[45] As a scholar, Yoder mirrors and grounds the commitment to faithfulness rather than efficacy through his conviction that a "Constantinian/Christendom" model of Christianity substitutes efficacy for fidelity in making moral judgments. He suspects that efficacy-based processes for making moral judgments are tantamount to denying that it is God who will make history come out right. It is not our duty to make history come out right; it is our duty to be obedient to the God who will do so. A consequentialist ethic, to Yoder's way of thinking, "abandons moral absolutes and is itself a product of the social experience which has taught Western Christians to think from a posture of the establishment, rather than from one of an excluded or persecuted minority."[46]

What insights might we take from these assessments of Day, King, and Yoder that can be generalized for thinking about how to narrate traditions as they move through time? At least the following three, which, when combined with those from earlier chapters in this book and in anticipation of the last chapter, round out the list of insights and implications to an even twenty.

First, we participate in the problems we want to solve. Human beings aren't computers; our outputs are neither fated by our inputs nor driven by the obligations of our programming. Within human bounds, we make choices about what we will work on, how hard we will work, how we will

---

[45] Martin Luther King, Jr., "Out of Segregation's Long Night: An Interpretation of a Racial Crisis," *The Churchman* (February, 1958): 8. In a nearly identical essay printed in another journal, King would include a sentence that has become famous and famously identified with him (although he recognizes that it came from elsewhere, though he does not name the abolitionist Theodore Parker as its source): "The arc of the moral universe is long, but it bends toward justice."

[46] John H. Yoder, "A Critique of North American Evangelical Ethics," *Transformation* 2.1 (January–May, 1985): 29.

approach that work, and what decisions we will make. We are, in a word, motivated. And such motivations – the things that drive us – are shaped by our encounters with the world around us, our desire to make sense of them, and our pursuit of solutions to the problems and pains with which the world confronts us. Unsurprisingly, pacifists are motivated, in part, by their experiences of violence (whether those experiences are immediate or mediated through stories, texts, and images) and the suffering that violence causes. They are also motivated by the conviction that such suffering can be addressed, relieved, and/or prevented. And Christian pacifists link both their concern about suffering and their conviction that such suffering can be addressed to faith in a God whose goodness and power reveal suffering to be unnatural, whose actions are consistently toward its alleviation, and whose will is that human beings participate, in our own human way, in that alleviation of suffering.

So: what motivates us? Disciplines as varied as evolutionary biology, social psychology, political philosophy, and systematic theology all offer significant and overlapping responses to that question. Yet certainly among the things that motivate us are our own feelings of discomfort, disquiet, disease, and disequilibrium, each of which produce a kind of suffering in us. We then seek redress for these sufferings. And, when we are thoughtful and attentive to the world around us, we recognize that we are not alone in these sufferings and that one of the ways we can pursue redress for our own pains is to work at addressing the sufferings of others. That is, we find in the world pains we also find in ourselves. This insight is revelatory in two ways. First, this insight shows that we are connected to those around us. And, second, it shows that we carry in our own lives connections to the causes of suffering.

Christian pacifists recognize the suffering caused by violence because they can empathize with the suffering caused by violence in others. They do so imperfectly, certainly: to empathize with another is also to recognize that we are not identical to that other. Yet they do empathize. Moreover, when they are reflexively attentive, they recognize that the sufferings of violence that they feel also link them to the causes of suffering in themselves and others. So thoughtful Christian pacifists don't pursue nonresistance or nonviolent resistance because they believe they will eliminate violence from their lives, let alone the world. They pursue these things because they recognize that they can't entirely eliminate violence from their lives, but the impossibility of eliminating violence doesn't mean they can't do something, or that they are released from obligations to God and neighbor to whom they are bound in faith-shaped relationships.

Yet violence is not the only cause for suffering in the world; we also face the sufferings that come with feelings of incompleteness and incoherence in our own thoughts, plans, and ways of engaging the world. For scholars at least, this means not only recognizing the imperfections in our own thoughts but also that our attempts to address such imperfections are, themselves, imperfect. For scholars who are historians, this means recognizing that they are bound up in the imperfections of the very narratives they tell about how the past has led us to the present. And because such imperfections are sources of suffering, we also recognize that our various thoughts, plans, and ways of engaging the world are causes for the sufferings of our own imperfections. To the degree that scholarship is one way we engage the world, expressing thoughts and plans, it also reveals the causes for the sufferings it attempts to address.

Earlier in this chapter, I suggested that even as Day, King, and Yoder escape many of the problems (the sufferings) of the conventional Christian pacifist narrative, at least as that narrative experiences them, they nevertheless tend to create new versions of those old problems. What I am now suggesting is that this is inevitable. We all repeat in our own work some version of the suffering we are attempting to address. As a participant in the sufferings they are attempting to address, Day, King, and Yoder aren't simply examples of a problem that pacifists or scholars (or pacifist scholars) face; they are examples of a problem we all face.[47]

This can sound like bad news. And it is, in part. It would be much easier on our psyches if we could live free from the sufferings we participate in causing and it could, perhaps, be a better world if such sufferings were

---

[47] Obviously, a moment of reflexive honesty leads me to note that this project also participates in the sufferings it attempts to address. The theology of traditions that begins the project is still too bound to both modern suspicions about traditions and also modern theological projects that treat history too immanently and offer "eras" – social imaginaries – through which to make sense of them. My accounts of the conventional narratives about the pacifist, just war, and just peacemaking traditions simplify them unduly (silencing some voices and giving others megaphones), and the narratives I propose to replace them are beholden to assumptions (on, e.g., the relation of thought and practice, the project of demythologizing, the willingness to separate the three traditions from each other) that do not begin with me but have shaped some of the problems we now face with them. It still blurs offering narratives about the way things really are with narratives that are strong misreadings of traditions in order to decalcify them and thereby make them more supple. At the end of the project – whenever that may be – my deepest hope is that I have offered ideas that provoke better ideas and practices rather than ideas that resolve the problems of bad ideas and practices and the sufferings they cause.

eliminated from the world. Yet it is also good news in at least three ways. First, attention to this reflexive problem stimulates us. That is, one of the forces that motivate our engagements with the world is the attempt to do something about the suffering we feel, especially as we recognize our own complicity in that suffering. Second, the fact that we continue to experience these things as suffering – including the suffering that comes with our awareness of complicity – suggests that we are not bound to treat such sufferings as fated or ultimately inevitable and it hints at the possibility that somewhere, somehow, there is relief. And, third, recognizing our complicity in the problems we would challenge helps us understand and empathize with those who benefit from those problems and whose conversions we seek. These three bits of good news are expressions of what Christians mean when they refer to the "good news of the gospel." And even as other religious traditions (and other a-religious traditions) may offer alternative expressions of and answers to the questions that these pieces of good news raise that need to be taken seriously, their continued existence as good news in themselves nevertheless offers not only motivation but stimulates conversation and grounds hope.

Recognizing that we participate in the problems we wish to solve – and that our participation in the problems we wish to solve grounds the shape of redemptive activity – is doubly important when shaping pacifist responses to climate-related conflict. Both pacifist and environmental projects – indeed, perhaps distinctively, pacifist and environmental projects – catch participants up in unavoidable systems of complicity. At structural levels, pacifists participate in cultural and political systems that not only can behave violently but even define themselves through violence (e.g., the modern nation state defining itself by its claims to a monopoly on legitimate violence): they may pay taxes that go toward military expenditures, watch violence on television, accept policing actions (if not military ones), and even serve in a limited range of roles within either the government or the military. At theoretical levels, pacifists may favor some forms of coercive action (e.g., forms of nonviolent resistance) without offering clear or compelling arguments about what makes coercive actions that don't involve physical force "nonviolent." At structural levels, those pursuing environmental sustainability participate in cultural, political, and economic systems that are destructive to the environment: they may rely on energy produced by burning fossil fuels, eat foods like beef that carry significant environmental costs, use household items containing toxic chemicals or rare resources that were manufactured in another part of the world and shipped to them, pay taxes that provide subsidies to energy-producers, etc. At theoretical levels, those pursuing environmental sustainability may favor international political arrangements (e.g., carbon taxes) that favor some countries over others or some living standards (e.g., those involving persons being paid a living wage in an industrialized country) that, were they applied to everyone on the planet, would significantly increase rates of resource depletion – and do so without offering clear and compelling arguments about what makes these arrangements and standards expressions of environmental elitism. Both violence and environmental destruction inevitably breed hypocrisy.

Yet as I've suggested above, complicity isn't all bad. Not only does it help us understand the complexity and reach of the systems we oppose, it can motivate engagement, give a basis for empathy, and signal our obligation to treat deficiencies and suffering as deficiencies and suffering rather than as normal or fated. Complicity in systems of violence and environmental degradation is one way we connect in an interconnected world. As attention to our interconnectedness to other human beings and to the nonhuman natural world expands as part of the shift into the Anthropocene, our ability to recognize and live into the ambivalences and impurities endemic to life on earth will signal our limits. When viewed theologically, this attention also has the potential of pointing toward new possibilities that diminish violence and promote sustainability. In a peculiar way, recognition of complicity can fund hope and, therein, point toward a future that is not yet rather than a past that is unrecoverable.

The second implication of this chapter follows from the previous one: the resources we have to address the sufferings we face have also helped to shape those sufferings. To the extent that the things we make then remake us, this is a corollary to the preceding insight and it complicates how those of us who would address suffering can move forward in time. Ignoring the origins and roles that our resources play in our sufferings can exacerbate them or induce new suffering. Yet so can attempt to either purify or reject those resources.

The danger of ignoring the sources and roles that our resources play in causing the suffering that we would address is, on its face, self-apparent. And even where it is not, liberation theologians and continental philosophers have so highlighted these dangers as to make rehearsing them here repetitive and derivative. I would point out, though, that at a generalized level, this is the danger that the myth of return repeats: treating the New Testament and the early church as not only normative but as providing unmitigated goods, the myth of return ignores both the distance between contexts and also the ambiguous goods that constitute the New Testament and early church. The New Testament is not only more ambivalent about violence and the use of force than the conventional narrative of Christian pacifism admits, but, as a historical document, it carries in its body the scars and weapons of its time: slavery condoned, men and women ranked, both acceptance of and resistance to imperial power, an incoherent mix of quietism and activism, etc. And the early church's pacifism not only grows out of its anti-Jewish sentiment but is shaped by a range of fictional narratives (about, e.g., the martyrs) and strident proclamations (about, e.g., the dangers of heresy and the need for purity) that harm its credibility in the world and its usefulness for the church. I have named these and other problems with the myth of return in earlier chapters. The more general problem with treating narratives as innocuous or wholly virtuous is that such an approach ignores the capacity of narratives not only to shape but to distort those whose lives are framed by them. The powers of narratives – like all powers – are good but ambiguous ones: narratives are capable of being used to harm as well as to heal. So, for instance, the conventional Christian pacifist narrative has funded utopian projects like those of Thomas Müntzer and John of Leiden in the 1530s, each of whom was influenced by the early Reformed peace churches and, like the writers of the New Testament, first anticipated an immediate eschaton and then inserted themselves into the narrative of the end of time. Both projects ended in the deaths of thousands.[48]

Attempts to reject resources also bring dangers. The modern project of self-creation – of intentionally leaving behind the burdens and trappings of history – includes the project of discarding traditions, or at least the power of those traditions to function authoritatively for disciplined new lives, in order to avoid the dangers and sufferings that the resources within traditions bring with them.[49] The concern, voiced succinctly by Audre Lorde, is that "the master's tools will never dismantle the master's house,"[50] and so our need is for different tools and a fresh start. To the degree that traditions provide a limited range of tools with which to

---

[48] See John Gray, *Black Mass: Apocalyptic Religion and the Death of Utopia* (New York: Farrar, Strauss, and Giroux, 2009).

[49] See, e.g., Jeffery Stout, *The Flight from Authority: Religion, Morality, and the Quest for Autonomy* (South Bend: University of Notre Dame Press, 1987).

[50] Audre Lorde, "The Master's Tools Will Never Dismantle the Master's House," in *Sister Outsider: Essays and Speeches* (Berkeley, CA: Crossing Press, 2007), 112. It is important to note that Lorde's statement, in context, is more subtle than the uses to which her statement has been put.

understand and construct our present context, this concern is genuine: how are we to escape the dangers that led those tools to be weaponized in the first place when we're using them now? The irony, though, is that Lorde's concern replicates the modern project: avoiding old tools and imagining that we can start from scratch on a new house with new tools is what modernity is all about. The tools at hand in modernity are likely to be the only tools available to us; attempting to escape or reject the traditions in which those tools come wrapped is not only fruitless but peculiarly self-indicting: the very act of rejecting a tradition is, itself, an act shaped by a dominant modern tradition.

Perhaps, instead, we need to think more carefully and creatively about using the old tools rather than looking for new ones? After all, contemporary power theorists have shown us that any tool can be weaponized, so rejecting the imperfect tools that are readily at hand in the pursuit of tools we do not yet see won't necessarily bring us any closer to the elimination of suffering caused by traditions and may only induce new suffering in us and for others. So, for instance, to the extent that the myth of return within the conventional narrative of Christian pacifism has been motivated by the rejection of traditions of thought that arose after Constantine, that narrative has been weakened and made less resilient in its ability to function in new contexts. When St. Augustine's thought, for instance, is rejected because it is linked to just war thinking, pacifists also lose access to his cautions against thoroughgoing apocalypticism and the dangers of the *libido dominandi*, both of which serve as warnings about self-delusion and misshapen pride.

A paradigmatic expression of the problem with rejecting resources is the pursuit of what literary theorist Kenneth Burke referred to as the project of debunking. He writes,

I think that the typical debunker is involved in a strategy of this sort: He discerns an evil. He wants to eradicate this evil. And he wants to do a thorough job of it. Hence, in order to be sure that he is *thorough enough*, he becomes *too thorough*. In order to knock the underpinnings from beneath the arguments of his opponents, he perfects a mode of argument that would, if carried out consistently, also knock the underpinnings from beneath his own argument. But at this important juncture, he simply "pulls his punch," refusing to apply as a test of his own position the arguments by which he has dissolved his opponent's position . . . since there comes a point at which he too must advocate something other, he *covertly* restores important ingredients of a thought that he has *overtly* annihilated.[51]

---

[51] Kenneth Burke, "The Virtues and Limitations of Debunking," *The Philosophy of Literary Form*, 3rd ed. (Berkeley: University of California Press, 1973), 171. Emphases his.

We might think of Burke as calling us to become "incomplete debunkers" when working with traditions: discerning and combating their evils as best we can but not in a way so thorough as to knock the underpinnings from beneath our own arguments. Incomplete debunkers pursue projects of mediating debunking even as they recognize their tendency (provided for them by the traditions of criticism they have inherited) to become complete debunkers. Debunking, after all, can itself be debunked when it is made the culminating step in a process of criticism; this is part of Burke's criticism of it. Since debunker and debunked can converse, they must share some something in common.[52] Yet when debunking is used to annihilate another position, it rejects all sides of that position, one of which must exist implicitly in the debunker's position. Thus, the debunker's own arguments fall victim to his or her criticisms of that other position and, as a result, debunkers must covertly incorporate parts of the rejected position into their respective positions. Because the resources of traditions participate in the suffering those traditions cause but are also the resources at hand for dealing with that suffering, critics of traditions ought to practice mediate debunking even as they try to attend to and ameliorate their own tendencies toward complete debunking. That is, as a mediating move, debunking does not seek to annihilate another position so much as recognize its ambiguities and deal with the consequences of that position as it uncovers them.

The resources within traditions express themselves in a variety of ways: customs and practices, structures and attitudes, narratives and silences. For most of us, at least, the most explicit way that traditions express themselves is through texts. We become most aware not only of the resources within traditions but their relation to other resources and to traditions themselves as we read about them. As such, one of the most important projects we can take on in recognizing and addressing the suffering that the resources of traditions create is through giving careful, critical attention to the texts we use: Notice what we read and how what we read shapes us. Notice which voices are absent from the text and pursue other texts in which those voices may be present. Attend to claims that the text makes about its origins and purposes and what those claims reveal about how the text positions itself in time. Attend to the way texts have been used as balms and as weapons. Explore how texts are related to other resources within traditions. The project of mediate debunking,

---

[52] See Donald Davidson, "On the Very Idea of a Conceptual Scheme," *Inquiries into Truth and Interpretation* (Oxford, UK: Clarendon Press, 1984): 183–198.

therefore, needs to be applied to how we read texts. Recognize. Reuse. Recycle.

In his book, *Peirce, Pragmatism, and the Logic of Scripture*, Peter Ochs offers a "strategy of pragmatic reading" that provides just such an application. Ochs begins by distinguishing two types of reading strategies. The first is the plain sense reading, in which the meaning of the text is described "within the *rhetorical* context of some body of received literature."[53] Plain sense readings assume that an author says what she means and writes to describe what she thinks is actually going on. Plain sense interpretations trust not only in the author's ability to do this, but in the possibility for the medium to convey the author's world/ideas/emotions in a broadly coherent and generally accurate manner.

However, the very trust that makes plain sense readings possible also makes them equivocal, confused, or contradictory. At some level, author, medium, and reader all carry biases and limits. Those biases and limits mean that representation will fail. Awkward seams in the text, holes in the writer's skills, and problems in the reader's interpretation will result from the failures of that plain sense reading.

Therefore, Ochs develops a second reading strategy to compensate for the failures of the first. The pragmatic reading of a text attempts to redress those failures by probing after meanings hidden in the plain sense "*for some particular context of interpretation.*"[54] That is to say, a pragmatic reading's success will turn on how well it resolves the problems of the plain sense reading for a specific group of interpreters.

Because pragmatic readings occur within particular communities, there is no single method of interpretation that can be mapped onto all texts in order to reveal their meaning. Instead, each community will address the deficiencies of a text according to its own set of rules and practices for reading. Regardless of the method, however, each community of readers searches out the intentions of the text's author as she attempted to make sense of and/or construct the world.

This community-specific process of pragmatic reading is complicated in two ways. First, the author's equivocation, confusion, or contradiction is mirrored in the system of symbols that constitute the text, making those symbols vague. Thus, the interpreting community has the task of addressing the vagueness of the symbols. Second, the community must also

---

[53] Peter Ochs, *Peirce, Pragmatism and the Logic of Scripture* (New York: Cambridge University Press, 2005), 6.

[54] Peter Ochs, *Peirce, Pragmatism and the Logic of Scripture*, 6–7. Emphasis his.

address the confusions of the author behind those symbols. That is, the interpreting community assumes that there is an author – a human being – behind the text who is deliberately trying to convey some message through those symbols, and that the confusions of the text are, in part, traceable to the confusions of the author.

To address the author's confusions, pragmatic readers must read not only texts but persons, trying to discern the way persons behave and communicate. Thus, "the pragmatic reading of a text is also a study of human character and its relation to public practice."[55] Rather than generalize "public" to include all persons, however, pragmatic readers recognize in the contextual nature of their reading that they ought not carry their reading too far beyond the public practice that gave rise to the writing. Pragmatic reading assumes that author and reader share (or would share) a common community. The community of interpreters counts the author as one of its own from whom it has something to learn even if it also has something to criticize.

Since most pragmatic readers are also writers, they are themselves involved in the process of reading their own work and attempting to correct those sections of equivocation, confusion, or contradiction. That is, they are continually revising earlier positions as they find within those positions aspects of the arguments that they oppose. Yet rather than rejecting those earlier positions, they practice the form of mediate debunking described above, trying to explicate their positions more carefully than they have thus far done. This process places pragmatic writers in a continued process of reclamation and refusal marked primarily by their sympathetic opposition to positions – including their own – that need to be debunked.

Even when they have carefully and thoughtfully engaged in this process over an extended period of time, Ochs argues, pragmatists will reach a point at which debunking fails, and this point will call for yet another reading strategy. At this point, the vagueness of the symbols is the product not of equivocations, confusions, or contradictions within the text, but instead the result of "a persistent vagueness that calls for yet another kind of pragmatic reading. This is a species of *definitional,* rather than corrective reading: one that, for some particular community on some particular occasion defines the meanings of inveterately vague symbols."[56] At some point, symbols, as part of the world, simply cannot describe that world

---

[55] Peter Ochs, *Peirce, Pragmatism and the Logic of Scripture*, 8.
[56] Peter Ochs, *Peirce, Pragmatism and the Logic of Scripture*, 9.

without remainder because too much of that world is beyond the processes of examination that are marked by symbol use in the first place. This is precisely because the processes of examination that involve symbol use are posited on certain assumptions about the world that cannot be undermined without undermining those processes. At the level of definitional pragmatic reading, the interpreting community is less interested in correcting an author than in learning to cope with the irremediable vagueness of the symbols by trying to put new symbols into play. The pragmatic reading of a text puts the interpreter in the position to "imagine that a *reason* for each interpretive movement may be located, metaphorically, *between* the text and its movement."[57] The "magic" of a pragmatic hermeneutic occurs when such imaginative reasoning bears the fruit of reaching conclusions about texts (and between them) that have practical bearings on how to read the texts and their authors and how to live in light of them.[58]

Ochs' strategy of pragmatic reading can, in principle, be applied to the non-textual resources of traditions as well. A kind of pragmatic ethnography may help us recognize the problems that the customs and practices of particular traditions carry with them, discovering their equivocations, confusions, ironies, and contradictions, and learn to correct the ones we can while living with the ones we cannot. A kind of pragmatic political theology may help us recognize the problems that the political, economic, and social structures shaped by particular traditions carry with them, discovering their incoherencies, manipulations, double-standards, and confusions, and learn to correct the ones we can while living with the ones we cannot. A kind of pragmatic architectonics may help us recognize the way the material products and services (and the processes by which we shaped them) that visibly identify particular traditions have, in turn, shaped us, discovering their uses and misuses, the potentials and limits of their flexibilities and functions, and their impact on us even as we learn to craft new things and old things in new ways while living with the ones that abide.

This approach, broadly construed, is the one that I have taken up in this project: offering a pragmatic reading of the history of Christian pacifism. I began by demythologizing the conventional narratives of the histories of

---

[57] Peter Ochs, *Peirce, Pragmatism and the Logic of Scripture*, 14.

[58] For further discussion of pragmatic reading strategies, see Mark Douglas, "Warp and Woof: Pragmatism in 20th Century Christian Ethics" (Dissertation, The University of Virginia, 2000).

this tradition in order to reveal both its plain sense meanings and the failings of those meanings to account for the various equivocations, lacunae, ironies, contradictions, and pluralities that inhabit it. These problems inhibit the tradition's abilities to function during the transition into an environmental age as we face new causes, exacerbations, types, and understandings of climate-shaped conflict. So, in light of these problems, I will momentarily offer a pragmatic reading of the Christian pacifist traditions – now plural – to address a particular set of problems (those associated with climate-shaped conflict) from within a particular community (the early twenty-first-century Western church). Along the way, I will undoubtedly repeat the errors of the conventional narratives because I, too, will be relying on those narratives as they have shaped my work. As such, I perceive of this project as neither a final argument nor the sole voice in the conversation. How could it be? Writing from one social imaginary while trying to envision another mandates tentativeness.

A pragmatic historiography of the sort I'm attempting may help us see not only the ironies, discontinuities, incoherencies, and multiplicities within the Christian pacifist tradition but the possibilities and continuities of that tradition as it has moved through time, revealing the myths that undergird the narratives of the tradition and offering an alternative account of the movements of the tradition(s) through time that still honor the power of such narratives to help us make sense of Christian pacifism while bending it to address the needs of today and tomorrow. If such an approach helps others make sense of climate-shaped conflict, of the history of Christian pacifism, of the movement of traditions through time, or of the role that theological perspectives might play in addressing contemporary issues of global import, then my pragmatic readings will have done as much as I could hope.

The final general implication of the ideas within this chapter is that attending to the multiplicity of voices and perspectives within traditions reveals the confusions within those traditions even as it makes those traditions supple enough to adjust to change. The previous chapter made the case for a tradition of Christian pacifism between the fourth and nineteenth centuries that is more continuous and inclusive than the conventional narrative – operating as it does within the myth of return – has recognized. John Mueller's book *The Remnants of War* makes the case that the idea of pacifism has reshaped western perspectives on war since the mid-nineteenth century, one implication of which is that the idea of pacifism has become politically respectable, even if the practices of pacifism haven't attained sufficient prominence in the policies of modern nation-states to make war unviable or unlikely. John Howard Yoder's book *Nevertheless* makes a case for dozens of contemporary and viable forms of pacifism, not all of which agree with each other. Dorothy Day's writings in *The Catholic Worker* bring into relief connections between economic systems and violence and the way pacifists must respond to those connections. The work of Martin Luther King, Jr. highlights the viability of pacifist practices as effective ways to bring about changes in societies that are not themselves pacifist. And this chapter has made the argument that the resources of a tradition are both ambiguously good and also necessary for traditions to move through time, especially as they move from one social imaginary into another. What is left for this section is to attempt to describe the relations between the ambiguity of a tradition – the way it causes suffering through faulty, restrictive, naïve, malicious, ironic, contradictory, plural, and incomplete uses of its resources even as it also makes possible our movement forward and improvements (intellectually, morally, and technologically) in time – and the multiplicity of voices that now clearly constitute the traditions of Christian pacifism.

A stereotypic conservative response to all this might suggest that multiplicity is the cause of moral ambiguity: a single perspective, treated as the dominant resource within a tradition, does not suffer from the contradictions and ironies that multiple perspectives create. The pacifist tradition needs a magisterium much as Roman Catholicism needs a Vatican. A stereotypic liberal response might suggest that multiplicity is the solution to moral ambiguity: shaping a marketplace of ideas in which everyone can be exposed to and argue about various visions of pacifism will prevent or mitigate restrictive, naive, and malicious uses of resources. The pacifist tradition needs a Habermasian theory of communicative action that shapes deliberative democracy. There is truth in both descriptions, at least to the extent that both descriptions locate real problems with the pacifist tradition and offer solutions to them that can address them. Yet as this paragraph suggests, each response attends to and attempts to solve some causes of moral ambiguity but, in the process, exacerbates others. In a world replete with ironies, each solution may also exacerbate the very problems it hopes to solve.

As an alternative to either of those routes, we might surrender the pursuit of a solution to the ambiguities of the Christian pacifist tradition, giving up whatever notions of uncompromising purity and/or unmitigated progress that motivate such a pursuit. The Kingdom of God is not only beyond our power to achieve; it's beyond our imaginations to emulate.

Peace is a genuine good, but under conditions of finitude and sin, it is always a human good, and as a human good, the various pacifist projects that pursue and promote it are always already caught up in the very strategic assessments and weighing of values that constitute the pursuit of all human goods.

In such a framework, the multiplicity of voices functions not so much as a variety of possible answers from which to choose as a range of strategies with which to work. To be clear: I am not arguing in favor of utilitarian forms of pacifism over against principled forms, nor, e.g., in favor of nonviolent resistance over against nonresistance, or socially engaged and prophetic forms of pacifism over against quietist and perfectionist forms. I am arguing that all forms of pacifism, once they are relieved of the burdens that come with being framed as or judged against an unambiguous good, become strategic. Sometimes, those strategies will look like holding fast to principles (for the coherence of community, for the consistency of witness, as a way of recognizing that some goods in some contexts are of such great value that affirming them must mean allowing violence rather than preventing it through the use of violence). At other times, those strategies will look like recognizing a goal, assessing possible strategies that might lead to that goal, and deciding that the practices of nonviolence are the most likely way to achieve that goal. In such a framework, the multiplicity of voices become expressions of the sheer range of resources available for us to work with when dealing with the causes of suffering because one voice/resource will not be enough.

Our first goal, then, ought not to be to pick from among the possible resources as if finding the right resource will mean we can address any suffering that comes along. Instead, it will be becoming more adept at using all the resources that are available to us. We ought not to be trying to get pacifism right so much as use pacifisms better. We need to become more familiar with them, more alert to their powers and their limitations, more practiced at using a wider range of them, and, perhaps above all, more versed in their histories: where did they come from? How have they been used? Towards what goods? Within what contexts? By what parties? With what consequences? In concert with what other resources? Over against what other alternatives? With what implications?

And our second goal is to develop the capacities for discernment that grow out of practiced use. What disciplines within the humanities and the natural and social sciences have we used in coming to understand the context(s) in which our decisions are being made and toward which they will be applied? How have we discerned which resources are appropriate for those particular contexts? What is the range of politically attentive possibilities available to us as we shape faithful actions in those contexts? How will we become aware of and address the deleterious consequences that may follow from our use of resources? As the range of the resources become more familiar, perhaps the pacifist tradition might even begin to shape a set of criteria comparable to those that the just war tradition has used in formulating its *jus ad bellum* and *jus in bello* criteria, albeit with an eye to the concerns of fidelity. These might include criteria like:

- Due fidelity: How do we understand the God to whom we are attempting to be faithful and whose call we are attempting to follow? How have we discerned that these actions are faithful expressions of Christianity as we best understand its message? What practices of discernment have we used in this process? How have we trained ourselves in these practices? What criticisms have been applied to such practices? And, perhaps, in an environmental age, will we learn to think of faith in non-anthropocentric ways?
- Appropriate authority: Are we the right people to be engaged in this action? Are there others with whom we should be in conversation prior to these actions? Where other people are advocating for alternative approaches, how will we discern between these approaches? And, perhaps, in an environmental age, who will speak for the nonhuman natural world?
- Fitting response: Among available types of pacifism, how have we selected the type of pacifism that is appropriate for this context? How comfortable (morally and functionally) are we with such an approach? What disciplines have we used in assessing the context(s) in which we are acting and how well do we understand and use those disciplines? And, perhaps, in an environmental age, how will we integrate this response with the demands of sustainability and creation-care?
- Vulnerability: What harms to ourselves, to others, and to the natural world are likely to follow from our actions? How vulnerable are we willing to make ourselves in pursuing these actions, recognizing that they could lead to our own harm? How vulnerable should we expect other people to be, recognizing that our actions and inactions could lead to their harm? Which people are being made vulnerable and do we owe them distinct treatment or attention because of their own social locations and/or histories? And, perhaps, in an environmental age, how (and how much) should we include the non-human natural world –

whether as a systemic whole or some of its discrete parts – as among the vulnerable?

- Confessional integrity: How will we recognize the costs of our actions? To whom will we be obligated as a result of our actions? How will we work to meet those obligations? Where we cannot meet those obligations, what consequences ought we be willing to assume? And, perhaps, in an environmental age, will our confessions sweep widely enough to recognize the costs to the planet for our actions and inactions in a way that can shape penance?

- Prospects for success: What would count as success in this context? Can these actions lead to that success? Who will assess what success looks like in this context? How do we remain honest in our assessment of such prospects in light of our tendencies for self-deception? And, perhaps, in an environmental age, how will we incorporate prospects for environmental sustainability and/or resilience within our goals?

- Publicity: To what degree have these practices led us to arguments that can be offered in larger public settings in their defense as faith seeks public understanding? How much of an obligation do we have towards others and to which others do we have particular obligations of publicity? And, perhaps, in an environmental age, how will we convey these arguments to those whose starting points for such debates are different than ours – particularly if we find ourselves arguing across social imaginaries?

This list is meant only to be suggestive; the point here is to note that once we recognize that all forms of pacifism have strategic value, we ought to then shape questions about assessing and using those forms and processes for addressing those questions. None of this is to say that the strategic value of any form of pacifism determines its worth. Not only would such an approach ignore the centrality of questions of fidelity for the Christian pacifist tradition but it would suggest that values that can be strategically assessed ought to trump those that hold obligatory power over us even where they may not seem to be strategically important. If anything, such non-strategic values help to reveal the very incompleteness of our moral sensibilities that the history of pacifism, tied as it is to questions of fidelity under conditions of sin and finitude, has brought forward.

It is, though, to say that we need richer understandings of the histories and varieties of pacifism. These richer understandings will not relieve us from continued projects of discernment, confession, and action that constitute the use of pacifist resources any more than a pragmatic reading strategy relieves texts of their ambiguities and failings. Just as no particular history or form of pacifism will "get it right," so no project of pursuing richer understandings of a history or form will get it right. Such richer understandings might, though, offer us slightly clearer lenses to help us glimpse something of the power of resurrection as it infiltrates into and seeps out from the proximate processes of history. They might remind us of a resilience in traditions that comes not from their own resourcefulness but from God's refusal to leave us entirely to our own devices. They might offer us cairns by which to locate not only the trails we have walked but a way for our next few steps. In the Anthropocene, our greatest need will not be to conform our actions to supposed ideal forms or to repeat the nostalgically framed arguments of earlier ages; it will be to learn new forms of established practices for faithful discernment with diverse others.

The next section of this volume offers just the start of such things, offering a theological framework for discernment and proposing a modified narrative of the history of Christian pacifism that doesn't so much remove the ironies, disjunctions, failings, multiplications, and incoherencies from that tradition as offer a reason for their existence while equipping us to use these human traditions in a world that is beyond human control and in which human beings can no longer be treated as the measure of all things.

PART III

RE-NARRATING THE HISTORY OF THE CHURCH AND NONVIOLENCE

"I know well enough what it is, provided that nobody asks me; but if I am asked what it is and try to explain, I am baffled."[1]

St. Augustine

"Christians should be oriented not by Newton's onto-theological grid but rather the biblical-historical narratives, and they should reconceive the world fundamentally temporally, as a duration. Christians are not other-worldly, but most fundamentally 'other-temporalitied.'"[2]

Charles Mathewes

---

[1] Saint Augustine, *Confessions*, trans. R. S. Pine-Coffin (London: Penguin Books, 1961), 264.

[2] Charles Mathewes, *A Theology of Public Life* (Cambridge: Cambridge University Press, 2007), 17.

7

Time and Tradition in a Theological Framework

Christianity is often thought of as a set of beliefs to which Christians assent. This almost (but not entirely) misses the point of the faith. Christianity isn't principally about what Christians believe, and for two reasons. First, such a claim tends to isolate beliefs from thought on the one side and from action on the other: believing is what one does when thought ends or before action begins. The Christian faith, though, binds the three – belief, thought, and action – together: thought shapes belief and belief drives further thought; belief leads to action and action tests belief; action restructures thought and thought disciplines action. Second, treating Christianity as a set of beliefs to which Christians assent places the community (or the individual) in the center of the narrative about what it means to be Christian, whereas Christianity finds its center not in the individual or the community but in the God whom Christians understand as the Creator, Redeemer, Sustainer, and Consummator of the universe. That is, Christianity finds its focus not in what Christians do but in what God does; not in who Christians are but who God is. Christians attempt to believe and think and act in light of that focus.

Why does this matter? First, it matters because it is de-centering. It shapes (or at least has the potential to shape) a perspective that can gain some critical purchase for thinking about/believing in/acting on matters of personal, social, and global import. It is hard to make sense of swirling complex systems when the only place one can find to stand is in the very middle of the whirled. Whether or not such a location actually makes for better thought/belief/action than other places in which one might stand is another question – but it is better to pursue an answer to that question in light of the insights that come at the conclusion of an analysis rather than simply being overly suspicious of the location in which the analyst stands. Second, it is encompassing. No aspect of human life – or, for that matter, any aspect of existence – is quarantined off from the questions and perspectives of the faith. As such, Christians try to do far more than straightforwardly pursue their varied and idiosyncratic relationships with God. Instead, they try to make sense of their individual lives, the lives of those around them, and the whole world through faith.

To get a sense of why all this matters for this project, I want to attempt to lay out a particular vision of time and space in which events like climate change and conflict occur and through which traditions like pacifism and environmental concerns like climate change become coherent. Indeed, I think it vital to lay out such a vision of time and space not only to clarify my own methodological approach but to make the Christian pacifist tradition more coherent while avoiding the temptation to make it so coherent that its use simply becomes a matter of plugging it, like a mathematical equation, into whatever problem we might face and reading the answer that comes out.

I begin the concluding section of this book with a quote by St. Augustine: When asked what time was, he famously noted, "I know well enough what it is, provided that nobody asks me; but if I am asked what it is and try to explain, I am baffled."[1] Augustine's point – one he would explore later in his work – was more than that the concept of time is difficult to visualize; indeed, that later work involved some fairly sophisticated visualization on his part. Instead, it was that the process of standing in time and trying to make sense of it – which is, in part, the process of telling history as we and it move into the future – always catches us up short as we face contradictions, incompletions, and aporias of all sorts. Part of the genius of Augustine (and Christianity, to my mind) is that he attempts to tell the kind of history that not only allows for such contradictions, incompletions, and aporias, but actually treats them as evidence in support of history as he tells it. To get at such a telling, however, it is good to take a step back and recognize that history is told through particular sets of lenses and that these lenses change over time.

---

[1] Saint Augustine, *Confessions*, trans. R. S. Pine-Coffin (London: Penguin Books, 1961), 264.

I TELLING STORIES ABOUT TIME

The modern telling of history is profoundly linear: one thing follows another through observable processes of cause and effect. No effects can be causes of things that happened earlier and causes cannot skip forward in time to bring about new effects without being mediated by all the time that stands between cause and effect. The beginning and ending of history look like its middle and everything is in time, but time itself is homogenous.[2] This is, as Charles Taylor argues, the way the disenchanted world of the secular age tells the story of time – a story so deeply engrained in our self-understandings that we struggle to imagine the story of time being told in any other way.[3]

Yet the story of time can be and has been told differently. To take one example, for Plato and those who followed him, the really real – the realm of ideal forms – stands outside of chronological time, unchanging and eternal. As such, we who live in time occasionally catch a glimpse of what the reality "outside time" is like when such forms show through their temporal approximations. What happens in time, then, is less real (and, therein, less perfect, less consistent, and less coherent) than what simply *is*, which is outside of time. Or, as another example, many cultures look back to a mythic founding time in which the order of things is established and to which those in the culture ritually return in order to establish their place in that order and to teach that order to others. In such contexts, founding time is neither equivalent with history (as in the modern conception of time) nor set apart from the rest of time (the way Platonic eternity is). Instead, founding time is made special and distinct from the rest of history. Through ritual, members of such cultures can loop back to find their own place in chronological time by finding it first in founding time. The conventional telling of the Christian pacifist narrative about its own history participates in a weak form of this version of history-telling through its myth of return.

The broader Christian tradition, influenced as it is by both Platonic and mythic visions of time and currently shaped by the modern understanding of time, tells yet a fourth story about time. Like the Platonic story, it recognizes that there is a reality beyond what is apparent in chronological

---

[2] Among philosophers, Walter Benjamin and those who rely on his thought including, in various ways, Charles Taylor, Benedict Anderson, and Ted A. Smith have most fully developed this modern understanding of time in order to criticize it. See Benjamin, *Illuminations* (London: Fontana, 1973).

[3] Here and in the succeeding paragraphs, I am drawing from Taylor, *Secular Age*, 54–59.

time and that this reality shows itself in occasional revelatory glimpses and at the peripheries of our vision. Unlike the Platonic story, though, it resists (sometimes more successfully than others) the urge to segregate time from eternity. Instead, it maps eternity down upon chronological time – or, more accurately, maps chronological time up into eternal time – such that the significance of the eternal has, can, and will show forth in the reality of the transient. The eternal God creates the world and all its elements good; God incarnates in the world, participating in the world of creatureliness; God is bringing about the transformation of the world into a fullness that is not yet; God's work and being bring about the consummation of this world into the Kingdom of God, which is eternal, and that eternity includes the temporal.

Like the story of founding time, Christianity envisions a world in which time can loop and jump such that we can make sense of our own location in time only by reference to another point in time. Unlike the story of founding time, however, the return is not to a point of origin, but to those points of significance in which the eternal most clearly manifested itself: creation, exodus, incarnation, crucifixion, resurrection, consummation (this last one, especially, isn't even technically a return so much as a participation in that which is not yet). This can be seen, for instance, in the rituals of the Eucharist: in eating bread and drinking wine, individuals are drawn into the creation story in which God causes grain and grapes to be brought forth, to the Last Supper Jesus shared with his disciples before being crucified, to the gathered community of the church from around the world and throughout time, and to the eschatological feast of the Kingdom of God. More than simply remembering or anticipating these events, Christians participate in them.

Like the modern story, Christianity envisions a world in which persons move forward in time as causes have effects and beginnings shape middles, which shape endings. Unlike the modern story, however, Christianity envisions time as purposeful in its forward movement, albeit in ways that are marked by fits and starts, with causes that have distant effects (in both past and future) and as something that cannot be made sense of if it is all that we regard. The eternity through which Christians finally make sense of time is not only our distant future but our ordering past and present reality. To say this differently, Christians believe we live in two times simultaneously but that the one through which we can make the most sense of the world around us is veiled from us and yet is being unfolded before us. Or, to say it even more differently, the Christian vision of time is such that we have to resist making too much sense of time because, short our completion in eternity, we do not yet see time as what God is making it into. Thus, as Charles Mathewes has helpfully put it, "Christians should be oriented not by Newton's onto-theological grid but rather the biblical-historical narratives, and they should reconceive the world fundamentally temporally, as a duration. Christians are not other-worldly, but most fundamentally 'other-temporalitied.'"[4] The world and its elements are, therefore, contingent: both real and valuable and caught up in a transformation through which – eventually – their full reality and value will become apparent.

Why this digression into an explication of the Christian vision of time? There are several reasons. First, no other aspect of the Christian tradition, its values, or its implications can really become coherent without it. The pacifist tradition as it has been developed in the Christian faith (not to mention the just war and just peacemaking traditions) only becomes coherent within this larger temporal framework. The same is true for Christian understandings of the value of the environment, which have changed over time in ways that express both continuity (e.g., stewardship) and discontinuity (e.g., deep ecology). Given that this book joins an exploration of the Christian pacifist traditions with inquiry into the value of the natural world, all within a context in which that natural world is changing, such a digression undergirds next steps.

Second, this vision provides leverage for thinking about how those traditions and values manifest themselves without getting seduced into what Ted A. Smith calls "narratives of progress and decline."[5] Narratives of progress suggest a consistent movement onward and upward toward greater goodness, truth, and beauty. Narratives of decline, on the other hand, describe a movement from the idyllic into ruins; from Eden to being expelled from the garden. The problem with both narratives, Smith points out, is that "they do not account for the complexities and discontinuities within [particular historical manifestations of practices], and that they do not recognize the indirect, ironic relationships between human projects and the saving work of God."[6] History is always entangled in creation, fall, redemption, and consummation. Teasing out the various ways God

---

[4] Charles Mathewes, *A Theology of Public Life* (Cambridge: Cambridge University Press, 2007), 17.

[5] Ted A. Smith, *The New Measures: A Theological History of Democratic Practice* (Cambridge: Cambridge University Press, 2007), 11.

[6] Smith, 11.

works in history must mean refusing straightforward or linear narratives of history.[7]

Depending on who is doing the telling, both stories about the pacifist tradition and anthropogenic climate change tend to be one or the other type of narrative. A pacifist like John Howard Yoder, for example, will argue that the tradition has grown from its early Jewish roots to become an increasingly important tool in making sense of why not to fight, even though its fitness for addressing the complexities of justice during times of war is, at times, stretched beyond helpfulness or coherence. Christian pacifists refer to the pre-Constantinian church as that community of disciples who better understood and lived out the radicality of Jesus's Sermon on the Mount and maintain that we ought to try harder to emulate that community – even though the bits of evidence we have from the early church are both highly reconstructed in order to make particular theological points and full of evidence of conflict and disparate visions of war and peace. The former claim progress; the latter describe decline.

Environmentalists speak of climate change "tipping points" in the near future from which there can be no recovery and after which life on earth will grow increasingly difficult[8] even as other scholars argue that, based on past experiences, human ingenuity will not only make human flourishing possible in this new warmer world, but that there are anticipatable and exciting benefits to climate change.[9] The former describe decline; the latter champion progress.[10]

---

[7] These narratives are not only attractive to many people because they simplify how we understand living in a complex world but because it is so easy for us to take delight in both our possibilities and our errors. One need only look at the rise and development of "disaster porn" – end-of-the-world movies and books; the endless looping of horrific events on cable news – to see the power of this voyeuristic side.

[8] Perhaps the most popular narrative of decline in this context is Robert Kaplan's famous 1994 *Atlantic Monthly* article, "The Coming Anarchy." That essay not only received a great deal of press and was passed around by a wide range of politicians, who relied on it in shaping their own opinions about the relationship between environmental damage and human security, it set a trajectory for understanding that relationship that is still bearing fruit. See Robert D. Kaplan, "The Coming Anarchy," *Atlantic Monthly* 273.2 (1994): 44–76.

[9] See, e.g., Gregg Easterbrook, "Global Warming: Who Loses – and Who Wins?" in *The Atlantic* (April, 2007). Available at: https://www.theatlantic.com/magazine/archive/2007/04/global-warming-who-loses-and-who-wins/305698/

[10] All of which suggests another, practical reason to avoid telling narratives of progress or decline: the natural world, especially writ on a global scale, simply doesn't respond to changes in straightforward and obvious ways. So, for instance, a warming world can lead to melting ice sheets on Greenland which, filling the Atlantic with cold freshwater, could disrupt the thermohaline conveyor (the ocean current system more commonly known as the "Gulf Stream" that helps keep the climate of Northern Europe warmer than it would

I want to tell a story about the pacifist tradition and its possible place(s) for helping address the kinds of conflict that climate change may either bring about or exacerbate. This story will include evidence of the kind of progress over time that comes about in a straightforward way: those of us who come later in time have the benefit of wisdom and examples from the past. It will not, though, suggest that such progress is inevitable, linear, or uniform. The tradition regresses as well as progresses (indeed, in my telling the tradition occasionally does both simultaneously). Additionally, I want to situate this story about the pacifist tradition into the context of anthropogenic climate change, but without undue hand-wringing about what people are doing to the environment or what the environment is going to do to us. Climate change is a reality, but its full story cannot yet be fully told. Possibilities and ironies, continuities and disjunctions, causes for grief and sources for hope all await.

All too often, the Christian church and of late the mainline and Roman Catholic churches in the West, especially, have tended to express a particular vision of hope in which the impending arrival of the Kingdom of God will resolve the conflicts and failings of the current world. This vision defers the activity of God into an unpredictable moment in the future while turning current conflicts and failings principally into signs that God's kingdom is not yet here. While it is obviously and ped-antically true that the Kingdom of God has not yet fully expressed itself, the linearity of this vision treats hope solely as a forward-looking virtue and the work of God as somehow at a lull. So, for instance, when these churches diagnose the crises of the present day (violence between persons, ecological destruction, collapse of the "traditional family," loss of mem-bership, etc.), they can point to very specific examples and statistics to support their diagnoses and around which to rally either troops or mour-ners. Yet the solutions they proffer – at least when they are trying to be theologically faithful to their larger vision rather than binding themselves to a particular (and particularly transient) political solution – tend toward platitudinous proclamations that "God is doing a new thing," that "God will not leave us bereft of the divine presence," or that "God is inviting us into His new work." Hope gets founded in abstractions even as diagnoses are founded in concrete statistics because the linear, homogenous vision of

otherwise be). The impact of global warming would, then, paradoxically be colder climates in Great Britain, the Scandinavian countries, and elsewhere in that region. (This event, dramatized, exacerbated, and sped up considerably, was the basis for the 2004 disaster movie "The Day After Tomorrow.")

time that marks modernity infects the church and inhibits its ability to say anything that is truthful, concrete, and hopeful. Only attention to possibilities and ironies, contradictions and disjunctions, indirections and complexities as themselves revelatory can help the church re-envision its understanding of the mighty acts of God during its time in the world – albeit in such a way that it must insistently use its peripheral vision. The story I want to tell about the pacifist tradition is hopeful, but not as an expression of divine activity deferred, of human activity sufficient, or as a signal that this is as good as it gets.

Third, this Christian vision of time helps me locate myself in it and therein resist the biggest temptation this work faces: to make *now* the key moment through which to understand time and the world's current place in it. The temptation is so great not only because of a natural impulse many of us feel to make ourselves and our places in time the centerpiece of existence – which may be a perpetual side to this temptation – but because *now* is a time of particular ferment with regard to both ideas about war and peace and understandings of the climate and its changes.

Toward that end, I pick up one more of Smith's phrases: an "eschatological angle of vision."[11] Smith uses the phrase to describe a perspective in which things and ideas, practices and values, plans and memories resist our ability to fully describe them with reference only to our current location in time and space and in which they gain more complete meaning only as we begin to glimpse their transformed character. They are both in need of and in the process of being redeemed. Redemption doesn't simply sit at the conclusion of their existence; it works upon them where we find them now, acting in both their death (that is, their failures and the pains they cause) and their transformation (their possibilities and their ability to be signs of promise for us). This angle of vision allows for mourning but not despair; gratitude but not slavishness; hope but not optimism; significance but not centrality. It lets *now* be "meaning-full" without suggesting that it somehow matters more or less than "then" or "later" because it binds past, present, and future up into the larger activity of God. To be entangled in history is to be entangled in the work of God. There is no more point in trying to extricate oneself from that work in order to objectively name its parts than there is in trying to extricate oneself from time in order to understand it.

[11] Smith, *The New Measures*, 12.

All of this is rather abstract and poetic and so may function as a way of escaping the painful realities and brutish prose of which both war and climate change consist.

To add concreteness to this project, I turn to Canadian philosopher Charles Taylor's understanding of a "social imaginary," which I find to be not only congruent with the theological vision of time I'm trying to describe but also diagnostically helpful in naming the particular changes that we are undergoing as we transition into an environmental age. Taylor first develops the idea of a social imaginary in his book, *Modern Social Imaginaries*. There, he describes social imaginaries as "the ways people imagine their social existence, how they fit together with others, how things go on between them and their fellows, the expectations that are normally met, and the deeper normative notions and images that underlie these expectations."[12] Social imaginaries are expressed by ordinary people through images, stories, and legends (rather than abstract ideas) and make possible "common practices and a widely shared sense of legitimacy."[13] They are complex and multilayered, bringing into rough coherence the ideas, practices, and background conditions (and the relations between them) through which people make sense of and act in the world around them, including the moral order. They also change over time as new ideas and practices gradually penetrate into and change existing social imaginaries. A social imaginary isn't simply the set of ideas that a particular society uses to order its common life (a "theory," though social imaginaries include theories), nor a lens through which a group of people see the world around them (a worldview, though they include worldviews), nor even a shared set of practices and the implicit agreements that have led to them (a *habitus*, though social imaginaries include them, as well). It is all of these plus their interactions plus the built environment – the stuff – that a given society creates and is shaped by. Given the way ideas, worldviews, habits, and technology all participate in the shaping of any tradition, Taylor's description of the social imaginary is especially *apropos*.

Building from Taylor, I argue that social imaginaries both stabilize/give coherence and continuity to incremental change over time and, when social imaginaries themselves change, manifest in disruptions and disjunctions. These latter transitions between social imaginaries occur during

---

[12] Charles Taylor, *Modern Social Imaginaries* (Durham, NC: Duke University Press, 2004), 23.

[13] Taylor, *Modern Social Imaginaries*, 23.

what I will refer to as "axial points" in history. Axial points are periods of transition between social imaginaries when the arguments that constitute traditions rise toward social consciousness because a tradition is being unsettled due to dramatic social change. A cursory reading of Western history highlights such axial points as the beginnings of the various ages into which that history is divided: the rise of Greek thought and its distribution around the Mediterranean through the conquests of Alexander, who not only wanted to control the lands around Greece but to change them to resemble Greek culture; the rise of the Roman Empire that followed about 300 years later and established Roman law and culture throughout much of Europe and the Middle East; the collapse of that empire about 500 years later; the medieval period (which could, perhaps, be subdivided into periods before and after its engagement with Islam); the age of exploration/colonization/conquest beginning in the fifteenth century; the age of revolutions marked by the English, French, and American revolutions; the modern age that follows and, now, something that some Continental philosophers, at least, refer to as "the postmodern age." As my subdivision of the medieval period begins to hint at, this timeline is entirely too simple. It misses the consistency of some ideas over long swaths of time, it overstates the impact of changes in governance and conceptions of the state in its telling, and it ignores the degree to which other histories – those that might focus on technological change, economic change, or religious engagement, for example – could be told in ways that, while not entirely undermining this way of dividing history, would certainly complicate it. Obviously, it also disregards the long and rich histories of non-Western cultures.

That said, this way of dividing up Western history is useful, in part because it does focus on who rules what and how they rule; in part because it orders history in ways that correspond to significant changes in social imaginaries; and in part because it helps to clarify why the conventional telling of the history of the pacifist tradition has grown around the myth of return. That myth typically arises most fervently during axial points in Western history, which is to say, during periods of transition between social imaginaries. The myth of return becomes a therapy through which pacifists find a way to move forward in time even as they are observing the theological incoherence of their own recent past. It isn't that pacifists suddenly and uniquely discover something that their predecessors have missed as they read the New Testament and attend to the early church. It is that they are struggling with how to make sense of the wisdom of those who had come before them when that wisdom had begun to seem less wise. And they were focused on ideas about war and peace because these axial periods are marked not only by conflict but by changes in thought about how to be faithful to the God they worship as they observe conflicts around them.

I have, to this point, been emphasizing the discontinuous/revolutionary character of how traditions change over time in my explanation of social imaginaries. I do so for three reasons. First, because this approach has been underemphasized by many scholars writing on the idea and history of "tradition" – which may reveal the degree to which their approaches, though critical of modernity's approach to understanding history, participate in that approach by emphasizing the accretionary, discrete, and pluralized characteristics of traditions themselves. Contrast this, for example, with Alisdair MacIntyre's claims about traditions as arguments extended through time, as he describes them in *After Virtue*.[14] In that book, his description of tradition serves a conservative role: rather than treat traditions as changing in disruptive ways, he treats disruptions – as expressed in arguments – as the center of traditions that move through time rather continuously. Traditions do, indeed, conserve. But they don't necessarily change in conservative ways.[15]

The second reason for emphasizing the disjunctive character of how traditions change over time is historical. This approach does a better job of accounting for the way history – and, especially, the history of discrete societies – moves forward in spurts and starts as a result of the advent of external pressures (new conflicts, new neighbors, etc.) and internal changes (new technologies, the creation and dispersal of cultural memes and particular schools of thought, etc.). Labeling particular ages (the axial, the medieval, the industrial, the information, etc.) and the trends/ ideas that characterize them is meant to do more than provide helpful mnemonics for schoolchildren learning history; it is meant to suggest that there are identifiable characteristics that mark certain periods of time as congruent with each other in a way that they are not congruent with the periods that come before and after them. Things change, but they do not change at a constant rate, and the changes do not allow succeeding periods to be congruent with their preceding ones.

---

[14] See Alisdair MacIntyre, *After Virtue: A Study in Moral Theory*, 3rd ed. (South Bend, IN: University of Notre Dame Press, 2007).

[15] To say that differently, much of the criticism directed at MacIntyre's concept of "tradition" (an argument extended through time) had to do with his claim that reason was tradition-dependent. My criticism, on the other hand, is that he never adequately explained how he thought arguments worked over time.

Finally, I have emphasized the discontinuous/revolutionary character of how traditions change for a theological reason: I believe such an emphasis better recognizes the way God works in history, as attested not only in Scripture and the history of the church but in a theological vision of time marked by disruption and revelation, tragedy and hope, the transience of all things and the permanence of God. The character of the transformation brought on by God includes loss and gain, death and rebirth, the sufferings of sin and the joys of presence, all as crucifixion and resurrection reverberate through time. God's saving work can feel so indirect and ironic because the redemption of time looks less like progress or decline than like death and resurrection and time's end is the promise of eternity – albeit an eternity that continually impinges on the present. To live in history is to live in light of a longing for something that is never fully realized in history while being regularly and surprisingly touched by blessing and caught by loss. In other words, history itself is on a kind of pilgrimage, and pilgrimages include journeys onto peaks and into valleys, surrendering things that are precious and receiving gifts along the way. Traditions are marked by discontinuity and irony because, short of the consummation of all things, everything is marked by discontinuity and irony.

This is not to say, however, that history consists of a series of restarts or that traditions disappear at axial points in history. At the same time that their limits highlight the distance between when ideas, practices, and technologies come into existence and when they're being applied, they also serve a conservative and stabilizing influence during times of transition. They do so by serving as a primary resource for finding, shaping, and laying the building blocks out of which new ideas and new practices emerge. Indeed, this is the great strength of understanding traditions as arguments extended through time: the very multivocality of traditions makes them sufficiently malleable to be reshaped for use in new times and places (and, as is often the case – especially with religious traditions – to beget a number of new sub-traditions where those in the arguments prefer leaving to winning). They may not look or sound the same, but Tradition 2.0 (or following) bears sufficient resemblance to its predecessor to be demonstrably part of the family. All of which suggests that traditions perdure precisely because they are capacious enough to contain and shape differences, though it is this very capaciousness that makes possible their disjunctive character when viewed over long swaths of time.

There are both historical and theological reasons for attending to the stability of traditions over time. The historical reasons need no rehearsal here; most of those who think about and write on traditions attend to them because they manifest themselves in broadly coherent ways across time and they value them precisely because they function as a stabilizing force throughout. The theological reason to recognize and value traditions is that they are signs that the God who acts in history is One and that God's desires for the world's welfare are consistent. Indeed, part of what this stability suggests is that the disjunctions, ironies, and indirections that constitute history's pilgrimage have more to do with our blindness about and resistance to that welfare than to any sense of capriciousness on God's part. Viewed through the eyes of faith, God does not leave us bereft of resources or of Godself. Stability, as much as discontinuity, marks the indirect way that the faltering and impure movements that constitute human projects are contained within and given momentum by the saving work of God.

Indeed, to get a sense of how traditions work, we need to attend to both discontinuity and stability over time – and to do so in the kind of bifocal way that lets us see both with only the slightest shift in our angle of vision. Only in this way can we keep clear in our minds that traditions are not so much *things* as *activities* in which we participate and, since it is we who are participating in them, we are carrying our own sensibilities, visions, possibilities, and failings into them, all the while remembering that they are activities that are simultaneously shaping us. Just as a bit of honest self-reflection on our parts will help us not only to be alert to the discontinuities and constancies, the ironies and possibilities in our own lives but to be aware, therefore, of our need to treat our lives with both tenderness and rigor, so we might learn to treat traditions as things in need of both judgment and grace. As Charles Mathewes notes,

We inherit our ability to reflect from our elders, and we come to see that their tools only imperfectly fit the problems we face. Hence, unless we wish totally to jettison our minds, we find ourselves compelled to work through that inheritance, accepting its imperfections (and, furthermore, accepting that our own solutions will cause our descendants similar problems), and this acceptance involves, indeed just *is*, in part, forgiveness. This is not false piety; it is simply the condition of being responsible in one's thought to one's predecessors.[16]

Learning to forgive traditions, we learn how to read them, how to appreciate them, and how not to hold them too tightly. At least from a Christian perspective, we learn a bit more about how God works in

---

[16] Charles Mathewes, *Evil and the Augustinian Tradition* (Cambridge: Cambridge University Press, 2001), 69.

history so that we can learn something about how God works in us as well. Toward that end, though, we treat traditions as shaped by the twin trajectories of discontinuity and stability.

As Chapter 5 suggests, one productive way to describe this mix of continuity and discontinuity is through attention to the centripetal power of questions basic to particular traditions and the centrifugal power of the answers to those questions that are given in particular places and times. One implication of this approach involves learning to recognize the questions basic to a particular tradition (much as I've argued that questions of fidelity are central to the pacifist tradition). The second implication is to recognize the importance of not confusing questions with answers. The third implication is to give careful attention to the transience of the answers to questions even while noting the way particular answers may shape the way successive generations ask basic questions. Rather than pursue these implications in detail at this point, I hope that Chapter 8 will demonstrate how these three implications play themselves out.

2 DISCERNING AND OUR PLACE IN TIME

Yet prior to that chapter, I need to make one further set of arguments about discernment. After all, if my larger theological claim about God's ways of acting in the world (and therefore in traditions) is to have any teeth, questions about how to discern God's actions in the midst of human activity – especially during times of crises brought on by the shift from one social imaginary into another – become especially pressing. Vitally, the eschatologically shaped theological vision of time that I am advancing here both complicates (because it mandates that an unsatisfying incompleteness and troubling timidity must sit near the heart of our processes of discernment) and makes possible (by offering us an eschatological angle of vision) such practices of discernment. It is to these processes of discernment that I now turn.

2.1 Discernment

My description of how traditions move through time – not only manifesting both continuity and discontinuity, but doing so in a (mostly) coherent and analyzable way – is at least *prima facie* defensible from within my argument that a Christian vision of time, in accounting for both the vicissitudes of human activities and the saving work of God, must account for both the stability and linearity of time (on the one hand) and the ironies, disjunctions, and indirections of history (on the other). My description and my argument are congruent. Yet how stable is "congruence" as a foundation upon which to build constructive thought?

Saying something stronger than "there is congruence" is tricky. On the one side, simply saying "The relationship between the two is only apparent through the lens of faith," though perhaps true, is not only terribly unsatisfying but gives short shrift to the complexity of faith and its engagement with the world. Any project using theological analysis to examine conflict and climate change should vehemently resist such simplification. On the other side, any attempt to turn the arguments of faith into a kind of proof for the empirical legitimacy of my argument above risks reducing this chapter into an apologetic for the superiority of a Christian vision of time – which would be, ironically, the very thing that an account of time that tries to attend to disjunctions and indirection should find impossible. Appeals to neither naive fideism nor blinkered empiricism will do.

Fortunately – if that word is even appropriate for this context – the question of how to read the relation between the movements of history and the work of God is not new to Christian theology. Indeed, it is as old as Christianity itself. Paul's relatively history-free but revelation-rich accounts of the good news of salvation for Jews and Gentiles through Jesus's crucifixion emphasize the work of God. The synoptic gospel's varied but history-rich narratives of who Jesus was and how God acted in/as a first century Palestinian man, however, are much less explicit than Paul's letters about how crucifixion (and resurrection) change that history.[17] The tension between the events of history and the work of God has never entirely disappeared, try though the church might to either conceal or resolve it.

The question, fundamentally, is one of revelation: how are we to understand God as acting in the world? One answer, given in various ways by theologians as diverse as Anselm, Thomas Aquinas, John Calvin,

---

[17] The work of Oscar Cullmann is of special significance here. His division of time into the period before Jesus and the period after is problematic in part because it remains beholden to the modern idea (as his subtitle hints at) that time moves in one direction and in a linear way (and, therefore, God works in one direction and in continuous ways). It is, nonetheless, important to note the way in which Cullmann brought questions about the relation between time and Christology to the fore for both biblical scholars and Christian theologians. See Oscar Cullmann, *Christ and Time: The Primitive Christian Conception of Time,* trans. by Floyd V. Filson (Philadelphia: Westminster Press, 1964).

and H. Richard Niebuhr, is that God is the one behind the many: God is the agent behind all other agents, the cause behind all other causes. Each of these theologians' approaches are shaped by surprisingly subtle thoughts on agency and are enjoying new vigor due to explorations in narrative theology, postmodern philosophy, and, perhaps somewhat surprisingly, contemporary research in theoretical physics.

Yet as subtle and distinct as these approaches are, all of them surface a common frustration: how to weigh between (or even talk about) contending claims concerning God's role in a particular event. Two devout Christians see the same thing – say, a hurricane striking an American city. One Christian says that the hurricane was caused by low barometric pressure over warm ocean waters that led to spinning winds energized by evaporating water. The hurricane's creation, path, and destruction of the city followed the laws of physics. God has so structured the universe as to conform to such laws, and God's actions in the midst of such destruction are either directed toward helping those who are suffering or bearing their suffering with them. Another Christian says that the hurricane was evidence of God's wrath on a city that refused to condemn the sins of its citizens. While most Christians would prefer some version of the former explanation to the latter, one of the troubling (and at times infuriating) problems with the latter is that it resists disproof.[18] That God is acting behind actions not only raises difficult questions about God's providence but, more pertinently in this instance, renders opaque any attempts at describing how God is acting behind actions.

Another answer to this question of revelation, this one given most explicitly by Paul Tillich but perhaps also – at least in weak versions – by Gregory of Nyssa, nominalists like William of Ockham, and mystics like Julian of Norwich, is that our understandings of God and God's actions exist only symbolically.[19] God acts as God in that which is not God through symbol; therefore, symbols participate in divine being. Yet

---

[18] Of course, concomitantly, it also resists proof.

[19] The claim that Gregory of Nyssa thinks about God in symbolic ways is, perhaps, the most difficult to make since (a) Gregory doesn't think in systematic ways about anything, including God; (b) the concept of "symbol" has been so identified with Tillich that it's hard to avoid memeric Tillichian overreadings of earlier theologians; and (c) the dominant approach to interpreting Gregory's work on the Trinity has been in terms of analogy, not symbol. There is, however, a strain of interpretation that resists the dominant approach and reads him much more apophatically and which opens him up to the "participates in but is not captured by" qualities of symbol-language. See, e.g., Sarah Coakley, *Powers and Submissions: Spirituality, Philosophy and Gender* (Oxford: Blackwell, 2002), 109–129.

symbols of God are not, themselves, divine. Symbols both point beyond themselves and participate in that to which they point.[20] Therein, symbols resist the infinite/finite dualism that underlies the question of how the eternal can participate in time by reminding us that "finite" cannot be the opposite of "infinite" if "infinite" is to have any meaning. In other words, "infinite" cannot be bounded by anything, including an opposite. Instead, the infinite captures up (*aufgehoben*) into itself not only the idea of the finite but the idea of opposition; it negates negation.[21] If God acts symbolically in the world, then there is quasi-agency to symbols: they manifest God but never without a not-God remainder and never in such a way that they manifest God in full.[22]

The move toward thinking about God's action in terms of symbols helps overcome the problem with thinking about God as the one behind the many in that we actually do see and therein can evaluate symbols. To the degree that symbols are made up of the stuff of existence and exist in time, they are available for anyone to engage. Yet whether symbols can carry the weight this kind of engagement loads upon them is another question. The "participate in/point beyond" polarity – or at least the insistence that we keep both poles in our heads simultaneously – has the effect of turning them into abstractions and turning God into a philosophical concept. Perhaps philosophers may find such a god interesting, but those who are struggling with deeply existential questions about how to discern God's actions in the midst of natural and human processes are hardly likely to be satisfied with the answers such an approach provides. Moreover, to the degree that symbols do point beyond themselves, their effect is only to defer or even complicate the problems with discerning the actions of the one behind the many. We may now have a common referent in the symbol we see but still disagree about the object in which it participates without a way to adjudicate that disagreement.

A third approach to the question of how to understand God's acting in the world is to resist answering it, or at least to resist giving too complete

---

[20] Paul Tillich, *Dynamics of Faith* (New York: Harper and Row, 1957), 41–43.

[21] Hegel's influence on Tillich is apparent here. Langdon Gilkey's influence on how I understand Tillich, including with regard to the symbol of God, is also apparent here. See Langdon Gilkey, *Gilkey on Tillich* (New York: Crossroad, 1990), 99–113.

[22] A far more complete exploration of the role Tillichian symbols might play in discerning God's being and actions in the world – one that takes the conversation through contemporary continental philosophy – can be found in Richard James Severson, *Time, Death, and Eternity: Reflecting on Augustine's Confessions in Light of Heidegger's Being and Time*, in the ATLA Monograph Series (Lanham, MD: Scarecrow Press, 1995).

an answer to the question. Beginning with Augustine,[23] this way of engaging the question dismisses neither the significance of discernment in making sense of God's actions in time nor the degree to which those actions are mediated. Yet rather than accepting the theological totalism of the one behind the many or the philosophical holism of symbolic activity, it intentionally refuses completeness. This refusal isn't the product of exhaustion; Augustinians don't throw up their hands and say "I quit" when confronted by the complex questions about discernment and mediation. Instead, Augustinians resist the exhaustive: they simply do not feel like they are in a position (or, rather, in a time) from which to answer questions about God's actions in anything other than partial, tentative, and halting ways that recognize not only that their answers are always up for further review and revision but that the processes of review and revision are actually affirmations. Augustinians take the answers of non-Augustinians seriously rather than simply dismiss them out of hand because the energy behind such revisions signals that such answers are on the way, eschatologically, toward completion.

Because this approach resists giving answers that are too complete, it regularly picks up components of the other two answers, inquiring into questions of both how to discern God's providential activity in the world and how to account for the mediated ways in which that providential activity happens. Unsurprisingly, many of the scholars I named above who represent other answers would call themselves Augustinians. As a result, this approach can sound like either of the other approaches at times; indeed, it can do so almost joyfully because it treats the kinds of questions they raise and the problems they manifest as opportunities to practice honoring the insights of others, training its own insights, and accepting mysteries that are currently beyond human wisdom. That is, it finds relief in the possibility that because these other answers are useful but wanting, there might be something still to come that will fulfill the wants to which their usefulness points. This is the eschatological remainder.

Because this approach can sound like the other two answers, though, it is important to stake out what differentiates the three. One way to do so is

---

[23] To be clear: the approach I'm describing here doesn't so much center on Augustine as begin with him. Not only are there failings with Augustine's vision of time and the work of God (for one thing, it makes time primarily a mental project), but Augustine's own thought has been a magnet for others thinking about time and much of what they have said so sticks to what he said that it's all but impossible to remove their thought to get at what is uniquely his. Those who go to the last book of *Confessions* looking for what I'm suggesting here are likely to be disappointed.

to name the source of the difficulties of revelation. The answer of "the one behind the many" tends to treat the difficulty of discerning what God is doing in the midst of history as the product of human failing: if we just were less self-absorbed (or could escape our own biases/were less afflicted by wrong/could look out without peering through the glaze of sin), we would be able to see what God is doing. "[W]hat can be known about God is plain to them, because God has shown it to them. Ever since the creation of the world his eternal power and divine nature, invisible though they are, have been understood and seen through the things he has made," writes Paul in the first chapter of Romans. "So they are without excuse; for though they knew God, they did not honor him as God or give thanks to him, but they became futile in their thinking, and their senseless minds were darkened." The correction to such a source of difficulty is redemption, the means to such correction is the cross, the centrality of the cross suggests that revelation is usually about God fixing what we've broken, and the human response is primarily confession.

The answer of "the symbol which participates in and points to God" locates the difficulty of discerning the work of God in history as the product of divine complexity. God, as God, can both fill a thing with her presence and remain distinct from or beyond that thing. It isn't so much that human beings, as human beings, are symbol-creators; it's that symbols are the gifts God gives us to make sense of the divine – but since the divine is beyond the human, those gifts are more mysterious than we can imagine. "For my thoughts are not your thoughts, nor are your ways my ways, says the Lord," writes Deutero-Isaiah in Chapter 55. "For as the heavens are higher than the earth, so are my ways higher than your ways and my thoughts than your thoughts." The correction to such a source of difficulty is either wisdom or mysticism (or the wisdom of the mystics), the means to such correction are educational and spiritual exercises, and the centrality of such exercises means, paradoxically, that the responsibilities for discerning the mysteries of God lie upon us.

The third approach, though, locates the primary difficulty of connecting God's actions to human history neither in human failing nor in divine complexity but in finitude. That is, the problem isn't first with our failings (which, for Augustinians, are parasitic upon our difficulty of living in time), nor with the mysteriousness of God (which, for Augustinians, isn't perceived as something that reveals our distance from God so much as something that grows out of the seemingly impossible closeness of God) but with the fact that we live in time. We're like the colloquial fish who has no idea what water is. We're so enveloped by time that we can't get any satisfactory grip on it in order to hold it up to the light for closer examination. The aporias of time – that it exists and yet doesn't; that it is measurable and yet measures; that it connects things and yet divides them – are, themselves, signals that we won't get time right. Rather than resolving it, we shape a narrative that incorporates and therein submits to the aporias. The correction to such a source of difficulty is transformation (which isn't really a correction at all because we're not so much being fixed as being changed). The means of such a transformation is resurrection, which serves as the starting point for the completion of all things. The centrality of the resurrection means that revelation is primarily about the fulfillment of promise. And the human response is primarily hope.

Obviously, those last several paragraphs generalize and overly separate: all three approaches recognize sin, mystery, and finitude; all three focus on the cross, wisdom, and resurrection; and all three confess, grow, and hope. The difference may lie in the starting points: do we hope because we recognize sin or do we recognize sin (at least as sin, rather than simply bad stuff that happens) because we hope? Do we take on the practices of faith because we might achieve the mind of God (or at least some beatific vision) or because practicing is simply what we're left to do while we await a transformation that promises us the full wisdom and presence of God? Do we pursue wisdom that leads us to God or that reveals just how much stands between us and God? The approaches need not be exclusive. Though generalizations, the distinctions are, hopefully, nonetheless helpful.

At the very least, the emphasis on finitude as the primary difficulty helps put the Christian narrative about God's work in time on more equal footing with other narratives because it emphasizes the aporetic qualities of time. Time, whether explored by Plato, Aristotle, Augustine, Hegel, Husserl, Heidegger, Ricoeur, or anyone else, catches the best philosophers and theologians up short. Ricoeur's answer, for instance – that there is a fundamental aporia behind all the others which is the difference between phenomenological and cosmological understandings of time and that that these two understandings are both woven into imaginative narratives, which ought, therefore, to be the focus of our attention – isn't so much an attempt to resolve the aporia as to honor the paradoxical within it.[24]

---

[24] See Paul Ricoeur, *Time and Narrative* (3 vols.). Trans. by K. Blamey and D. Pellauer (Chicago: Chicago University Press, 1990).

In fact, Ricoeur and Augustine, in spite of their differences (and, for that matter, Ricoeur's criticisms of Augustine), share this important insight: the aporias of time aren't puzzles in need of solution but signs in search of significance. For Augustinians, at least, the signs point to both our time-embeddedness, with all the limits such embeddedness implies, and the possibility that there is something (that Augustinians call eternity) more than time and that completes time. The way time matters to us and how time works through us aren't things in which we can fully find meaning, but that it matters to us *that* time matters and that we feel time working through us reveals that time really is – or at least is becoming – meaningful.

Eternity doesn't begin where time leaves off (history isn't what happens on the way to eternity) and it isn't of a different realm than time (history isn't just one thing after another in which nothing of eternal significance happens). Instead, eternity brings all time – past, present, and future – to consummation. Eternity is changing time (or, rather, perhaps time is changing into eternity). As such, the aporias of time don't primarily signal our failures to understand time (though they also do that) so much as reveal time's incomplete transformation. We get hints of eternity in the midst of time because time has never been left to itself; indeed, we experience these hints because we time-bound creatures are, ourselves, being transformed into something eternal. Time's completion and our completion come together; likewise, times' aporias and our finitude come together as well. Yet at least until we and time are completed, we don't get solutions; we get visions and these visions surprise and shock us. They're partial and strange; wonderful and painful. We experience them, Paul writes, as the groans of creation during labor pains (Romans 8:22). They signal that the aporias of time are not simply things "out there" to examine, but in us to experience.[25]

In saying these things, I'm not so much trying to present a confessional statement as offer a phenomenological explication. The test for this approach to thinking about how God acts in the world isn't the compiling of empirical data. Nor is it a defense of the internal coherence of a particular theological vision. The test – always partial and always revisable – is whether we find this way of understanding the way God acts in history to be congruent with our experiences of history's movement through time even as we participate in that movement. Or, said

---

[25] My thanks to Ted Smith, who let me talk the last several paragraphs through with him and reminded me of the passage from Paul's letter to the Romans.

differently, it is enough that my theological explanation of the movement of time through history and my description of how the pacifist tradition has changed over time are congruent with each other because there is no other way to consider their relationship. When we bring theological or philosophical explorations of time into contact with explanations or theories of history, the most we can ever look for is congruence. But to look for such congruence is enough because, at least to the degree that we are honest about our own timeliness (and our discontentedness with it), congruence can express a great deal, giving voice to both the possibilities and impossibilities of making tighter connections than declaring two things "congruent."[26] We are, in as literal a way as I can give voice to, living within the ellipsis of time (neither presented with the full narrative nor lacking the sense that there is something more to the narrative that is present to us), marked as we are by our sense that something has been omitted and that the omission not only matters, but is shaping how we read what comes after.

To get a sense of the significance of congruence, consider the incongruities of two other ways of reading history theologically. One way of reading it would be to treat all evidence of improvement or progress (whether that means closer relations between faith and political power as Eusebius suggested in the fourth century or the expansion of rights to reach more subjects as John Locke might have suggested in the seventeenth century or even the increased effectiveness of nonviolence to change societies as Martin Luther King, Jr. argued in the twentieth) as evidence about how God is at work in history. Even setting aside the problem that such approaches tend to baptize the desires of those who hold such perspectives, such an approach re-enacts narratives of progress without accounting for the disjunctions, contradictions, contractions, and upheavals of history. Narratives of progress, popular though they have been, fail to deal with the complex movements of history and, therein, fail the test of congruence.[27]

---

[26] Taking this thought further, the next step would be toward developing a pragmatics of time and eternity in which the meaning of a thing is found in its usefulness in helping us do the hard work of growing in an understanding of ourselves and the world around us. That, though, is not my purpose in this chapter. Instead, it might be understood as the purpose of the book. Pragmatics, after all, develops in the insistence that we move into constructive work when engaging in history (that is, that the purpose of reading history is for our current context), and that such engagement is always centered in the need to address the suffering we find in that context (which suffering we both find in ourselves and recognize our role in causing).

[27] Narratives of decline repeat this failure, only in a more pessimistic register.

Another way of reading history would be to treat change as meaningless: history is "just one damn thing after another," a vale of sorrows from which the Christian goal is escape. Though now perhaps more popularly associated with the fundamentalisms of twentieth-century rural America – a vision given voice to in hymns like "I'll Fly Away" and "This World Is Not My Home" – this theological vision has repeatedly manifested itself in the history of the church. Some early Christians like Tertullian apparently thought history served no purpose other than to give evidence of the fall from which we need to be redeemed. Some forms of medieval Christianity (the Bogomils, the Cathars) expressed their opposition to the incarnation and earthly things, including the workings of history. Placing God (and human connections to God) outside of time, this way of reading history undermines the very claims about revelation, the incarnation, and divine sovereignty that have given Christianity meaning. Therein, obviously, this approach fails to deal with the complex movements of God in time and, as a result, fails the test of congruence.

The deeper question, though, is about the shape of congruence, not its existence. How is a telling of history in which traditions transition between periods of comparative stability and growth and periods of upheaval and change a better tale than, for example, a dispensationalist one in which God occasionally steps in to change the rules for divine–human and human–human relations but otherwise lets the world run? An answer to that question is itself theological, and has to do with the possibilities and limits of human actions as well as the capacities and actions of God.[28]

Begin by inverting the question: rather than "How do we get God into history?" we might ask, "How do we get a history adequate to God's story?" Let that inversion shape the claims that history is properly God's, not our possession, and that we are properly God's, not our own. History

[28] The theological answer to dispensationalism is rather quick and easy: dispensationalism relies on the idea that God changes the rules on occasion and is provided by those who think that now that God has changed the rules to favor them, God is done with rule-changing. So, for example, some Christians think the church has replaced Israel as God's chosen community because with Jesus, the rules about how to relate to God changed for good. The problem with this approach is that it relies on a vision of God which is both theologically troubling ("Is God so fickle and are God's promises worth so little?") and existentially threatening ("If God changed the rules to favor us and, in the process, withdrew favor from some other group to whom he promised favor, what would keep him from changing the rules and withdrawing favor from us?"). For a more developed theological exploration of the problems with dispensationalism, see Kendall Soulen, *The God of Israel and Christian Theology* (Minneapolis: Fortress Press, 1996). Dispensationalism isn't the only way to shape a vision of history that is congruent with a theology of God's work in time, though.

conforms to God's purposes. Because of that, nothing that we do can ultimately deter God's history from working itself out. Join to that the claims that (a) we struggle to discern how God is working God's purposes out; and (b) in that struggle, we regularly either overstate our role in making that history or overtly try to control it ourselves.

Because history is God's, we cannot make it ours, and our attempts to make it so will fail. Because we are God's, though, our attempts to make history ours will fail in ways that reveal that our projects to control history are not so much alternatives to God's history as perversions of it. That is, because we can't make history, we can't destroy it either. Instead, we can at worst misunderstand our roles in it and in misunderstanding those roles, attempt to pursue our roles in it badly. We have visions that are partly but not wholly clear; we promote ideas that are partly but never wholly pure; we act in ways that are partly but never wholly good. Our anxieties and the resulting overreach disrupt vision, thought, and action. The history we try to make, then, is a distorted expression of the history that God is making.

None of this is to deny or mitigate the danger and damage of our overreachings: we need not develop the worst vision of sin and evil to account for the worst expressions of them. History is filled with actions – innocuous, unthinking, petty, often driven by small vices and banal motives – that have produced horrific results. Indeed, part of what makes those horrors so horrible and recurrent is that we seduce ourselves by making our visions of their causes darker in order to account for our revulsion of them without understanding that the horrors were not necessarily the goals of those who contributed to perpetuating them – and that we, too, could do things that lead to horrors. Instead, my point is that our failings are parasitic on God's good work. As Roman Catholic philosopher Robert Johann noted, "[S]ince making things normally takes longer than destroying them, the shorter our temporal perspective for viewing historical events, the more our history will consist of destruction, catastrophes, battle, murder, and sudden death."[29] The temporal limits of our perspective shape our failure to see through destruction, catastrophe, and horror and discover a larger vision of God's grace-filled work with time.

Our historical projects, then, are nourished by the grace of God because even at their worst, they can never fully resist that grace, but, driven by our anxieties and attempts to escape those anxieties, they are also perversions of the good that God wills. Our projects of attempting to make history contribute to its progress(es) and our distorted understandings of how to

[29] Robert O. Johann, *Building the Human* (New York: Herder and Herder, 1968), 71.

make that history contribute to its collapses. God's actions in bringing history to fullness express themselves both through our projects and do so in spite of our failings. God's response to the failings of such projects is not their rejection but the hard transformations through which their perversions are destroyed and the projects redeemed. We experience periods of stability and progress as evidence of God's favor upon our actions (though we might better understand them as God's favorable actions through us) and we experience periods of chaos and disruption as evidence of God's absence (though we might better understand them as God's judgments upon us, keeping in mind that God's judgment expresses itself through our transformation, not our annihilation). Or, to say all this differently, it is because history is God's that our traditions move through time in both continuous and disruptive ways. God both drives and saves us from disruptive change. Congruence is not evidence of weakness; it is profound evidence of the powerful and mysterious ways in which God works.

Yet why pursue this topic, anyway? What do these reflections get us? Only this: recognizing that those who are reading this book may not share the same theological perspectives I have (and may, by their own accounts, say not only that they have no theological perspective at all but that we should be distrustful of any perspective that is theologically shaped, especially when it comes into contact with world events), it would be easy to let my historical descriptions of the movement of pacifism through time stand on their own and leave the rest of this book to the academic ghettos in which theology often finds itself. Much of the book, after all, offers an argument for a way of understanding how traditions move through time that is mostly free of theological baggage. I intend this analysis of how traditions move through time to be an invitation to read the whole book as a theological project. It could be that the non-theological readers will find resources there that help them in their non-theological work. It could even be that in the finding of those resources, they may experience that flash of discovery and meaning that is the very stuff of revelation – the very way that the eternal God reveals himself in time. If that happens, it won't be so much because of the brilliance of my insights but because any words or insights, finite as they are, can be revelatory of God. To paraphrase Walter Benjamin, every word is a small gateway in time through which the Messiah might enter.[30]

---

[30] "For every second was the small gateway in time through which the Messiah might enter." Walter Benjamin, *Selected Writings, vol. 4: 1938–1940*, H. Eiland and M. W. Jennings, eds. (Boston: Belknap Press, 2003), 397.

8

Re-narrating the Christian Pacifist Tradition

Having demythologized[1] the Christian pacifist tradition in the preceding chapters – though in a way that laid groundwork for a remythologized Christian pacifist tradition – and then offered a way of viewing history through the very type of theological lens that I would expect from the telling of a *Christian* pacifist tradition, the way is now clear and the responsibility now pressing to offer my own narrative of the history of Christian pacifism. This new narrative, I suggest, not only attends to many of the best insights of the preceding narrative but accounts for insights, practices, and communities that are underregarded within it. More importantly, this new narrative is more durable and open to new expressions in the face of the various new concerns, ideas, crises, and identities that are being shaped in the environmental age.

I offer this narrative in the form of a confession. This is not to suggest that I am advocating for a new creed to which Christians should offer adherence. Such an approach would confuse faith with agreement and be

---

[1] Here, I am using the term "demythologized" to mean something other than the project of unearthing the objective and publicly discernable/agreed upon facts about its history (*contra* the way, e.g., that Rudolph Bultmann claimed to have demythologized early Christian narratives) as a way of complicating its too-simple (and therefore insufficiently resilient) and self-congratulatory (and therefore insufficiently theological) narrative. Instead, I am demythologizing in order to fund a new mythology that not only better accounts for historical data but also offers meaning and structure to those who would take up the beliefs and practices of nonviolence as fundamental commitments for how they will live. Neither is this a project of dismantling nor deconstructing that narrative. My hope is not to leave the narrative in bits and pieces lying around unconnected but to reshape it toward something that is contemporarily helpful, theologically coherent, and can grow out of the better insights – hidden though I sometimes think they are – of that narrative.

eye-rollingly ironic, given the emphasis on questions of fidelity that I have suggested constitute the heart of the Christian pacifist tradition. Nor am I offering it as a series of statements about orthodox belief in the face of heretical challenges. Such an approach would not only mandate attention to a wide range of Christian doctrines that need not be addressed here but would threaten to further reify a division between beliefs and practices that won't be sustainable in an environmental age. Nor is it the case that other narratives of the Christian pacifist tradition are not confessional. Some are – though the theological coherence of those confessions warrants a closer review of the sort I've pursued in this book. Instead, I offer this narrative of the history of Christian pacifism in this form because confession is the vernacular of the church when it attempts to describe its own history as that history is caught up in the work of God.

I will begin by offering the narrative in its brief version, much as I offered the conventional narrative of the history of Christian pacifism in this book's opening chapter. Following the narrative, I'll offer a gloss on that narrative that teases out reasons to think about the history of Christian pacifism in the way that I am suggesting here. The new narrative goes like this:

In the beginning, when God initiated the creation of the world, God began God's great projects of bringing order out of primordial chaos and peace out of primordial violence.[2] Among God's creations were human beings, who not only participate in these great projects because they find their identities in God but because God commanded them to care for creation. Where human beings work for order and peace within creation, they express their unbreakable and immeasurable relationship with their creator as faith. Where human beings pursue chaos and violence against creation, they test that relationship and reveal how disordered their faith is. Even when acting in the best expressions of their faith, human beings face the tensions of pursuing two goods – order and peace – as creatures who are bounded by the conditions of creation, including limits within the non-human natural world and their own finitude. And when pursuing relationships that ignore or deny their identities in God, their creaturely roles in God's work in history, or their own continuity with the rest of creation, human beings exacerbate the sufferings caused by chaos and violence.

After centuries of human beings working toward both order and peace and also chaos and violence, God became human, revealing the significance of the divine–human relationship to God, the costs of finitude, chaos, and violence for the

---

[2] To be explicit: I am making a theological claim about origins that is attentive to Scripture (including minority voices that link creation narratives to earlier conflict narratives of the ancient Near East such as the Babylonian *Enuma Elish*) but also to scientific accounts, including those associated with the origins of the universe and the origins of species.

planet, and a fresh vision of creation as it is consummated in perfect order and peace, which is the Kingdom of God. The church is a particular community called to pursue this fresh vision, and it has done so in ways that manifest the complexities of its faith, its failures to understand its relationship with God, and its continued obligations toward the work to which it has been called. Throughout its history, the church has borne halting witness to its faith in God and its commitments to order and peace. When it has lacked political power, it has tended to make faith-based arguments for peace because its capacity to pursue order was limited. When it has had political power, it has tended to make faith-based arguments for order, sometimes ignoring its obligations to pursue peace. Where it has ignored its place in creation, it has failed to bear faithful witness to the one God who creates and recreates. Throughout its history, though, the church has never been left without witnesses for peace and for order.

Among these witnesses, God has always raised up individuals and communities who have expressed their faith though a commitment to nonviolence; in so doing, they have been martyrs, goads, teachers, prophets, leaders, and guides. These expressions of faith have always come in particular contexts and they bear the imprints of those contexts. Attempting to harmonize all these expressions is futile: the movement of traditions through time is marked by both continuity and change, and the project of discerning one's place in time is difficult. Since understanding when they live is among the most difficult tasks of human existence, these persons and groups have sometimes confused their present with their future. At other times, they have blurred their future with their past. In all times, they have measured the state, the church, their own communities, and even themselves against their (partial but faithful, distorted but hopeful, and idiosyncratic but loving) visions of the Kingdom inaugurated but still awaiting completion and found them wanting. Sometimes, these judgments have led them to withdraw; at other times, these judgments have led them to confront; at still other times, these judgments have led them to reach out.

During the modern age, their witness became increasingly plural, prominent, and successful in both obvious and subtle ways. In spite of their best impulses and loftiest language (and like their more bellicose brothers and sisters in faith), both premodern and modern pacifists have largely ignored the impact of the natural world in shaping the conditions that lead to violence. At the beginning of the twenty-first century, they are seeking more capacious language, more developed practices, more attentive expressions of justice, and more resilient ways of connecting with others both within and outside the church. As they enter the Environmental Age, they will yet again need to develop these capacities in new ways as they rediscover their connections to the rest of creation and look toward the Kingdom of God that is "already but not yet" constituted by peace and order joined in harmony. In the providence of God, such new ways are already revealing themselves, especially in the majority world, and offering glimpses of a peaceful Kingdom that is already but not yet.

Before providing a gloss on the various parts of this new narrative, I want to offer three brief comments about it as a whole. First, language about both creation and time shows up throughout the narrative. A narrative about the history of Christian pacifism for the environmental age should emphasize both space (the creation around us) and time and, where possible, reveal the links between them. Human beings exist in particular places and times; a narrative that helps them make sense of when they live has to attend to where they live as well – and attending to where they live means attending not only to the cultures they have created but to the natural world as well. Understandings of their locations in time and space may vary across social imaginaries, but human beings never cease to live in particular places and times.

Second, order and peace play a prominent role throughout the narrative but do so in tensive ways. In some contexts, the pursuit of one involves the pursuit of the other; in other contexts, the pursuit of one involves the sacrifices of the other. Whether cooperating or competing, they express themselves politically. Together, they signal a plurality of goods from the very beginning of the narrative and resist any attempt to elevate one good over all others. As such, the two terms can also stand in for a range of other tensively related sets of terms (e.g., competition and cooperation, justice and love) whose dynamism resists permanent forms of relationship.

Third, in its confessional form, this narrative of the history of Christian pacifism begins before history and ends after it. This telling of the tradition locates it within a larger theological framework of the work of God. It is perfectly possible to offer a narrative about the history of Christian pacifism without recourse to a theological framework – and as I offer a gloss on this narrative below that picks up important figures, movements, and forms in that history, I would hope that persons working from either an atheological framework or the pacifist framework of another religious tradition will find my arguments provocative if not compelling. However, I am more interested in trying to get Christian pacifists to describe their own history differently because pacifism is more meaningful when it is manifest in practices, some of which will be useful in the Anthropocene. The point of this book isn't simply to write about the history of Christian pacifism; it is to shape a narrative of that history – a mythology – that can carry the wisdom of Christian pacifism into the future.

With those preliminaries out of the way, I turn to the text in its particulars.

I BEGINNINGS

Beginning this narrative with creation achieves a series of benefits. First, it lashes the story of Christian pacifism to the breadth of Scripture. "In the beginning," after all, are not only the opening words of Genesis but of John's gospel as well. Christian pacifists have turned to Scripture throughout history as a guiding authority for their lives and actions; moving away from Scripture is highly unlikely. Yet all too often, they have unduly and unnecessarily restricted the range of texts available to them to a collection of New Testament texts with an occasional dip into the Old Testament (e.g., the vision of the peaceable kingdom in Isaiah 11). To the degree that Christian pacifists retain their various commitments to Scripture as authoritative for interpreting and expressing their witness of nonviolence, it is better that they express those commitments through attention to the fullness of Scripture – including the whole of the Hebrew Scriptures – lest they simultaneously reduce the resources available to them and invert their relationship to Scripture through proof-texting, making it do what they want it to rather than doing what the God they find in Scripture calls them to do.[3]

---

[3] It is suggestive in this regard that scholars who locate themselves within the traditions of the historic peace churches have given little sustained attention to the doctrine of creation. While one reason for this is the relative paucity of systematic theologies that have arisen from within the radical reformation wing of Protestantism (and where those systematic theologies do exist, treatments of creation tend to be brief and fairly conventional), this relative absence is counterintuitive, given the degree to which those in the peace churches are so connected to the land. One text – perhaps an exception that proves the rule – is Calvin Redekop, ed., *Creation and the Environment: An Anabaptist Perspective on a Sustainable World* (Baltimore: Johns Hopkins University Press, 2000). Even there, though, the editor notes that "[t]he Anabaptist/Mennonite tradition has developed a unique, though not totally consistent, philosophical and ethical position regarding the creation" (9). Representative of the thought in that book is Walter Klaassen's conclusion that

[i]t was the need to survive and not the love of the land that produced the expertise and care for the land for which Mennonites became famous. I make this judgment because nowhere in the literature on Mennonite agriculture do I find that their care of the land was motivated by any biblical imperative to care for the creation or that to love God means to love the land. The tradition of living without weapons in a dangerous human world was consciously derived from Scripture... Not so the care of the land.

Walter Klaassen, "Pacifism, Nonviolence, and the Peaceful Reign of God" in Redekop, *Creation and the Environment*, 142–3. This has had not only theologically but morally troubling implications, including the degree to which the peace churches accepted the doctrine of discovery in the Americas – a doctrine that they are only recently working to dismantle. See, e.g., "Dismantling the Doctrine of Discovery" at https://dofdmenno.org/ for more on this work. Accessed on May 25, 2017.

Second, it reminds those who would tell the story of Christian pacifism that their story does not arise *de novo* with Jesus. The earliest church – the church that is so valorized in the conventional narrative of Christian pacifism – understood the Old Testament as their Scripture and found in it both vision and resources. Pulling the narrative of Christian pacifism back into the Old Testament helps subvert supersessionist tendencies in the tradition and pushes toward greater recognition of the ambivalences and silences in the New Testament text about violence. Pulling the narrative of Christian pacifism back into the creation story also helps subvert isolationist tendencies in the tradition and pushes toward greater recognition of other (non-Christian) expressions of pacifism with which pacifists may not only find common cause but common moral, theological, and even scriptural starting points. The early church may, by historical necessity, be the starting point of the Christian pacifist tradition but it ought not be the starting point for the way Christian pacifists describe their tradition.

Third, it locates the work of Christian pacifism within the work of God and the history of Christian pacifism within a larger narrative of salvation history. That is, this narrative finds its theological heart not in the life of Jesus but in a Trinitarian vision of God and God's relation to the world, simultaneously reaffirming that Jesus is fully God as well as fully human and that God and God's work can best be viewed through the lens of Jesus's life, death, and resurrection. While this shift from a Christocentric to a theocentric vision of history complicates how pacifists might understand the work of God (as they must deal not only with difficult Old Testament texts as part of their tradition rather than foreign to it but also with troubling historical events as occasions of divine action), it also more closely aligns the narrative of the history of the Christian pacifist tradition with that tradition's theological commitments. While narrative complexity increases, so does theological fidelity. Since questions about fidelity are at the heart of the Christian pacifist tradition, this theocentric shift expands Christian pacifists' ability to address those questions.

Fourth, it provides a trajectory for the narrative of the history of Christian pacifism – a moral arc to history – that both undermines the troubling myth of return that has sustained the conventional narrative of Christian pacifism and also undergirds an eschatological frame of reference through which to make sense of Christian pacifism. That is, the Christian pacifist tradition is initiated at creation and is completed at the end of history; between those two points in time, it is always journeying. As it continues along that journey, it will both gain and lose things along the way, some to its great benefit and some that cost dearly. Paradoxically, then, situating the Christian pacifist tradition within a theocentrically framed construal of time has the effect of treating the tradition as human: shaped by past events and with the potential to address future ones, it is peripatetic in its movement from past through present to future, never quite assured of its own footing in its movement through time or secured through its own efforts against the transient qualities of history. Relieved of the impossible burdens of providing an eternal "right answer" to questions of fidelity or an acontextual set of morally pure practices by which to respond to violence, the tradition becomes not only more clearly human but more fully humane.

Fifth, it recognizes a multiplicity of goods in the world and the difficulty of negotiating among them without surrendering any of them. Peace is a good but can't be sustained over time without a commitment to order. Order is a good but won't be valued without a commitment to peace. Peace and order are both goods but not goods that should come at the expense of justice. Somehow, divine love both judges the limits of these goods even as it unites and transforms them. The tensions between these goods not only reveal the difficulties inherent in negotiating among contending moral visions for dealing with complex problems but also fund the possibilities for discovering new and fitting ways through which a tradition can address those same problems. I have emphasized peace and order in this narrative partly for contextual reasons (climate change introduces new levels of chaos to human existence and chaos feeds violence) and partly for a theological one: the pursuit of both of them can be understood as expressions of fidelity. Where their pursuit is sundered from larger questions of fidelity, an emphasis on either peace or order can devolve into the reification of particular actions disconnected from matters of agency and social location. Where their pursuit is oriented by larger questions of fidelity, however, peace and order are both relational goods; they shape possibilities for community and empower projects of just love.[4]

Finally, beginning the narrative of the history of Christian pacifism with creation links human history with the history of the non-human natural world. The events of human history – the movements of peoples,

---

[4] I would suggest, incidentally, that treating peace and order as goods within the order of relationship may have the effect of bypassing unhelpful contemporary debates about whether the first sin is disobedience (Adam and Eve eat forbidden fruit) or violence (Cain kills Abel), since both disobedience and violence are expressions of bad faith and rejections of relationship.

discoveries of new technologies, political alignments and realignments, changing economic systems and the movements of goods and services, the conflicts and resolutions of conflicts that such events produce, etc. – are all subject to the resources and forces of the natural world. These links tend to be underexplored in the construction of historical narratives and under-valued in assessments about change over time. Evolutionary adaptations, seasonal stability and variations, access to natural resources, biodiversity in ecosystems, storms and periods of calm, climatic changes, etc.: all of these have shaped how human beings have moved through time. Moreover, human beings, as participants in natural systems, have expressed their connections to the natural world in manifold ways. To take but one example, evolutionary biology has demonstrated that some primate species, at least, have been successful over time not only because they outcompeted other species for resources but because one of the distinctive features of their competitive success was the ability to coop-erate with each other. As such, both violence and cooperation have been a part of human existence from the beginning. Violence may be innate in human societies but it is also optional in them. While it is overly simplistic to say that violence and cooperation are two alternative and opposed paths from which to choose when faced with the struggle to survive and that pacifists have chosen the latter, it is nonetheless the case that the potential for pacifist responses to violence and potential violence are seemingly hardwired into human beings.[5]

2 JESUS AND THE EARLY CHURCH[6]

Locating the beginning of the Christian pacifist tradition in creation rather than the New Testament need not undermine the centrality of either the

---

[5] To be clear, I am not equating cooperation with pacifism. Pacifism is a commitment to nonviolence, not to cooperation, and it is possible to be uncooperative in nonviolent ways (as acts of nonviolent resistance amply demonstrate). More importantly, cooperation is not a wholly good thing, as it has shaped patterns of in-group preferencing that, over time, have led to violence. As demonstrated in both archaeological and anthropological data, conflict within and between hunter-gatherers has existed for as long as there have been hunter-gatherers. Following Azar Gat, I would note that "the argument here is not that *all* hunter-gatherers invariably fight. Human societies – be they hunter-gatherer, agricultural, or industrial – have lived in peace for longer or shorter periods… Yet most societies observed to date have engaged in warfare from time to time, including the simplest hunter-gatherers." Azar Gat, *War in Human Civilization*, 15–16.

[6] This section, especially, might be read as the summation of a set of challenges to Stanley Hauerwas and the vision of Christian ethics he has laid out in, among other places, *The Peaceable Kingdom: A Primer in Christian Ethics* (Notre Dame: University of Notre Dame

New Testament or Jesus as he is described there for the tradition. It does, though, add complexity to the tradition's Christological focus by viewing Jesus not only as a model (though certainly also that), or an initiator of an alternative way (though certainly that as well), but as a divine response to the violence and chaos that threaten creation and its flourishing.[7]

While sometimes lifted up as a moral exemplar, the Jesus described in the New Testament isn't necessarily a great model for pacifists if they are expecting moral clarity about how to live in the world. There are too many instances of disconcerting stories (e.g., Jesus overturning tables and driving moneychangers out of the Temple, as in Mark 11) to idealize him. There are too many ambiguous teachings to simplify him. For example, in Matthew 5:39, Jesus says, "Do not resist an evildoer. But if anyone strikes you on the right cheek, turn the other also." Is he advocating nonresistance – as a plain sense reading of the text suggests – or nonviolent resistance, as some interpreters have suggested since being struck on the right cheek could mean being insulted more than being injured and so turning the other cheek is a rejection of the insult and a reaffirmation of one's moral standing and value?[8] There are too many deferrals of identity (e.g., when Jewish leaders bring Jesus before Pilate, in Luke 23, they condemn him for saying he is the Messiah – which he does not do in that gospel – and when Pilate asks him if he is the king of the Jews, he responds, "You say so.") and self-proclamations of unique identity (e.g., John 14:6–7: "I am the way, the truth, and the life. No one comes to the Father except through me. If you know me, you will know my Father also") to singularize him. And there are too many diverse proclamations by others about him (e.g., Paul describing him as a second Adam whose

---

Press, 1983). I would hope, though, that it is also read in light of an appreciation for Hauerwas's work, even where it goes in directions quite different from those he has advocated.

[7] Shifting from "Beginnings" to "Jesus and the Early Church" gives opportunity for a misreading of my argument that I need to eliminate here. I do not mean to suggest that pacifists skip past the Hebrew Scriptures as resources for practices and understandings of nonviolence. Indeed, in both Chapter 2 and the "Beginnings" section, I explicitly reject such a move. There are resources aplenty in the Hebrew Scriptures for those who espouse nonviolence. How could there not be? Jesus and the earliest church relied on those texts. Instead, treat "Beginnings," "Jesus and the Early Church," and later sections in this chapter not so much as a chronology of the history of Christian pacifism as touch-points for making sense of that history. And treat the Bible, in all its complex wholeness, as an authority to which those who would make sense of "Beginnings," "Jesus and the Early Church," etc. can turn.

[8] See, e.g., Walter Wink, *Jesus and Nonviolence: A Third Way* (Minneapolis: Fortress Press, 2003), 10–15.

act of righteousness leads to justification and life for all in Romans 5) to support a single, theologically coherent, and biblically grounded view of Jesus as moral exemplar. As the range of above passages suggests, there are so many Jesuses in the New Testament, each one the product of a complex mix of remembered events, transmitted narratives, and theological projects, that he is more likely to be a cipher than a model for anyone who would ground an ethic in Jesus's life and teaching.

Moreover, to the extent that Jesus's role as model is reduced to treating him as a moral exemplar, pacifists risk a problematic theological inversion wherein reference to Jesus becomes a means of highlighting their own righteousness. Through the peculiar logic characteristic of inwardly curved selves, linking Jesus's holiness to his morality and then identifying one's own morality with that of Jesus tempts one to assume that one is also holy like Jesus. Fortunately, Christian pacifists have largely resisted this temptation: the very stringency of a purely pacifist ethic resists both perfection as a standard and assumptions of moral rectitude as honest self-assessments.

Yet even where most Christian pacifists have resisted this temptation, the very stringency of the pacifist ethic can create its own moral aporia by treating pacifism in idealistic terms, elevating peace above other goods such that it becomes the defining moral quality of Christian life. Yet peace, while a great good, is not obviously different in kind from other goods in Christian life. Prioritizing peace in one's moral engagement does not absolve one of the costs and consequences that come with ignoring or downplaying the pursuit of other goods in attempting to live faithfully. Said differently, Christian pacifists may and even should consistently pursue nonviolent approaches to conflicts, but in doing so, they do not avoid responsibility for the costs – to themselves and to others – that nonviolent approaches entail. People suffer because of pacifist approaches and not all those who suffer have explicitly or even tacitly volunteered for such suffering by choosing to be pacifists. The point here, again, is not that people should avoid being pacifists; those who have chosen nonviolence as a way of life model a morally exemplary way of living. It's that such a choice carries costs, and being a moral exemplar does not relieve one of the responsibilities that come with those costs. Pacifism, though morally exemplary, is still a human way of living. Pacifists may live without resort to coercive violence; they may not live without regret.

To situate Christian pacifism within the larger context of God's creation is to recognize that human actions occur within a context in which predation, disease, consumption and its attendant increase in entropy, energy transfer, mutation and natural selection, impersonal but vital physical forces, scarcity, natural variability, population growth and decline, finitude, and the interconnectedness of things are all conditions of existence. They are not conditions of sinful existence – though sinful actions can follow from these things – but existence itself. A theological account of the human movement through time still needs to account for the ever-expanding wisdom of the natural sciences and the diagnostic power of the social sciences. Historicizing either Eden or a post-creation fall from grace does neither. That same theological account recognizes not only the inescapability of tragedy but the subjective qualities of tragedy (the same event that harms some benefits others), the complexity of tragedies (so often a peculiar mix of human agency and natural forces), and one's complicity in the trage-dies of others. Such a theological account concedes that while some tragedies might be prevented, others reduced, and still others miti-gated, tragedies recur because flourishing – human and otherwise – comes at a cost.

As the world transitions into an environmental age, the complexity and interconnectedness of existence both grows and becomes more apparent – as do the realities of tragedy and complicity. One person choosing to eat a fast-food hamburger rather than a locally sourced salad has a negligible impact on the world, but the decision still increases greenhouse gasses. One couple choosing to live in a neighborhood with a good elementary school for their children means becoming a two-car family and adding pollution to the system. One small clothing business choosing to compete with larger corporations while paying employees a living wage means importing cloth and materials at the lowest possible prices even though that cloth is produced in majority-world factories with histories of human rights abuses. One municipality wishing to promote single-stream recy-cling to reduce solid waste signs a deal with a company that buys recycled materials, ships them to China for sorting and renewal, and regularly ships the same materials back to landfills because they contain excluded items. One country trying to raise its citizens' standards of living signs a trade agreement with a dozen other countries, some of whom use their taxes to support a war abroad. While the responses to all of these examples – and countless more – can include working to create more just, peaceful, and sustainable ways of living, the notion that a commitment to nonviolence is the starting point to such work isn't so much wrong as immaterial (who would advocate for a violent response to owning and driving a second car?) and the notion that any of the decisions involved in any of these examples can be wholly separated from their environmental costs and the attendant political consequences is naïve.

What, then, might it mean to think of Jesus as a model if moral exemplarity isn't the starting point? Perhaps it might have something to do with the complexity and value of living a life of faith in a world full of tragedies. In other words, the first thing Jesus models for pacifists in an environmental age – and, I would argue, in any age – is his fidelity to God. Jesus displays this fidelity not only or even primarily in his willingness to suffer nonviolently for a world in which people suffer the costs of imperfectly pursued, improperly valued, importunately demanding, and immorally envisioned multiple goods. Instead, he displays fidelity in his belief that God will leave neither him nor the world finally bereft of Godself and that God's will is toward flourishing, not suffering. Such a faith is capacious enough to encompass, "not my will but yours be done" (Luke 22:42), "My God, my God, why have you forsaken me?" (Matthew 27:46), and "It is finished" (John 19:30). Such a faith may incorporate obedience but also transcends it because it is suffused with a capacity for dynamic and growing intimacy rather than a commitment to static and ordered relationships. Such a faith treats doubt as a means for refining one's loyalties and replaces the question, "Do you believe?" with "Given that everyone believes in something, what is worth believing in?"

Jesus is the model for Christian pacifists in this regard because he reminds them that pacifism, at its core, is an expression of fidelity rather than a pattern of moral engagement. This kind of fidelity, in a complex world that is tragic, sinful, and nevertheless suffused by divine grace, is complicated. Following Jesus, Christian pacifists ask, "How am I to understand this world and my role in it?" "What is God doing in the world right now and how am I being called to respond to that work?" "By what means might I come to discern what God is calling and commanding me/us to do?" "Where and when do I find myself in God's story right now?" They then link the answers to those questions to the sorts of practices of nonviolence that are fitting for that time and place. Jesus chose not to appeal to God to send more than twelve legions of angels down in his defense not because he was unable to do so (Jesus's question was rhetorical) or because use of the sword is wrong (if so, why was the sword there in the first place?) but "all this has taken place, so that the scriptures of the prophets may be fulfilled" (Matthew 26:56).

The practices of pacifism, then, are expressions of faith as it is manifest in particular times and places and they will not always look the same. In one time and place, voting can be a pacifist practice because voting is the means by which nonviolent transitions of state power occur even if voting does implicate the voter in the decisions of the state; in another time and place – a U.S. congressman voting to authorize the President to use force – it clearly is not. In one time and place, driving a military ambulance can be a pacifist practice even if it does mean taking an oath to defend the state; at another time and place – when that oath also means swearing ultimate allegiance to the military or its leader – it is not. In one time and place, an organized sit-in at a cafeteria in the Jim Crow South can be a pacifist practice because it is a form of protest against racist policies that does not harm other patrons; in another time and place – a sit-in that blocks the entrance to a hospital's emergency room because abortions are performed there – it is likely that harm is going to follow for those who need access to that ER. Treating Jesus as a model of faithfulness not only inserts discernment into the center of pacifist practices pursued in a complex world; it develops a more clearly Chalcedonian Christology within which to recognize both Jesus's full humanity (what and how did Jesus believe?) and full divinity (what and how has the church believed things about Jesus?).

One way this richer sense of how to treat Jesus as model bears fruit is that it clarifies how pacifists might go about thinking of Jesus as an initiator of a new, alternative way. Pacifism did not begin with Jesus. As historians of pacifism have pointed out, Jesus wasn't the first person to resist the temptation to use violence coercively.[9] Though perhaps the church begins with Jesus, the intentional establishment of a community of believers committed to nonviolence is not unique to Christianity. Nor is it clearly the case that Christians engaged in a unique set of pacifist practices, gave unique reasons to be pacifists, or oriented their pacifism around a unique set of norms. While the early church's apocalypticism shaped a worldview in which pacifism may have been valued, that worldview wasn't Jesus's so much as it was the church's response to Jesus's life, death, and resurrection. What, then, would it mean to treat Jesus as inaugurating a new and alternative way marked by pacifism and what are the larger qualities of this new way?

The conventional narrative of the history of Christian pacifism argues that the new way is marked by the centrality of a counter-narrative: The world favors violence; we favor pacifism. The world favors strength; our

---

[9] Among many resources here, see Mark Juergensmeyer, "Nonviolence" in *The Encyclopedia of Religion, vol. 10*, Mircea Eliade, editor in chief (New York: Macmillan Pub. Co., 1987), 463–468. This entry includes a helpful bibliography covering nonviolence not only in history but throughout the world religions at its conclusion.

strength is made perfect in weakness. The world is driven by fear; we are commanded to love. The world is oriented around death; we believe in life eternal. The world is shaped by empires; we look to the coming Kingdom of God. The world says, "Caesar is lord"; we confess that Jesus is Lord, etc. Instead, though, it might be clearer to say that the alternative way is shaped by the revelation that it is the world's narrative that is "counter," not the church's. To the degree that the early church understood Jesus's Lordship not in abstract or spiritualized terms but in ways consistent with Israel's confession that "Yahweh is Lord," then the early church's claim was that the world belonged to Jesus – that "[t]he earth is the Lord's and all that is in it, the world and those who live in it" (Psalm 24:1). That confession carried within itself the implicit claim that the church does not need to let "the world" dictate the terms of their relationship.[10] One of the reasons, after all, that the apologetic was the primary rhetorical form of the early church was that the apologists believed that argument could carry the day. Their theological vision not only grounded a better way to live in the world but offered a narrative that was a truer way to understand the world than the narrative that the world told about itself. The early church didn't think of itself as participating in an alternative reality; it thought that it was participating in reality.

The alternative way that Jesus inaugurates, then, is not expressed in a counter-narrative in which the "powers and principalities" of Ephesians 6:12 are actually in charge but in a dominant narrative in which "in him all things in heaven and on earth were created, things visible and invisible, whether thrones or dominions or rulers or powers – all things have been created through him and for him. He himself is before all things and in him all things hold together" (Colossians 1:16–17). The new way is a way of looking out and seeing not evil but grace. Pacifism gains coherence in such a vision because in it, Christians need be neither stoic heroes nor tragic victims in the face of the vagaries and suffering of the world. Relieved of the burden of bringing light into the world and the pain of fleeing the corrupting power of that world, pacifist responses to violence in the world become expressions of confidence about the future and hope in the immediate return of Jesus. For the early church, pacifism is a strategic response not because it cannot win through use of force but because it need not worry about winning. In Jesus, God has already won. For the

---

[10] For a lengthier treatment of this idea of the church as having a counter-counter narrative, see my *Confessing Christ in the Twenty-first Century* (Lanham, MD: Rowman and Littlefield, 2005).

early church, pacifism is a faithful response not because it is the only way to avoid apostasy but because one will not be judged based on whether one has gotten one's religious actions right. For the early church, pacifism is an alternative way of living in the world not because the world is setting the terms of engagement but because God has revealed the poverty of any terms the world would demand.

This insight of the early church is of paramount importance in the twenty-first century. In an environmental age, the church will need to resist the temptation to equate "new way" with "alternative way." Environmental issues neither respect borders nor honor small groups who get it right; there is no place to escape these issues and no use in providing a prophetic witness to the surrounding world that isn't also an invitation for the world to join in the project of seeing itself as part of the creation that God is transforming.[11]

As such, Christian pacifists must see their actions in an environmental age as invitational and the range of pacifist practices as wide. March not to protest against but to bring on board. Write not to decry but to encourage. Build alliances rather than tribes. Practice confession. Vote on behalf of future generations and a nonhuman natural world that can't vote for themselves. Listen, but also, buy local. Eat less meat. Drive less. Purchase and support cleaner forms of energy. Reduce, reuse, and recycle. Recognize that complicity is the shadow side of the degree to which we are connected to each other. They must also link all these things to a hopeful way of living and a graceful way of seeing.

In the face of the enormity of the global dangers associated with climate change and environmental degradation, such practices may seem so paltry as to be useless. Were they engaged as solutions to those dangers, they

---

[11] One place for the church to proclaim witness to this new way in an environmental age is to relieve itself of tendencies to spiritualize the Kingdom of God or to flee the world via a theology of the rapture. The contemporary fascination with rapture-theology is not only a modern heresy (it arose in the nineteenth and early twentieth centuries); it is a dramatic misrepresentation of good news and betrayal of biblical texts. So, for instance, where 1 Thessalonians 4:16–17 notes that when Jesus returns from heaven, those "who are alive, who are left, will be caught up in the clouds ... to meet the Lord in the air; and so ... be with the Lord forever," it isn't actually suggesting that Christians will be removed from a condemned world. Instead, the Greek suggests that Christians will "meet the Lord in the air" in order to escort him back to the earth and show him around – to display what they'd done with his stuff while he'd been away. A passage often used to argue about why we shouldn't care about the earth turns out to have an implicit warning about our obligations to take care of it. See Steven Bouma-Prediger, *For the Beauty of the Earth: A Christian Vision for Creation Care*, 2nd ed. (Grand Rapids: Baker Academic, 2010), 69–71.

would be. Yet this new way – the alternative to the alternative – functions not as a set of solutions so much as a time of rehearsal. The practices are practice for a time that is not yet, a time in which peace and order are perfectly expressed and the threats of violence and chaos are no more. Between now and then, expressions of peace and order are partial, conflicted, and ambiguous and practicing at them means not only recognizing this but attending to the implications that come with it.

Surely, there can be no context in which to express this alternative-to-the-alternative vision than war. War threatens life, stability, hope, and, at its largest scales, the very planet. It also threatens to normalize pain and suffering; to measure success though destruction; to dehumanize both others and self. In the face of such threats, the vision of a world shaped in love, governed in hope, and transformed by grace functions as a prod – as a nagging and insistent claim that war is not normal, that triumph will not be measured out through violence, that the goods violence brings are temporary, and that the promises war makes for wellbeing are lies. As pacifists live into their alternative-to-the-alternative way of living, they remind the world of these things.

The pacifist Christology revealed in and undergirding my narrative of the history of Christian pacifism treats Jesus as model (but as a model of faith) and as the initiator of a new alternative way of living (but as an alternative to the alternative) by thinking of Jesus as a divine response to suffering, including the suffering caused by violence and chaos. Indeed, a cursory read of Scripture suggests that most, if not all, revelations of God are responses to suffering and that much of this suffering is driven by violence and chaos. Even to the degree that Christians think of Jesus's life, death, and resurrection as a response to sin, the connections between sin, violence, and chaos are apparent: sin, after all, doesn't simply clot the soul, it affects the body as the body is subjected to forces that harm it. Neither sin nor the sufferings it causes triumph, though. The divine response to suffering that is Jesus' life, death, and resurrection signals God's commitment to the divine–human relationship and bears witness to God's will that creation – including human beings – flourish. Said differently, not only pacifist Christology but the history of pacifism is oriented around Jesus's life, death, and resurrection.

Thinking of Jesus as a model of faith, as initiating an alternative-to-the-alternative, and as a response to suffering provides theological rigor to a pacifist Christology but it also makes it significantly more vertiginous. Being faithful is trickier than being good if only because faith is less palpable. Seeing one's narrative as alternative-to-alternative risks devolving into contrariness. Thinking of Jesus as response to suffering means facing – and feeling – suffering. That the early church struggled to make sense of all this is unsurprising. That the early church did not begin in or maintain consensus about all this was inevitable. That the early church functioned in a variety of contexts – each with its own range of resources and threats – as it struggled to make sense of and live into all this helps make sense of the ambiguities, disagreements, and silences that constitute its first hundred and fifty years of an existence in which it promoted peace and order in a world where violence and chaos remained existential threats. That it was successful in so doing – particularly in light of the fact that it was competing with other religious answers to the questions that such a Christology raised – signals both the breadth of its genius and the limitations of its answers and it at least hints at the continuing presence of God not only in its midst but at work in the wider world.

3 THE HISTORY OF PACIFISM IN THE CHURCH: 150–1850 C.E.

This side of eternity, the church's successes in addressing its deep questions about Jesus, peace, order, the Kingdom of God, faithfulness, the authority of Scripture, and the significance of creation (and others) have been substantial but partial. Its answers, while not fleeting, are always partial, deeply contextual, continually under review, and the sources of debates and divisions. It follows that the history of Christian pacifism bears the markings of these successes and their limits. It also follows that this history, in its own complicated ways, bears witness to both stability and change over time: traditions persevere because they provide durable resources for thought, practice, and structure and they change because those resources only imperfectly address the needs of new times and places.

One reason for the durability of the Christian pacifist tradition has been its continued focus on Jesus as model of faith, inaugurator of an alternative-to-the-alternative, and divine response to suffering. What does it mean for us to have faith like Jesus? What does it mean to have faith in Jesus and what are the implications of that faith? If Jesus is God's clearest and most powerful response to suffering, how is God now at work in a way that is consistent with the ways of Jesus while also bringing about a new thing inaugurated through Jesus? What does a life lived after and in light of Jesus look like? These are not only deep questions of faith; they shape a narrative and a range of practices that have been conditioned by the contexts in which those questions have been answered. One reason for the changes in the tradition over time has been the changes in the contexts in which those questions were answered. And one reason for the irregularity of those changes has been that history moves through time in complicated ways. All this was discussed in earlier chapters as a way of both criticizing the conventional narrative of the history of Christian pacifism and also suggesting that the Christian pacifist tradition is more complicated, more ambivalent, and richer than the conventional narrative suggests:

- Christian pacifism grew in the soil of anti-Jewish sentiment.
- Christian pacifism's focus on purity and identity shaped patterns of interaction that would later nourish the church's pursuit of political power and recourse to the threat and use of coercive violence.
- Christian pacifists have a far wider range of conversation partners and resources than they have tended to recognize – including many partners and resources they have rejected.
- Christian pacifism has existed throughout the history of the church in, e.g., the monastic traditions, various heretical movements (Cathars, Fraticelli, Waldensians), and the daily practices of countless Christians (especially women) for whom recourse to arms was not a viable option.
- Christian pacifism, as it arose in the historic peace churches, was, in part, a response to large social transformations brought about during the Reformation and has to do with both obvious changes (e.g., renewed attention to Scripture and new ways to read it; the rise of the modern nation-state) and less obvious ones (an apocalyptic sensibility in the face of so much change), and these churches drew from resources and communities that preceded them (including the Hussites and Lollards). Moreover, the peace churches were not the only groups to advocate for pacifism; as Heiko Oberman notes, "nearly all the emerging intellectual elite north of the Alps – be they an Erasmus, a Luther, or a Zwingli – went through a phase of pacifism that was to remain part of their dream of a new society."[12]

---

[12] Heiko Oberman, *The Two Reformations: The Journey from the Last Days to the New World*, edited by Donald Weinstein (New Haven: Yale University Press, 2003), 18. That Erasmus and Zwingli went through pacifist phases is far more evident to me than that Luther did.

- Christian pacifism as a form of political action exploded in both the range of approaches and the political success of its ideas after the latter half of the nineteenth century.

Left out of those earlier chapters, though, has been the role that climatic change has played in all this history. This section fills in that history.

It must begin by reiterating something noted much earlier: that climate change does not *cause* violence or responses to violence any more than it controls any other aspect of the movements of history. Instead, climate change shapes the conditions for violent and nonviolent actions because climate change plays a role in shaping the way history moves. Volcanic eruptions, for instance, don't cause wars. They can, though, lead to cold summers, which can lead to failed crops, which can lead to the pursuit of other sources for food, which can lead to violence or decisions to avoid violence. To make sense of the impact of climate on conflict, one needs to get away from thinking in simple cause-effect relationships. Indeed, perhaps the first lesson to learn from paleo- and historical climatologists is that causation is a far more complex idea than modernist approaches suggest.[13] If that is the first lesson, the second equally vital lesson to learn from them is that natural forces ought not be written out of narratives about why societies change. The causes of transition from one social imaginary into the next are complex and multifaceted and include the advent of novel ideas, the creation of new technologies, the occurrence of impactful events, and the reshaping of established practices. If contemporary climate change reveals nothing else, however, it reveals that natural forces also drive such transitions.

A brief rehearsal of major climatic changes begins to reveal just how much ancient and modern Christian history – typically understood through attention to either political systems or social structures – is shaped by significant climatic events.

In the fourth century B.C.E., the ecotone between the continental and Mediterranean zones in Europe shifted north. Celtic tribes, which were well established in Italy at the time, were outcompeted by Rome, which based its agricultural systems around a few major crops harvested to feed the cities. Better fed and agriculturally more stable than the societies

---

[13] In this, climatologists share something with theologians who have, throughout history, attempted to address questions about how God works in the world – whether through Thomas Aquinas's notion of four causes (final, formal, material, efficient), Calvin's notion of first and second causes, Hans Urs von Balthasar's notion of theodramatics, or some other approach.

surrounding it, Rome began to exert influence outward and, over the course of the next few hundred years, Rome conquered Carthage (its great Mediterranean rival) in the mid-third century B.C.E., moved into France, and forced the Celts north. Celtic and Gallic reaction to Roman incursion included violent attacks and the establishment of increasingly settled communities north of the Alps. In 59 B.C.E., Julius Caesar played upon Roman fears of the Celts to support his drive through France and into Britain and Germany, thereby giving him grounds to establish himself as emperor and initiating the *Pax Romana* within which Christianity would arise and spread. Those climatic conditions – marked by warmth and extensive growing seasons – would continue into the sixth century, when the Mediterranean zone shifted back south and Roman power receded with it.

Christian interactions with Rome were always fraught, complex, and pluriform (as earlier chapters have suggested), but there is little doubt that the extensive Roman Empire provided resources for the spread of the faith throughout the empire and, after Constantine, gave stability and then centrality to the faith, especially in the cities. When, in the sixth century, centralized Roman power receded to be replaced by greater power at local, rural levels as the Middle Ages came into being, Christianity would, itself, change. Celtic Christianity – never really under Roman control – would prosper. The church would split between East and West. Distinct monastic communities would arise in the East, the West, and the British Isles. The decline in the centralized political power of Rome was mirrored in the decline of the centralized power of the church in Rome.

The decentralization of the church is hardly surprising when one attends to the sudden arrival of the Late Antique Little Ice Age in the sixth century. Climatic data shows that in 535 C.E., a huge volcanic eruption (or several) led to crop failure, global famine, and, most probably, the Plague of Justinian.[14] The period of colder temperatures, smaller harvests, and the spread of disease that this eruption initiated would last for about 130 years and contribute to the changes that the Roman Empire and Christianity experienced. Where centralized power could not

---

[14] See Brian Fagan, *The Long Summer*, 208 ff. See, also, Ulf Büntgen et al., "2500 Years of European Climate Variability and Human Susceptibility," *Science,* vol. 331 (February 4, 2011): 578–581. Available online at https://www.uibk.ac.at/geographie/forschung/den dro/publikationen—pdf-files/2011-buentgen-et-al-science—somb.pdf. Accessed on November 12, 2018.

maintain its hold on the empire and cities could not rely on crop abundance to sustain them, local control and increasingly rural and feudal forms of political control would predominate. Likewise, the pacifist impulses within the church would shift in increasingly communal (e.g., monastic) and local (i.e., expressed through the practices of politically powerless small communities) ways even as the natural conditions that make violence more likely (e.g., diminishing natural resources, the spread of disease, the forced movement of peoples) and their concomitant political implications (e.g., strained political agreements, diminished military control) increased. To reiterate: climatic change does not cause violence, nor does it determine responses to violence. Yet it can play a dramatic role in both. As Francis Ludlow notes, "Suggesting climate caused complex events in human history like the fall of empires is controversial... Ultimately [though], there can be very little doubt that these sorts of abrupt climatic events place great stress on societies, and can sometimes tip them over the edge."[15]

Said differently, the apparently receding centrality of pacifism for the Christian church in the centuries after Constantine (which has been treated in the conventional pacifist narrative as the product of the church's embrace of the state's power) might also be read as the consequence of the recess of centrality more generally for the church and the increasing difficulty for persons to make their way in a world of famine, disease, and diminished order. Yet these difficulties were not a permanent fixture of the Middle Ages any more than pacifist practices were nonexistent during that same time. Pacifist impulses, imperfect though they were, pulsed through the Middle Ages in ways both obvious (e.g., in the monastic reforms) and subtle (chivalric codes emerging in the twelfth century that linked knights across ethnic differences and established a warrior caste that also forbade violence against certain categories of people).

It is a sign worth interpreting, moreover, that between the early church and the advent of the radical reformers, the historians of Christian nonviolence focus on religious orders (e.g., the Franciscans), sects (e.g., the Waldensians, beginning in the twelfth century), or individuals (e.g., Peter Damian in the eleventh century). Even the counter-examples reinforce this pattern: the Peace of God (~975 C.E.) and the Truce of God (~1050 C.E.)

---

[15] Francis Ludlow, quoted in Penny Sarchet, "125-Year Mini Ice Age Linked to the Plague and Fall of Empires" *New Scientist* (February 8, 2016). Available at www.newscientist .com/article/2076713-125-year-mini-ice-age-linked-to-the-plague-and-fall-of-empires/. Accessed on March 3, 2017.

neither wholly prohibited violence nor were especially successful in preventing conflict – although both stimulated popular imaginations and did sometimes successfully limit violence for a period.[16] Yet too much attention at any of these points can undermine larger Christian pacifist arguments. Religious orders recognized an obligation toward nonviolence on the part of their members but not for the wider church, distinguishing between higher and lower standards of conduct such that laity could participate in wars while clergy could not.[17]

Between 900 C.E. and 1300 C.E., western Europe prospered during the Medieval Warm Period. As Brian Fagan notes,

In an era long before long-range weather forecasting, everyone, whether king or noble, warlord, merchant, or farmer, was at the mercy of the cycle of heavier rainfall and drought, savage gales and perfect summer days. They were unwitting partners in an intricate climatic gavotte between the atmosphere and the oceans. But, especially between A.D. 800 and 1300, the dance slowed slightly into a measured waltz, where summer warmth and more settled conditions tended – and one stresses "tended" – to be the norm. The gyrations of climate change slowed momentarily. Europe changed profoundly.[18]

This four-hundred-year period was enormously important in the history of Christianity. It was marked by monastic reform (including the rise of the mendicant orders) and the flourishing of scholarship. Anselm of Canterbury, Peter Abelard, Bernard of Clairvaux, Peter Lombard, Roger Bacon, Albert the Great, and Thomas Aquinas, among others, are all products of this age. Such reform was, itself, made possible by the comparative ease of growing crops through which to directly (via available foodstuffs) and indirectly (via taxes) support the monasteries and those novel new institutions for education, the universities. It was marked by new debates between church and state (e.g., the investiture controversy; the east/west split within the church in 1054) as the powerful scrambled to control growing wealth by gaining greater ecclesial and political power. It

---

[16] Rowan Williams's approach to the Truce of God is representative: "Of course, [the Truce of God] was never observed for any length of time with much consistency; and in retrospect its mixture of naïve earnestness and cynicism is rather funny (very characteristic of the Church somehow ...). But it is more than a comical bit of mediaeval eccentricity. Behind it lay the recognition that for baptized Christians, sharers in the Body of Christ, to be in a state of war with one another was horrible and ridiculous." Rowan Williams, *The Truce of God* (Grand Rapids, MI: Eerdmans Pub. Co., 2005), 25.

[17] See James F. Childress, "Moral Discourse about War in the Early Church." *Journal of Religious Ethics* 12.1 (1984): 2–18.

[18] Brian Fagan, *The Great Warming: Climate Change and the Rise and Fall of Civilizations* (New York: Bloomsbury, 2008), 6–7.

was also marked by both the crusades (beginning in 1095) and the Peace and the Truce of God (beginning in 989).

Though distinct in time and place, attention to these latter sets of events – the Crusades and the Peace and Truce of God – help explain the impact of climate on attitudes toward violence in the church. The former were made possible not only because there were resources available to fund and feed armies but because the Medieval Warm Period shaped expanded capacities for movement and cultural interactions and the reinvigoration of great European cities. French, British, Scandinavian, German, and Slavic nobility and ecclesial leaders found common cause and were able to tax persons throughout Europe to fund their military campaigns in the Middle East.[19] The latter were made possible not only (or necessarily even primarily) because of the church's commitment to nonviolence but because the acquisition of the growing wealth made possible by crop yields – wealth that went to the church and the nobility – could be better protected if it wasn't being fought over. As Michael Frassetto notes, the councils that shaped the Peace of God "were held to limit violence done to the clergy, churches, and even the poor, to define the nature of and relationship between orders of society, and, merging with the broad eleventh-century reform movement, to restore the right order of the world."[20] In other words, those councils define what might be thought of as protean social contract theories of the sort that would arise hundreds of years later as much as they are more broadly understood within the pacifist tradition as affirmations about the value of peace and the theological vision of human beings as having intrinsic worth.

[19] Brian Fagan reports that "[i]n 1327 alone, church officials reported a special Crusade tax of about 1,400 pounds (650 kilograms) of ivory, which would have required the killing of some two hundred walruses" in Greenland. Fagan, *The Great Warming*, 104. Crusading was expensive. Marcus Bull argues that "a lord or knight intending to fund his journey to the East would have had to liquidize assets to the value of four or five times his annual income" and uses this argument, in part, to suggest that lords and knights went east for ideological rather than economic reasons since they would be unlikely to recover their costs through wealth won in the Levant. Under-regarded in Bull's argument is the recognition that lords or knights had the resources available to make the trip at all: they could go east for ideological reasons because they could afford those ideological reasons. They could afford to because it was possible to accrue wealth during the Medieval Warm Period. See Marcus Bull, *Knightly Piety and the Lay Response to the First Crusade: The Limousin and Gascony, c.970–c.1130* (Oxford: Clarendon Press, 1993), 5.

[20] Michael Frassetto, "Ademar of Chabannes and the Peace of God," in *Where Heaven and Earth Meet: Essays on Medieval Europe in Honor of Daniel F. Callahan*, ed. Michael Frassetto, Matthew Gabriele, and John D. Hosler (Leiden: Brill, 2014), 122–123.

The Crusades and the Peace and Truce of God also serve as examples of a larger argument: that growing abundance as well as scarcity can shape prospects for both violence and nonviolence. Growing affluence – in this instance, affluence made possible through agricultural bounty and the ability to trade goods across distances – has the potential to shape conditions that lead to violence and to violence-avoidance. Where climates change, they can bring about concomitant changes in economic fortunes. And where economic fortunes change, decisions about whether to engage in violence are likely to follow. Said differently, neither scarcity nor affluence, per se, are as likely to lead to decisions about whether to act violently as are relative changes in scarcity and affluence – and climate change drives changes in economic fortune.

More centrally, they suggest a deeper connection between choices toward violence and choices toward nonviolence. Change – whether technological, political, or economic; whether toward flourishing or hardship; whether at very local or global levels – is disordering.[21] Such disordering surfaces deep questions that have both existential and political qualities, including, at least for those in Christian traditions, questions about the presence and work of God and appropriate human responses to God as a response. And among available answers to such questions as they are played out politically are those that favor violence and those that advocate for nonviolence. Said differently, violent and nonviolent practices don't arise from distinct and opposing political, social, or intrapersonal origins so much they express different responses to the changes that are reshaping understandings and deployments of those origins.

Economic changes – not to mention technological, political, and religious ones – would reshape the world even as all these changes were, in turn, shaped by life during the Little Ice Age[22] between 1300 and 1850. In 1258, one of the largest volcanic events in the past 10,000 years happened in Indonesia. The global spread of ash blocked sunlight, altered weather

---

[21] For a thorough set of essays on the Peace of God movement in the context of larger social changes, see Thomas Head and Richard Landes, eds., *The Peace of God: Social Violence and Religious Response in France around the Year 1000* (Ithaca: Cornell University Press, 1992), especially R. I. Moore's "Postscript: The Peace of God and the Social Revolution," pp. 308–326.

[22] The term "Little Ice Age" refers, variously, to the period between 1300 and 1850 – that is, after the close of the Medieval Warm Period – and to a particularly cold period – or, rather, set of cold periods between the sixteenth and nineteenth centuries that are marked by three distinctly colder periods: 1650 and after; 1770 and after; and 1850 and after. For purposes of this chapter, the variation between dates is less important than noting the impact of cold periods on western Christianity as it engaged questions of war and peace.

patterns, caused crop failure, and led to widespread famine. One third of the population of London died.[23] It was the beginning of the end of the Medieval Warm Period. Over the next five hundred years, climatic patterns would vary but temperatures would remain consistently lower than those of either the preceding five hundred years of bounty or the times that would follow. Europe would seek new sources of resources abroad to replace those that were disappearing at home, splinter into nation-states and myriad forms of Christianity, engage in the so-called "wars of religion" and develop modern political forms, pursue industrialization, and be decimated by various famines and plagues.

The rate and volume of climatic and social change during this period makes even a summary of significant events connected to the history of Christian pacifism difficult, let alone a discussion of the ways that these events are related to changes in climate. Certainly, significant climatic and climate-related events would include the Great Famine of 1315–17, the eruption of Kuwae in 1452–53, a series of famines in western Europe in the 1690s, and the eruption of Tambora in 1816, the "year without a summer." Other, subtler, climatic events would include the storms that destroyed the better part of the Spanish Armada in 1588, the dry wind that helped lead to the great fire of London in 1666 (which Protestants accused Catholics of starting and helped lead to the Popish Plot), and the great storm of 1703 that decimated southern England and much of its navy (which Daniel Defoe described as divine judgment on England for its military failures against Catholics during the War of Spanish Succession).[24] A bad winter in 1788 in France followed by a very hot summer and a large hailstorm on July 13, 1788, decimated cereal crops that year, shaped conditions that led to the bread riots of 1789, to Marie Antoinette's "Let them eat cake," and to the French Revolution. All of these climatic events either had or were perceived at the time as having an impact on various large and small conflicts in Europe.

Moreover, as these climatic events shaped conflicts in Europe, they also shaped the movements of pacifist thought. Take, for example, the movement of pacifist thought out of northern Switzerland and southern Germany in the sixteenth century. In the middle of the century, the Swiss Brethren left northern Switzerland for Moravia. Conventional

---

[23] "Mass grave in London reveals how volcano caused global catastrophe," *The Guardian* (August 4, 2012). Online. www.theguardian.com/uk/2012/aug/05/medieval-volcano-disaster-london-graves. Accessed on February 24, 2017.

[24] See Daniel Defoe, *The Storm* (London: Penguin Classics, 2005).

wisdom links this movement to persecutions faced by the Brethren at the time.[25] Undoubtedly, persecutions played a prominent – if not the dominant – role in this migration. It is, nevertheless, worth noting that pacifism in the region arose in the 1520s during a few warm years that were left behind over the next few decades during a long period of colder temperatures, advancing Alpine glaciers, and decreasing rye and grape yields (along with concomitant increases in prices on the basic foodstuffs of bread and wine), especially after a severe drought in 1540.[26] Politico-religious forces encouraged migration, but the chance to leave behind struggling farms and weak local economies and till the rich Moravian soil almost certainly exerted forces as well. The Swiss Brethren's willingness to "convert" to Hutterite suggests that maintaining the integrity of their particular religious vision was not the only factor in play in the move – as does the fact that they chose a specific direction in which to migrate.

Or, as another example, the changing sea levels in the early seventeenth century drove Dutch land reclamation and stimulated new farming methods in the first half of the seventeenth century, which in turn reshaped markets across the channel in England. Those reshaped markets – especially when combined with the great plague of London in 1665 and the great fire of London just after that – contributed toward new strains on the British economy. Owing Sir William Penn money at the time, King Charles II repaid the debt by granting Sir William's son, William Penn, land in what would become Pennsylvania – and the younger Penn brought his group of Quakers with him to that land, establishing an early and prominent pacifist enclave in the so-called New World.

The larger point is not to link specific climatic events to specific moments in the history of Christian pacifism. Some of the movements and figures bear so little correlative evidence of the impact of climate as to make connections impossible. For instance, the writings of Erasmus in the early sixteenth century, most notably *The Education of a Christian Prince*, are so obviously impacted by developing humanist political thought that

---

[25] See Cornelius Krahn, Harold S. Bender, and John J. Friesen. (1989). Migrations. *Global Anabaptist Mennonite Encyclopedia Online*. Retrieved 31 March 2017, from http://gameo.org/index.php?title=Migrations&oldid=143668.

[26] See Christian Pfister and Rudolph Brazdil, "Climatic Variability in Sixteenth-Century Europe and Its Social Dimension: A Synthesis," *Climatic Change* 43 (1999): 5–53. Fascinatingly, Pfister and Brazdil also point to literature linking changes in climate to patterns of witch-burning (as women were accused of being witches because they controlled the weather).

identifying climate-linked causes to those writings, *per se,* is a fool's errand. Instead, the point is to note that the roughly 500-year period of the Little Ice Age was also momentous in the history of Christian pacifism in the west. Groups (e.g., the Lollards, the Mennonites, the True Levellers, the Quakers) and individuals (e.g., Erasmus, Conrad Grebel, Bartolome de Las Casas, Robert Barclay, David Dodge, Lucretia Mott) sprang up and spread their convictions about Christian pacifism throughout the world. These groups and persons were not, in their writings and other actions, responding to environmental changes. They were, however, responding to social, political, and ecclesial forces that themselves arose in part as responses to the Little Ice Age.[27]

That so little research has been done on the connections between climatic events and the social and political history of the period is due, in part, to the ways war itself moved away from being so literally earth-bound during that time. With the rise of the modern nation-state in the west and all that rise entailed (the concurrent development of international law, reshaped concentrations of wealth and power and new economic and political apparatuses by which to collect and maintain them, new technologies – including Francis Bacon's three novelties of gunpowder, ocean navigation, and the printing press – eroding tribal identities and growing national/ethnic ones, the splintering of Christianity, etc.), not only did the reasons for war change but the types of war and understandings of war changed as well. The traditional resources over which wars had been fought – especially lands good for hunting, then herding and agriculture – receded in importance in the face of the explosion of non-land-bound resources. As Azar Gat notes,

> . . . although modernity was built upon the earlier gradual evolution of technology and social organization, it at the same time constituted a crossing of a threshold. . . The interrelated growth, from early modernity, of a global trading system and commercial capitalism, centered in Europe, generated a chain reaction that was to spark off industrialization – all within a few centuries – unleashing an unprecedented, exponential rocketing of both wealth and power . . . [such that] productive capacity and military might now became [*sic*] closely related.[28]

War was changing in ways that made it revolve less around natural resources even as Western societies were paying less attention to (and feeling less dependent upon) the natural world. As a result, not only were

---

[27] For an extended treatment of the period, see Brian Fagan, *The Little Ice Age: How Climate Made History 1300–1850.*

[28] Gat, *War in Human Civilization,* 446.

there fewer connections between climate and violence, but the capacity to see those connections was also diminishing.

Nor is the point to make the history of Christian pacifism contingent on environmental change. Pacifists have been shaped by a wide variety of forces and events, not the least of which are their own reflections on and convictions about the way the gospel expresses itself in their individual and collective lives. It is, though, to suggest that when we ignore the impact of climate on history, we unnecessarily and unduly truncate the range of forces that shape history, including the history of Christian pacifism.[29] This lacuna becomes even more pronounced in the face of the last century and a half, a period in which pacifism flowered and we slowly became more aware of the need to attend to the natural world. It is to this period that I now, briefly, turn.

4 THE MODERN HISTORY OF PACIFISM: 1850 TO THE PRESENT

Modernity conceals war from those who live during it. As Hans Joas has argued, the worldview of liberalism that arises in the West during modernity, when combined with the advent of social sciences, has had the effect of promoting ideas about the universalizability of human goods, the centrality of peace in maintaining stability, and the progressive quality of human history.[30] These ideas didn't so much end wars (some of the most destructive wars in human history were fought during this time period, after all) as make them more difficult to understand. For instance, modern conceptions of war revolve around questions having to do with the state's supposed legitimate monopoly on violence. Thus, not only do questions

---

[29] The disconnect between attention to pacifism and environmental issues does not go one way, incidentally. The most comprehensive text on religion and ecology contains no mention of war, conflict, peace, or pacifism (in spite of the impact of war on the environment and the degree to which pacifists have extended notions of peace into the natural world). And it contains a mere two sentences on the historic peace churches in the United States – and then only to note that they have an alternative economic system: "In the eighteenth and nineteenth centuries, a few sects, such as the Shakers (Quakers), the Harmony Society, the Mennonites, and the Amish settled in rural America to escape having to compromise religious norms with the economic transformation underway in Europe. They established communal-property economies, Christian communisms before Marx lashed the term to atheism, where care for others was central." See Willis Jenkins, Mary Evelyn Tucker, and John Grim, eds., *Routledge Handbook of Religion and Ecology* (New York: Routledge, 2017), 405.

[30] See Hans Joas, *War and Modernity*, trans. By Rodney Livingstone (Cambridge, UK: Polity Press, 2003).

about violence by non-state actors cause problems for modern international relations theory and historians of premodern history alike, but the linkage between the state and violence biases understandings of violence toward a preoccupation with the state as the primary player in matters of conflict. Unsurprisingly, modern pacifist historians and their critics have linked concerns with violence to concerns with the state such that taking a stand against violence implied taking a stand against the idea of the state.[31]

Such concealment has not been universally negative. Shorn of obligations to treat war as a natural and therefore inevitable component of human existence, the idea that war is an idea gave rise to the possibility of thinking and acting in ways that were neither driven by assumptions about an inevitable recourse to violence nor convinced that violent means were the best ways to achieve social and international flourishing. As suggested in Chapter 6, the varieties of Christian pacifism exploded during this period, as did their efficacy in bringing about personal, communal, social, and international change. Building on a rapidly expanding and diversifying history, those who speak of and write on Christian pacifism at the beginning of the twenty-first century don't simply address matters of war and peace. They carry their work into advocating for community revitalization, challenging economic inequities, addressing social divisions caused by race, gender, and sexual orientation, defending human rights, undergirding international law, pursuing competencies in intercultural and interreligious engagement, advancing new communication strategies, and defending natural resources.

Modernity has also concealed the natural world from those who live in it. At mundane levels, industrialization, urbanization, and global capitalism hide from us the sources of the natural resources on which we depend: food comes from supermarkets, not gardens. At conceptual levels, the natural world is treated as an inert and separable entity from human beings: rather than seeing ourselves as dynamic components of the natural

---

[31] This assumption, for instance, is shared by both H. Richard Niebuhr in *Christ and Culture* when he includes the peace churches in the "Christ against culture" portion of his typology and John Howard Yoder, who challenges Niebuhr's typology in "How H. Richard Niebuhr Reasoned: A Critique of Christ and Culture." Yoder resists Niebuhr's easy elisions of "culture" with "state" and being against violence with opposing the state but still maintains an idea that the church can be understood, in part, by the degree to which it is not "the state" (rather than not being "the market" or "the family" or "humanity" or any number of other categories through which humans order and make sense of their lives).

world, we see it primarily as a source of resources for us. History books are filled with prominent figures, important political events, and technological advances rather than significant climatic events. Diurnal rhythms are ordered by the clock rather than the sun; time is experienced in human-sized units rather than seasonal or geological ones; domesticated animals are pets rather than co-laborers; death – that most universal of natural events – is tucked away from us behind the closed doors of institutions like hospitals and nursing homes.

Again, such concealment has not been universally negative. The natural world is unflinching in giving and taking without regard to human need or sympathetic appeal. For all its failings, capitalism has lifted billions of people out of conditions in which they lived hand-to-mouth by creating wealth that did not depend on immediate access to natural resources. The proliferation of energy sources (fossil fuels, nuclear, solar, etc.) has expanded the possibilities for human beings to live in comfort, see the world, and reach for the stars. Modern medicines and medical technologies can alleviate many of the cruelest and most treatable diseases.

Yet these exercises in concealment have come with costs. Among them has been our failure to recognize the complex causal relationships between changes in the natural world and human conflicts (at least in part because so many of us resisted recognizing the causal relationship between the way we lived and the changes in the natural world we induced). We are entering the Anthropocene not only because of the changes we have induced but because we hid those changes from ourselves.[32]

One symptom of these costs has been the failure to recognize that Christian pacifism proliferates after the nineteenth century because it can: the world was again warming and the conditions for both increasing abundance and social change were ripe. As the climate warmed at accelerating levels due to the human production of greenhouse gases, it shaped conditions for disorder that revitalized the types of questions Christian pacifists ask and the practices that responses to those questions enlivened.

What is concealed can also be revealing. The story of the history of Christian pacifism I'm offering here helps to uncover two paradoxical qualities that grow through the twentieth century. The first of these is that pacifism grows in scope, reach, and power during a period of unparalleled violence. The wars since the beginning of the twentieth century (including

---

[32] Increasingly, climatologists locate the beginning of the Anthropocene in the postwar period. See Paul Voosen, "Anthropocene Pinned to Postwar Period," *Science* Vol. 353; Issue 6302 (August 26, 2016): 852–853.

global conflicts – WWI and WWII, the Cold War, the unhelpfully named and pursued War on Terror – and related regional ones) brought about more death and destruction than any comparable period of human history. So why were violence and nonviolence both expanding at the same time?

The conventional answer to that question is that encounters with violence motivated the search for alternatives: having seen the costs of war, human beings worked ever more diligently in the pursuit of alternatives to it. The United Nations serves, perhaps, as an institutional embodiment of this answer. Yet the U.N. (and its quasi-predecessor, the League of Nations) also embody the failings of this answer. Although it has inhibited war and mitigated some of the effects of war, the U.N. hasn't ended war and, as wars have continued, it has itself deployed armed peacekeeping forces. Moreover, some of the most troubling failings associated with these peacekeeping forces have come when those forces did not engage violently in the protection of vulnerable populations in Serbia and Rwanda, just to name two examples. The pursuit of peace has itself led to violence.

Moreover, the conventional answer fails to address the question of why nonviolent practices haven't consistently arisen as responses to violence at other points in human history. Not only in Western history, but in the global history of violence, wars have not consistently led to pacifist practices. History suggests that wars have consistently if not inevitably led to new wars. As such, pursuing peace is not the fundamental human response to violence. Instead, a wide range of socio-political and conceptual conditions need to be in place for pacifism and its attendant practices to arise.[33]

A better answer is offered by John Mueller in his work as described in Chapter 6: by the end of the American Civil War, Westerners increasingly viewed war as an idea instead of a natural (or even virtuous) condition of human existence. As an idea, it could be argued against and even rejected. In this answer, the reason for the twinned rise of violence and nonviolence in the twentieth century is that as war became an idea, it necessarily became a contested political idea, albeit one in which arguments for war can also carry the day. And when such arguments do carry the day, they do

---

[33] The work of R. Scott Appleby may be of use in this context as he argues for the way both religious violence and religious movements for reconciliation spring from common sources. See R. Scott Appleby, *The Ambivalence of the Sacred: Religion, Violence, and Reconciliation* (Lanham, MD: Rowman and Littlefield, 2000).

so in more dramatically damaging ways because recourse to violence would now be intrinsically bound to ideologies. When wars are over resources, the cost/benefit calculus of whether to fight for those resources was not only manageable but could lead to the answer, "This is not worth it." Resources have value and wars have costs. Weighing out value against cost provides an amoral answer to the question of whether to go to war. When wars are ideologically driven, however, such calculus loses its utility. Ideas are not fungible. What is the value of national identity, political liberty, ethnic purity, religious obligation, or commitment to an ally? How are such values to be weighed against war's costs? This is not to say that ideological forces were not in play in shaping conflicts prior to the modern period; clearly, they were. It is, though, to say that ideologies increasingly took center stage as primary causes for conflicts as other reasons for fighting – particularly those having to do with scarce resources – receded.

Of course, this still leaves open the questions of why, after the American Civil War, war became an idea and peace, as an idea, could outpace war? The answers to those questions, I would suggest, is that they could. Advances in human technologies, shifting demographic patterns, changes in political systems, and the rising power of capitalism around the world all combined to not only expand the types and range of human goods (therein reducing some scarcities) and increase the interdependence of human activities (thereby making war more initially costly to any group that would choose it), but to expand the range of conversation partners thinking about war and peace and to increase access to information about events around the world. Globalization, in short, made wars less likely and worse – and globalization is a product of this time.[34] Conditions were conducive to the spread of pacifist thought. So it spread.

Yet all these advances are, in part, the product of changing climatic conditions as the world warmed. The Little Ice Age had come to an end and was being replaced with increasingly warmer temperatures. As Fagan points out, "[t]hanks to modern instrumentation and vast computer databases, we know that global mean surface temperatures have risen between 0.4 and 0.8°C since 1860, and 0.2 and 0.3°C since 1900 in some parts of the world. Summer temperatures are now equal to the mean readings of the Medieval Warm Period."[35] With this warming came

---

[34] See, e.g., Roland Robertson, *Globalization: Social Theory and Global Culture* (London: Sage Publications, 1992), esp. Ch. 7.
[35] Fagan, *The Long Summer*, 250.

expanded access to resources, especially basic foodstuffs, which allowed human beings to give increased energy to other pursuits. Environmental change does not cause other changes (whether in political, technological, or economic systems). It does, though, catalyze such changes.

This answer to the reason for the simultaneous growth in attention to peace and violence also helps reveal the second paradox of war and peace in the twenty-first century: pursuit of the goods that have led to peace now leads us toward violence. For the first time in human history, human activity – the very activity manifested in the varied political, technological, and economic changes of the twentieth century – now drives large-scale environmental change. Internal combustion engines, industrial agriculture, and the rise of megacities (in concert with population growth and the discovery of new types of resources) are both products and primary causes of climate change. Climate-shaped conflict is a consequence of the very forces that contributed to the proliferation of pacifisms.

This is, clearly, bad news. Not only is it yet another example of how unintended consequences undermine the intended goals of noble projects but it illustrates the internal failings of narratives of progress. Where pacifism is valorized as a unique good and its attendant practices are treated as beyond reproach – that is, where peace is treated as a pure good rather than a messy human good and where pacifism is offered as a panacea to the world's violence – it can undermine its own best insights. Where pacifism and its practices are extolled by those (primarily in the global north) who have a wide range of resources at their disposal – including resources that are either associated with pacifist practices such as boycotts or are preconditions for pacifist practices such as ample time for reflection and slow-moving practices – the unequal distribution of unintended consequences means that those with the fewest resources are also most vulnerable to the greatest ravages of climate change and climate-shaped conflict.

Yet it is not wholly bad news, since unintended consequences need not be wholly negative. The proliferation of Christian pacifisms since the end of the nineteenth century also suggests that pacifism and pacifist practices have increasing capacities for resilience. One of the unintended consequences of the increasing depth and breadth of pacifism and pacifist practices is that pacifists are situated to experiment with a variety of different pacifist strategies in the face of new causes, types, and understandings of war in the Anthropocene. It is worth noting, for instance, that cities – which are particularly vulnerable to climate change and violence – are, when thoughtfully designed, also better at inhibiting both climate change and violence because they house so many resilient processes.[36] While water may be the resource over which the fiercest conflicts emerge, it is also a resource around which persons of divergent ideological impulses can converge.[37] Unsurprisingly, pacifists of the twenty-first century are increasingly linking their practices to the very types of imaginative projects (including but certainly not limited to the thoughtful city planning and the pursuit of nonpartisan goods) that preoccupy those most concerned with climate change.

Such resilience demonstrates the power of the myth of pacifism I am offering here. Christian pacifism has not disappeared over time because the questions of fidelity that drive its movement through time not only endure but become especially pressing in the face of changing social imaginaries like the one we are experiencing as we move into the Anthropocene. Moreover, although questions relating faith and action expand beyond pacifism's core questions of fidelity, attention to the deep connections between peace and justice in Christian thought – especially as they are expressed in concern for those who are suffering – suggests that emerging forms of pacifism may provide uniquely valuable strategies for addressing climate-shaped conflict. The very capacity to reinvent ideas and practices relieves Christians of the overwhelming urgency that clogs any narrative that cannot imagine change and therein inhibits progress (no matter how temporary, tentative, or incomplete such progress may be).

Said more theologically, the proliferation of pacifisms since the nineteenth century suggests that God has not left Godself without a witness in a world that is peculiarly filled with failures and possibilities. Perhaps this is what eschatology, for now, looks like: hints of the eternal amid the temporal; glimpses of grace amid suffering; fresh possibilities amid failed narratives; resurrection always responding to crucifixion. Moreover, because the God attested to in the Scriptures has shown a preferential option for the poor and oppressed – and because one manifestation of this has been that the poor and oppressed are situated to understand the systemic forces that inhibit the flourishing of creation – the proliferation

---

[36] See Jonathan F. P. Rose, *The Well-Tempered City: What Modern Science, Ancient Civilizations, and Human Nature Teach Us About the Future of Urban Life* (San Francisco: Harper Wave, 2016).

[37] A recent paper in *Science* not only demonstrates the need to address water issues in the twenty-first century (revealing a tremendous spike in water conflicts over the last decade) but suggests that water policy could be a place for nonpartisan agreement in the United States. See Peter H. Gleick, "Water Strategies for the Next Administration," *Science* Vol. 354, Issue 6312 (Nov. 4, 2016): 555–556.

of pacifisms has connected Christian pacifists to persons and movements around the world who bring unique insights and practices oriented toward creation's flourishing.[38] It isn't simply that God is bringing about God's kingdom; it is that some of the profoundest glimpses of that kingdom happen in the majority world and, therefore, some of the most imaginative new practices of nonviolence and creation care happen in those places as well. In the long term, the future of Christian pacifism is the peaceful Kingdom. At the dawn of the Anthropocene, it is in the joining of the global north with the majority world – which is also where the future of environmental ethics lies.[39]

[38] See, among others, Willis Jenkins, *The Future of Ethics: Sustainability, Social Justice, and Religious Creativity* (Washington D.C.: Georgetown University Press, 2013) for a much more thoughtful and detailed explication of this phenomenon. See also Jenkins et al., *Routledge Handbook of Religion and Ecology* for global religious perspectives on ecology.

[39] Literature on Christian pacifism as a global phenomenon is growing, albeit slower than one might hope. Among texts, one of the better overviews is Maria Pilar Aquino, "Religious Peacebuilding" in Andrew R. Murphy, ed., *The Blackwell Companion to Religion and Violence* (Malden, MA: Blackwell, 2011). Other texts would include Fernando Enns, Scott Holland, and Ann K. Riggs, *Seeking Cultures of Peace: A Peace Church Conversation* (Telford, PA: Cascadia Pub. House, 2004); Karikottuchira Kuriakose, ed., *Terrorism, Religion, and Global Peace: From Concepts to Praxis* (Piscataway, NJ: Gorgias Press, 2012); Michelle LeBaron and Venashri Pillay, *Conflict Across Cultures: A Unique Experience of Bridging Cultures* (Boston: Intercultural Press, 2006); and Theron F. Schlabach and Richard T. Huges, eds., *Proclaim Peace: Christian Pacifism from Unexpected Quarters* (Urbana: University of Illinois Press, 1997).

Afterword

I suffer from a disease called keratoconus that affects my left eye. A kind of myopia, keratoconus makes the cornea in my left eye cone out instead of bow out; as a result, my vision in that eye is blurry, difficult to measure, and sometimes doubled. Fortunately, my keratoconus is stable and, with a special contact lens or through a good set of prescription eyeglasses, my sight can approach 20/20. Shortly after being diagnosed with the disease, I ordered a new set of eyeglasses. The optometrist told me that he could make lenses that would be appropriate for my eyes, but first he would need to make the tool that he would use to make the lenses. This is, roughly, what I have been doing with this book: making the tool to use to make the lenses through which pacifists might see climate-shaped conflicts and thereby begin to address them.

Hopefully, the tool that is this book serves its own purposes. It helps Christian pacifists retell their own history in a way that is attentive to its connection to the rest of the natural world. It offers a narrative to non-pacifists that, even if not so compelling as to convert them to the ways of nonviolence, still helps them understand and engage Christian pacifism more carefully and charitably. It models a useful type of theologically attentive critical historiography. Maybe it can do even more.

In his famous 1967 essay, "The Historical Roots of Our Ecological Crisis," Lynn White lay the blame for the ecological crisis at the feet of western Christianity: "Especially in its Western form, Christianity is the most anthropocentric religion the world has seen ... Christianity, in absolute contrast to ancient paganism and Asia's religions (except, perhaps, Zorastrianism), not only established a dualism of man and nature but also insisted that it is God's will that man exploit nature for his proper ends."[1] His arguments about the dualism between human beings and the rest of the natural world implicit in Christianity were so compelling to so many people that even those who disagreed with his conclusion at more granular levels still conceded the larger argument to him. As someone who writes on religion and ecology, I've consistently struggled with the choice between answering his criticisms and giving them oxygen by answering them. The idea that modernity, with its anthropocentric biases and mechanistic sensibilities, simply continues a bastardized version of Christianity is, on my read, simply wrong. Francis of Assisi may be an ecological saint, but his opposite number is Francis Bacon, not Tertullian, Thomas, or Calvin.

Perhaps this book hints at a way past debates with White. Rather than addressing White's claims about the human/nonhuman dualism within Christianity, perhaps we should be attending to the dualism implicit in modern historiographic projects (of which White's is an archetype) between the natural and the political. Ecological change and political change have always come together; modern myths that exclude the natural in their preoccupation with the political, much like modern myths that exclude the organic in favor of the mechanistic, are simply wrong. Our response should be the production of more accurate and relevant myths.

The myth I produce in the previous chapter attempts to do just that. It encapsulates the work of the whole book, arguing for a different history of Christian pacifism that is both more accurate to the movement of that tradition through time and more relevant to the needs of the world during the Anthropocene. If I have created something that is at the very least provocative and, maybe even compelling, I will be grateful and this book will have served an important purpose.

Yet read another way, this book is largely a project of space-clearing. The dominant conventional myth of the history of Christian pacifism – a myth that is, at best, awkwardly suited to address climate-shaped conflicts – needs to be contested so that Christian pacifists can better engage those conflicts. I'm less interested in creating a better myth of Christian pacifism than I am in putting that new myth to work addressing the myriad crises of war in a warming world. The book I have wanted to write is not this one; it is the book that picks up where this one leaves off. How will Christian pacifism respond to violence caused by the movements

---

[1] Lynn White, "The Historical Roots of Our Ecological Crisis," in *Ecology and Religion in History*, edited by David and Eileen Spring (New York: Harper and Row, 1974).

of climate refugees, the competitions over increasingly scarce basic resources like grains and water, the political destabilizations of new pandemics, and other politico-ecological crises? Writing that book is, I hope, in my near future.

Yet before writing it, I have one other book to write. The conventional myth of the history of Christian pacifism isn't the only conventional myth that needs to be re-written. Conventional myths about the history of Christian just war and just peacemaking also need attention. In a world facing climatic crises and drenched in religion, those two traditions – or, perhaps, more accurately, one tradition and one sub-tradition – will, along with Christian pacifism, play roles in addressing climate-caused conflicts.

Toward that end, treat the current text as Volume One in a three-volume series in which each book grows out of its predecessors. This volume develops a theologically shaped critical historiography through which to make sense of the movement of traditions through time. Using the history of Christian pacifism as a kind of extended case-study, it argues that traditions move through time in neither linear nor random ways and that contemporary narratives about traditions are shaped by problematic modern mythologies, including, notably, the modern disregard of deep connections between political and natural events. In this volume, I argue that traditions find their continuities in distinct sets of questions (so, e.g., the Christian pacifist tradition centers around questions of fidelity) but that answers to those questions are shaped by the particular socio-historical contexts in which the questions are asked and that, therefore, answers given in one time and place may not be coherent or helpful in a different time and place. Questions exert a centripetal force on traditions, and answers to those questions exert a centrifugal one.

Volume Two grows out of that historiographic work in order to re-narrate Christian just war and just peacemaking traditions. Where the central questions of the Christian pacifist tradition have to do with fidelity, the central questions of the Christian just war tradition have to do with anthropology (e.g., What are people like? Who counts as a person like us? What social structures should people construct in order to live with each other?) and the central questions of the just peacemaking tradition have to do with efficacy (e.g., what goods and goals can we achieve and what processes can we put in place to achieve them?). All three sets of focal questions are theological and all three assume the importance of the other traditions' questions. Yet by attending to the unique focus of each tradition's questions – and exploring how those questions and their answers have moved through time – the first two volumes will, by their conclusions, have re-narrated the three traditions in such a way that they may be useful in understanding and addressing the kinds of climate-shaped conflict that we face in the Anthropocene. I suspect, moreover, that the oppositions between the three traditions will increasingly blur in such conflicts, so it is better to have all three in place and interacting with each other.

Having shaped the three traditions toward such usefulness in the first two volumes, the way is clear for the book I most want to write: one in which I attend to contemporary and impending climate-shape conflicts through the insights of this and the next book. In that third book, I will give much closer attention to the way persons in the environmental age may answer the questions that drive these three traditions and through which Christians address violence. Volume Three, then, is a project of constructive political theology. What does fidelity to the God revealed in Jesus Christ mean when climate change means refiguring the relation between God and creation – a relation in which "God and creature make up one complex reality?"[2] What political structures might be constructed to deal with climate-shaped conflict as it signals the end of the age of the Westphalian nation-state, and who/what will be included among those to whom those structures are beholden, as a theological anthropology in which human beings can be separated from the rest of creation breaks down? How will human beings understand agency when climate change simultaneously reveals their collective capacity to transform the whole world and their individual inability to make a significant difference in the world around them, and what can count as effective action in light of modified understandings of agency? These and others are the questions of Volume Three.

To some, this three-book series may sound like a project of prognostication – the unjustifiable musings of a futurist that refuses to live in his own time. It is not. Not only are the patterns of climate-shaped conflict already in play, but climate has played a role in past conflicts in fairly patterned ways: the future is already present and past is prologue. If anything, it is those of us who have been working in the ethics of war and peace over the past decades without giving attention to environmental issues who have been thinking of ourselves in ways out of time – and now, quite possibly, we are running out of time as a result.

---

[2] Niels Henrik Gregersen, "Christology," in Michael S. Northcott and Peter M. Scott, eds., *Systematic Theology and Climate Change* (London: Routledge, 2014), 37.

Bibliography

Appleby, R. Scott. 2000. *The Ambivalence of the Sacred: Religion, Violence, and Reconciliation*. Lanham, MD: Rowman and Littlefield.

Aquino, Maria Pilar. 2011. "Religious Peacebuilding." In *The Blackwell Companion to Religion and Violence*, edited by Andrew R. Murphy. Malden, MA: Blackwell, 568–593.

Bainton, Roland H. 1960. *Christian Attitudes Toward War and Peace: A Historical Survey and Critical Re-evaluation*. New York: Abingdon Press,

  1957. *What Christianity Says about Sex, Love, and Marriage*. New York: Association Press.

Barnes, Timothy David. 1971. *Tertullian: A Historical and Literary Study*. Oxford: Clarendon Press.

Barth, Karl. 2012. *Church and State*. Macon, GA: Smyth and Helwys.

  1975. *Church Dogmatics*, 2nd ed., vol. I, part 1. Edinburgh: T&T Clark.

Bartlett, David. 2003. *What's Good about This News? Preaching from the Gospels and Galatians*. Louisville, KY: Westminster-John Knox Press.

Bauman, Clarence. 1985. *The Sermon on the Mount: The Modern Quest for Its Meaning*. Macon, GA: Mercer University Press.

Becker, Adam H., and Annette Yoshiko Reed, eds. 2007. *The Ways That Never Parted: Jews and Christians in Late Antiquity and the Early Middle Ages*. Minneapolis: Fortress Press.

Bellah, Robert et al. 2007. *Habits of the Heart: Individualism and Commitment in American Life*. Oakland, CA: University of California Press.

Benjamin, Walter. 1973. *Illuminations*. London: Fontana.

  2003. *Selected Writings, vol. 4: 1938–1940*, edited by H. Eiland and M. W. Jennings. Boston: Belknap Press.

Bertschamann, Dorothea H. 2014. *Bowing Before Christ – Nodding to the State? Reading Paul Politically with Oliver O'Donovan and John Howard Yoder*. London: Bloomsbury.

Biggar, Nigel. 2013. *In Defense of War*. Oxford: Oxford University Press.

2009. Specify and Distinguish! Interpreting the New Testament on "Non-Violence." *Studies in Christian Ethics* 22.2: 164–184.

Boulton, Wayne G., Thomas D. Kennedy, and Allen Verhey. 1994. *From Christ to the World: Introductory Readings in Christian Ethics*. Grand Rapids: Eerdmans.

Bouma-Prediger, Steven. 2010. *For the Beauty of the Earth: A Christian Vision for Creation Care*, 2nd ed. Grand Rapids: Baker Academic.

Boyarin, Daniel. 2004. *Border Lands: The Partition of Judaeo-Christianity*. Philadelphia: University of Pennsylvania Press.

Brock, Peter. 1992. *A Brief History of Pacifism: From Jesus to Tolstoy*. Syracuse: Syracuse University Press.

1998. *Varieties of Pacifism: A Survey from Antiquity to the Outset of the Twentieth Century*. Syracuse: Syracuse University Press.

Brown, Dale W. 1986. *Biblical Pacifism: A Peace Church Perspective*. Elgin, IL: Brethren Press.

Brown, Peter. 2013. *The Rise of Western Christendom: Triumph and Diversity, A.D. 200–1000, Tenth Anniversary Edition*. Oxford: Wiley-Blackwell.

Brueggemann, Walter. 2001. *Peace*. St. Louis: Chalice Press.

Bull, Marcus. 1993. *Knightly Piety and the Lay Response to the First Crusade: The Limousin and Gascony, c.970–c.1130*. Oxford: Clarendon Press.

Büntgen, Ulf, et al. 2011. "2500 Years of European Climate Variability and Human Susceptibility." *Science* 10.1126 (January 13). http://science.sciencemag.org/content/early/2011/01/12/science.1197175 (accessed on March 3, 2017).

Burckhardt, Jacob. 1949. *The Age of Constantine the Great*. New York: Pantheon Books.

Burke, Kenneth. 1973. "The Virtues and Limitations of Debunking." In *The Philosophy of Literary Form*, 3rd ed. Berkeley: University of California Press.

Byler, Dennis. 1989. *Making War and Making Peace: Why Some Christians Fight and Some Don't*. Scottsdale, PA: Herald Press.

Cadoux, C. John. 1982. *The Early Christian Attitude to War*. London: Headley Bros. Publishers.

Cahill, Lisa Sowle. 1994. *Love Your Enemies: Discipleship, Pacifism, and Just War Theory*. Minneapolis: Augsburg Fortress Press.

Carter, Craig A. 2001. *The Politics of the Cross: The Theology and Social Ethics of John Howard Yoder*. Grand Rapids: Brazos.

Castelli, Elizabeth A. 2004. *Martyrdom and Memory: Early Christian Culture Making*. New York: Columbia University Press.

Cheney, Dick. 1993. "Defense and Environmental Initiative." *Forum* (September 1990). Quoted in William D. Palmer, "Environmental Compliance: Implications for Senior Commanders." *Parameters* (Spring): 81.

Childress, James F. 1984. "Moral Discourse about War in the Early Church." *Journal of Religious Ethics* 12.1: 2–18.

Clement of Alexandria. 1983. *Exhortation to the Greeks* X.100.2, in Louis J. Swift, ed., *The Early Church Fathers on War and Military Service*. Message of the Fathers of the Church 19, Thomas Halton, general editor. Wilmington, DE: Michael Glazier, Inc., 52.

Clough, David L., and Brian Stiltner. 2007. *Faith and Force: A Christian Debate about War*. Washington D.C.: Georgetown University Press.

Coakley, Sarah. 2002. *Powers and Submissions: Spirituality, Philosophy and Gender*. Oxford: Blackwell.

Cobb, L. Stephanie. 2008. *Dying To Be Men: Gender and Language in Early Christian Martyr Texts*. New York: Columbia University Press.

Cochran, David Carroll. 2014. *Catholic Realism and the Abolition of War*. Maryknoll, NY: Orbis.

Culliton, Joseph T., ed. 1982. *Non-violence – Central to Christian Spirituality: Perspectives from Scripture to the Present*. New York: Edwin Mellen Press.

Cullmann, Oscar. 1964. *Christ and Time: The Primitive Christian Conception of Time*. Trans. by Floyd V. Filson. Philadelphia: Westminster Press.

Cunningham, Lawrence. 2011. "Christian Martyrdom: A Theological Perspective." In *Witness of the Body: The Past, Present, and Future of Christian Martyrdom*, edited by Michael L. Budde and Karen Scott, 3–19. Grand Rapids: Eerdmans.

Curry, Andrew. 2011. "Fall of Rome Recorded in Trees." *ScienceNOW*, Jan. 13. http://news.sciencemag.org/sciencenow/2011/01/fall-of-rome-recorded-in-trees (accessed on January 14, 2011).

Dalby, Simon. 2009. *Security and Environmental Change*. Malden, MA: Polity Press.

Davidson, Donald. 1984. "On the Very Idea of a Conceptual Scheme." In *Inquiries into Truth and Interpretation*. Oxford, UK: Clarendon Press.

Digeser, Elizabeth DePalma. 1999. *The Making of a Christian Empire: Lactantius and Rome*. Ithaca: Cornell University Press.

Douglas, Mark. 2005. *Confessing Christ in the Twenty-first Century*. Lanham, MD: Rowman and Littlefield.

2000. "Warp and Woof: Pragmatism in 20th Century Christian Ethics." Ph.D diss., The University of Virginia.

Drake, H. A. 2000. *Constantine and the Bishops: The Politics of Intolerance*. Baltimore: Johns Hopkins University Press.

Dula, Peter. 2004. "The 'Disavowal of Constantine' in the Age of Global Capital." In *Seeking Cultures of Peace: A Peace Church Conversation*, edited by Fernando Enns, Scott Holland, and Ann Riggs, 62–77. Telford, PA: Cascadia Publishing House.

Dula, Peter, and Chris K. Huebner, eds. *The New Yoder*. Eugene, OR: Cascade Books, 2010.

Dungan, David L. 2007. *Constantine's Bible: Politics and the Making of the New Testament*. Minneapolis: Fortress Press.

Dunn, Geoffrey D. 2004. *Tertullian*. New York: Routledge.

Easterbrook, Gregg. 1980. "Global Warming: Who Loses – and Who Wins?" *The Atlantic*, April. www.theatlantic.com/magazine/archive/2007/04/global-warming-who-loses-and-who-wins/305698/ (accessed on August 13, 2018).

Efroymson, David P. 1977. "The Patristic Connection." In *Antisemitism and the Foundations of Christianity*, edited by Alan Davies. New York: Paulist Press.

1980. "Tertullian's Anti-Jewish Rhetoric: Guilt by Association." *Union Seminary Quarterly* 36.1 (Fall): 25–37.

Egan, Eileen. 1999. *Peace Be With You: Justified Warfare or the Way of Nonviolence*. Maryknoll, NY: Orbis.

Eliade, Mircea. 1959. *Cosmos and History: The Myth of Eternal Return*. New York: Harper and Bros.

Enns, Fernando, Scott Holland, and Ann K. Riggs. 2004. *Seeking Cultures of Peace: A Peace Church Conversation*. Telford, PA: Cascadia Publishing House.

Fagan, Brian. 2009. *The Great Warming: Climate Change and the Rise and Fall of Civilizations*. New York: Bloomsbury.

——— 2001. *The Little Ice Age: How Climate Made History 1300–1850*. New York: Basic Books.

——— 2004. *The Long Summer: How Climate Changed Civilization*. New York: Basic Books.

Ferguson, Everett. 2014. *The Early Church at Work and Worship, vol. 2: Catechesis, Baptism, Eschatology, and Martyrdom*. Eugene, OR: Cascade Books.

Ferguson, John. 1978. *War and Peace in the World's Religions*. New York: Oxford University Press.

Fiala, Andrew. 2015. *The Peace of Nature and the Nature of Peace: Essays on Ecology, Nature, Nonviolence and Peace*. Boston: Brill.

Finger, Thomas N. 2004. *A Contemporary Anabaptist Theology*. Downers Grove, IL: Intervarsity Press.

Fox, George. *Works*, vol. 1. 1831. Quoted in G. Amoss, "George Fox: An Exhortation to Friends in the Ministry." www.qis.net/~daruma/exhortation.html (accessed on September 29, 2015).

Frassetto, Michael. 2014. "Ademar of Chabannes and the Peace of God." In *Where Heaven and Earth Meet: Essays on Medieval Europe in Honor of Daniel F. Callahan*, edited by Michael Frassetto, Matthew Gabriele, and John D. Hosler. Leiden: Brill.

Fredriksen, Paula. 2008. *Augustine and the Jews: A Christian Defense of Jews and Judaism*. New York: Doubleday.

Gat, Azar. 2005. *War in Human Civilization*. New York: Oxford University Press.

Gilkey, Langdon. 1990. *Gilkey on Tillich*. New York: Crossroad.

Gleditsch, Nils Petter. 1998. "Armed Conflict and the Environment: A Critique of the Literature." *Journal of Peace Research* 35, no. 3: 381–400.

Gleick, Peter H. 2016. "Water Strategies for the Next Administration." *Science* 354, no. 6312 (November): 555–556.

Gray, John. 2009. *Black Mass: Apocalyptic Religion and the Death of Utopia*. New York: Farrar, Strauss, and Giroux.

Greenman, Jeffrey P., Timothy Larsen, and Stephen R. Spencer, eds. 2007. *The Sermon on the Mount Through the Centuries: From the Early Church to John Paul II*. Grand Rapids: Brazos Press.

Gregersen, Niels Henrik. 2014. "Christology." In *Systematic Theology and Climate Change*, edited by Michael S. Northcott and Peter M. Scott. London: Routledge.

Gustafson, James. 1981. *Ethics from a Theocentric Perspective*. Chicago: University of Chicago Press.

Harink, Douglas. 2003. *Paul Among the Postliberals: Pauline Theology Beyond Christendom and Modernity*. Grand Rapids, MI: Brazos Press.

Harnack, Adolph. 1981. *Militia Christi: The Christian Religion and the Military in the First Three Centuries*. Trans. by David McInnes Gracie. Philadelphia: Fortress Press.

Hauerwas, Stanley. 1981. "The Moral Authority of Scripture: The Politics and Ethics of Remembering." In *A Community of Character: Toward a Constructive Christian Social Ethic*. Notre Dame: University of Notre Dame Press.

1983. *The Peaceable Kingdom: A Primer in Christian Ethics*. Notre Dame: University of Notre Dame Press.

1981. *Vision and Virtue*. Notre Dame: University of Notre Dame Press.

2001. *With the Grain of the Universe: The Church's Witness and Natural Theology*. Grand Rapids: Brazos Press.

Hauerwas, Stanley, et al., eds. 1999. *The Wisdom of the Cross: Essays in Honor of John Howard Yoder*. Grand Rapids: Eerdmans.

Hays, Richard B. 1996. *The Moral Vision of the New Testament: A Contemporary Introduction to New Testament Ethics*. San Francisco: Harper San Francisco.

2009. "Narrate and Embody: A Response to Nigel Biggar, 'Specify and Distinguish'." *Studies in Christian Ethics* 22, no. 2: 185–198.

Head, Thomas, and Richard Landes, eds. 1992. *The Peace of God: Social Violence and Religious Response in France around the Year 1000*. Ithaca: Cornell University Press.

Heering, G. J. 1943. *The Fall of Christianity: A Study of Christianity, the State, and War*. New York: Fellowship Publications.

Helgeland, John, R. J. Daly, and J. Patout Burns. 1985. *Christians and the Military: The Early Experience*. Philadelphia: Fortress Press.

Hershberger, Guy Franklin. 1969. *War, Peace, and Nonresistance*. Scottsdale, PA: Herald Press.

Holmes, Arthur F., ed. 1975. *War and Christian Ethics: Classic and Contemporary Readings on the Morality of War*. Grand Rapids: Baker Academic.

Homer-Dixon, Thomas F. 1999. *Environment, Scarcity, and Violence*. Princeton: Princeton University Press.

Hornus, Jean-Michel. 1980. *It Is Not Lawful for Me to Fight*. Trans. by Alan Kreider and Oliver Coburn. Scottsdale, PA: Herald Press.

Hsiang, Solomon, M., Meng, Kyle C., and Cane, Mark, A. 2011. "Civil Conflicts Are Associated with the Global Climate." *Nature* 476 (August): 438–441.

Hunter, David G. 1994. "The Christian Church and the Roman Army in the First Three Centuries." In *The Church's Peace Witness*, 161–181, edited by Marlin E. Miller and Barbara Nelson Gingerich. Grand Rapids: William B. Eerdmans.

1992. "A Decade of Research on Early Christians and Military Service." *Religious Studies Review* 18, no. 2 (April): 87–94.

Iosif, Despina. 2013. *Early Christian Attitudes to War, Violence and Military Service*. Piscataway, NJ: Gorgias Press.

Jacobs, Andrew S. 2008. "Jews and Christians." In *The Oxford Handbook of Early Christian Studies*, edited by Susan Ashbrook Harvey and David G. Hunter, 169–185. New York: Oxford University Press.

Jenkins, Willis. 2013. *The Future of Ethics: Sustainability, Social Justice, and Religious Creativity*. Washington D.C.: Georgetown University Press.

Jenkins, Willis, Mary Evelyn Tucker, and John Grim, eds. 2017. *Routledge Handbook of Religion and Ecology*. New York: Routledge.

Joas, Hans. 2003. *War and Modernity*. Translated by Rodney Livingstone. Cambridge, UK: Polity Press.

Johann, Robert O. 1968. *Building the Human*. New York: Herder and Herder.

Johnson, James Turner. 1981. *Just War Tradition and the Restraint of War: A Moral and Historical Inquiry*. Princeton: Princeton University Press.

1987. *The Quest for Peace: Three Moral Traditions in Western Cultural History*. Princeton: Princeton University Press.

Johnson, Roger A. 2009. *Peacemaking and Religious Violence: From Thomas Aquinas to Thomas Jefferson*. Eugene, OR: Pickwick Publishers.

Juergensmeyer, Mark. 1987. "Nonviolence." In *The Encyclopedia of Religion, vol. 10*, edited by Mircea Eliade, 463–468. New York: Macmillan Publishing Company.

Justin Martyr. 2003. *Dialogue with Trypho*, 27.4, trans. by Thomas B. Falls. Washington D.C.: Catholic University of America Press.

Kaplan, Robert. 1994. "The Coming Anarchy." *The Atlantic Monthly* 272, no. 2: 44–76.

Klaassen, Walter. 2000. "Pacifism, Nonviolence, and the Peaceful Reign of God." In *Creation and Environment: An Anabaptist Perspective on a Sustainable World*, edited by Calvin Redekop, 139–153. Baltimore: Johns Hopkins University Press.

Koontz, Theodore J. 1996. "Christian Nonviolence: An Interpretation." In *The Ethics of War and Peace: Religious and Secular Perspectives*, edited by Terry Nardin, 169–196. Princeton: Princeton University Press.

Krahn, Cornelius, Harold S. Bender, and John J. Friesen. 1989. "Migrations." *Global Anabaptist Mennonite Encyclopedia Online*. http://gameo.org/index .php?title=Migrations&oldid=143668 (accessed on March 31, 2017).

Kreider, Alan. 2003. "Military Service in the Church Orders." *Journal of Religious Ethics* 31, no. 3: 415–442.

Kroeker, P. Travis. 2005. "Is a Messianic Political Ethic Possible? Recent Work by and about John Howard Yoder." *Journal of Religious Ethics* 33, no. 1: 141–174.

Kunstler, James Howard. 2006. *The Long Emergency: Surviving the End of Oil, Climate Change, and Other Converging Catastrophes of the Twenty-First Century*. New York: Grove Press.

Kuriakose, Karikottuchira, ed. 2012. *Terrorism, Religion, and Global Peace: From Concepts to Praxis*. Piscataway, NJ: Gorgias Press.

LeBaron, Michelle, and Venashri Pillay. 2006. *Conflict Across Cultures: A Unique Experience of Bridging Cultures*. Boston: Intercultural Press.

Ledegang, Fred. 2014. "Eusebius' View on Constantine and His Policy." In *Violence in Ancient Christianity: Victims and Perpetrators*, edited by Albert C. Geljon and Riemer Roukema, 56–75. Leiden: Brill.

Leithart, P. J. 2010. *Defending Constantine: The Twilight of an Empire and the Dawn of Christendom*. Downer's Grove: IVP Academic.

Lenski, Noel. 2016. *Constantine and the Cities: Imperial Authority and Civic Politics*. Philadelphia: University of Pennsylvania Press.

Levinas, Emmanuel. 1969. *Totality and Infinity: An Essay on Exteriority*. Trans. by Alphonso Lingis. Pittsburgh, PA: Duquesne University Press.

Long, Michael G., ed. 2011. *Christian Peace and Nonviolence: A Documentary History*. Maryknoll, NY: Orbis.

Lopez, Admiral T. Joseph, USN (Ret.). 2007. "On Climate Change and the Conditions for Terrorism." In *National Security and the Threat of Climate Change*. Alexandria, VA: The CNA Corporation.

Lorde, Audre. 2007. "The Master's Tools Will Never Dismantle the Master's House." In *Sister Outsider: Essays and Speeches*, 110–113. Berkeley, CA: Crossing Press.

Lovin, Robin. 1995. *Reinhold Niebuhr and Christian Realism*. New York: Cambridge University Press.

Luz, Ulrich. 1989. *Matthew 1–7: A Continental Commentary*. Trans. by Wilhelm C. Linss. Minneapolis: Fortress Press.

MacCulloch, Diarmaid. 2013. *Silence: A Christian History*. New York: Penguin Books.

MacIntyre, Alisdair. 2007. *After Virtue: A Study in Moral Theory*, 3rd ed. South Bend, IN: University of Notre Dame Press.

Madigan, Kevin J., and Jon D. Levinson. 2008. *Resurrection: The Power of God for Christians and Jews*. New Haven: Yale University Press.

Markus, Robert. 1990. *The End of Ancient Christianity*. Cambridge: Cambridge University Press.

Martin-Schramm, James B. 2010. *Climate Justice: Ethics, Energy, and Public Policy*. Minneapolis: Fortress Press.

Mathewes, Charles. 2001. *Evil and the Augustinian Tradition*. New York: Cambridge University Press.

———. 2007. *A Theology of Public Life*. Cambridge: Cambridge University Press.

McDonald, Lee Martin. 1993. "Anti-Judaism in the Early Christian Fathers." In *Anti-Semitism and Early Christianity: Issues of Polemic and Faith*, edited by Craig A. Evans and Donald A. Hagner, 215–252. Minneapolis: Fortress Press.

McMullen, Ramsay. 1963. *Soldier and Civilian in the Later Roman Empire*. Cambridge: Harvard University Press.

Michael, Robert. 1994. "Antisemitism and the Church Fathers." In *Jewish-Christian Encounters Over the Centuries: Symbiosis, Prejudice, Holocaust, Dialogue*, edited by Marvin Perry and Fredrick M. Schweitzer. New York: Peter Lang.

Middleton, Paul. 2006. *Radical Martyrdom and Cosmic Conflict in Early Christianity*. London: T&T Clark.

Mill, John Stuart. 1986. *On Liberty*. Buffalo, NY: Prometheus Books.

Miller, Marlin E., and Barbara Nelson Gingerich, eds. 1994. *The Church's Peace Witness*. Grand Rapids: Eerdmans.

Moss, Candida R. 2012. *Ancient Christian Martyrdom: Diverse Practices, Theologies, and Traditions*. New Haven: Yale University Press.

———. 2013. *The Myth of Persecution: How Early Christians Invented a Story of Martyrdom*. New York: HarperOne.

Mueller, John. 2004. *The Remnants of War*. Cornell, NY: Cornell University Press.

———. 1989. *Retreat from Doomsday: The Obsolescence of Major War*. New York: Basic Books.

Nation, Mark Thiessen. 2006. *John Howard Yoder: Mennonite Patience, Evangelical Witness, Catholic Convictions*. Grand Rapids: Eerdmans.

Nicholson, Oliver. 1999. "*Civitas Quae Adhuc Sustentat Omnia*: Lactantius and the City of Rome." In *The Limits of Ancient Christianity: Essays on Late Antique Thought and Culture in Honor of R. A. Markus*, edited by William E. Klingshirn and Mark Vessey, 7–25. Ann Arbor: University of Michigan Press.

Niebuhr, Reinhold. 2008. *The Irony of American History*. Chicago: University of Chicago Press.

———. 2005. "Why the Christian Church Is Not Pacifist." In *War and Christian Ethics*, edited by Arthur Holmes, 301–313. Grand Rapids, MI: Baker Academic.

Northcott, Michael S. 2016. *A Political Theology of Climate Change*. Grand Rapids: Eerdmans.

Nuttall, Geoffrey F. 1958. *Christian Pacifism in History*. Oxford: Basil Blackwell.

Oberman, Heiko. 2003. *The Two Reformations: The Journey from the Last Days to the New World*, edited by Donald Weinstein. New Haven: Yale University Press.

Ochs, Peter. 2011. *Another Reformation: Postliberal Christianity and the Jews*. Grand Rapids: Baker Academic.

———. 2005. *Peirce, Pragmatism and the Logic of Scripture*. New York: Cambridge University Press.

Ollenburger, Ben C., and Gayle Gerber Koontz, eds. 2004. *A Mind Patient and Untamed: Assessing John Howard Yoder's Contributions to Theology, Ethics, and Peacemaking*. Telford, PA: Cascadia Publishing House.

Orr, Edgar W. 1958. *Christian Pacifism*. Ashingdon, England: C. W. Daniel Company, Ltd.

Pfister, Christian, and Rudolph, Brazdil. 1999. "Climatic Variability in Sixteenth-Century Europe and Its Social Dimension: A Synthesis." *Climatic Change* 43: 5–53.

Pohlsander, Hans A. 2004. *The Emperor Constantine*, 2nd ed. New York: Routledge.

Prodi, Paolo. 2014. "Corruption in the Church: An Age of Constantine?" In *Corruption*, edited by Regina Ammicht Quinn, Lisa Sowle Cahill, and Luis Carlos Susin, 69–80. London: SCM Press.

Ramsey, Paul. 1961. *War and the Christian Conscience*. Durham, NC: Duke University Press.

Redekop, Calvin ed. 2000. *Creation and the Environment: An Anabaptist Perspective on a Sustainable World*. Baltimore: Johns Hopkins University Press.

Regan, Richard J. 1996. *Just War: Principles and Cases*. Washington D.C.: Catholic University of America Press.

Reichberg, Gregory M., Henrik Syse, and Nicole M. Harswell, eds. 2014. *Religion, War, and Ethics: A Sourcebook of Textual Traditions*. New York: Cambridge University Press.

Reimer, A. James. 2001. *Mennonites and Classical Theology: Dogmatic Foundations for Christian Ethics*. Kitchener, ON: Pandora Press.

2014. *Toward an Anabaptist Political Theology: Law, Order, and Civil Society*, edited by Paul G. Doerksen. Eugene, OR: Cascade Books.

Reuther, Rosemary Radford. 1974. *Faith and Fratricide: The Theological Roots of Anti-Semitism*. New York: Seabury Press.

Ricoeur, Paul. 1990. *Time and Narrative* (3 vols.). Translated by K. Blamey and D. Pellauer. Chicago: Chicago University Press.

Robertson, Roland. 1992. *Globalization: Social Theory and Global Culture*. London: Sage Publications.

Rogers, Will, and Jay Gulledge. 2010. "Lost in Translation: Closing the Gap Between Climate Science and National Security Policy." Washington D.C.: Center for a New American Security, April. https://s3.amazonaws.com/files.cnas.org/docu ments/Lost-in-Translation_Code406_Web_0.pdf?mtime=20160906080151 (accessed on November 12, 2014).

Rorty, Richard. 1989. *Contingency, Irony, and Solidarity*. New York: Cambridge University Press.

Rose, Jonathan F. P. 2016. *The Well-Tempered City: What Modern Science, Ancient Civilizations, and Human Nature Teach Us About the Future of Urban Life*. San Francisco: Harper Wave.

Saint Augustine. 1961. *Confessions*. Translated by R. S. Pine-Coffin. London: Penguin Books.

Schlabach, Theron F. 2006. "Guy F. Hershberger's *War, Peace, and Nonresistance* (1944): Background, Genesis, Message." *Mennonite Quarterly Review* 80 (July): 293–4.

Schlabach, Theron F., and Richard T. Huges, eds. 1997. *Proclaim Peace: Christian Pacifism from Unexpected Quarters*. Urbana: University of Illinois Press.

Schleitheim Confession. Translated by John Howard Yoder. www.anabaptistwiki .org/mediawiki/index.php/Schleitheim_Confession_(source) (accessed on November 5, 2015).

Schwartz, Regina. 1998. *The Curse of Cain: The Violent Legacy of Monotheism*. Chicago: Chicago University Press.

Sevenster, J. N. 1975. *The Roots of Pagan Anti-Semitism in the Ancient World*. Leiden: E. J. Brill.

Severson, Richard James. 1995. *Time, Death, and Eternity: Reflecting on Augustine's Confessions in Light of Heidegger's Being and Time*. Lanham, MD: Scarecrow Press.

Shandle, Matthew A. 2011. *The Origins of War: A Catholic Perspective*. Washington D.C.: Georgetown University Press.

Sider, E. Morris, and Keefer Jr., Luke, eds. 2002. *A Peace Reader*. Nappanee, IN: Evangel Publishing House,

Skarsaune, Oskar. 2007. "Apologetics in the Early Church." In *Religion Past and Present: Encyclopedia of Theology and Religion, vol. 1*, edited by Hans Dieter Betz et al., 318–320. Boston: Brill.

Slattery, W. Michael. 2007. *Jesus the Warrior? Historical Christian Perspectives and Problems on the Morality of War and the Waging of Peace*. Milwaukee: Marquette University Press.

Smith, Ted A. 2007. *The New Measures: A Theological History of Democratic Practice*. Cambridge: Cambridge University Press.

Smither, Edward L., ed. 2014. *Rethinking Constantine: History, Theology, and Legacy*. Eugene, OR: Pickwick Publishers.

Soulen, Kendall. 1996. *The God of Israel and Christian Theology*. Minneapolis: Fortress Press.

Stout, Jeffrey. 2004. *Democracy and Tradition*. Princeton, NJ: Princeton University Press.

  1987. *The Flight from Authority: Religion, Morality, and the Quest for Autonomy*. South Bend: University of Notre Dame Press.

Sun Tzu. 1971. *The Art of War*. Translated by Samuel B. Griffith. New York: Oxford University Press.

Tanner, Kathryn. 1997. *Theories of Culture: A New Agenda for Theology*. Minneapolis: Fortress Press.

Taylor, Charles. 2004. *Modern Social Imaginaries*. Durham, NC: Duke University Press.

  2007. *The Secular Age*. Boston: Harvard University Press.

Tertullian. 1950. "Apology 50." In *Tertullian: Apologetical Works and Minucius Felix Octavius*, translated by Rudolph Arbesmann et al., 123–126. Washington D.C.: The Catholic University of America Press.

  2011. "On Patience." In *Christian Peace and Nonviolence: A Documentary History*, edited by Michael G. Long, 23. Maryknoll, NY: Orbis.

Tillich, Paul. 1957. *Dynamics of Faith*. New York: Harper and Row.

Tilly, Charles. 1990. *Coercion, Capital, and European States, A.D. 990–1990*. Cambridge, MA: Basil Blackwood.

Trouillot, Michel-Rolph. 1995. *Silencing the Past: Power and the Production of History*. Boston: Beacon Press.

United Nations Intergovernmental Panel on Climate Change. 2014. *Climate Change Synthesis Report Summary for Policymakers*. www.ipcc.ch/pdf/assessment-report/ar5/syr/AR5_SYR_FINAL_SPM.pdf (accessed on September 16, 2016).

U.S. Agency for International Development. 2009. Office of Conflict Management and Mitigation. "Climate Change, Adaptation, and Conflict: A Preliminary Review of the Issues." Washington, DC: Government Printing Office.

U.S. Department of Defense. 2010. *Quadrennial Defense Review Report*. Washington, DC: Government Printing Office.

  2014. *Quadrennial Defense Review Report*. Washington, DC: Government Printing Office.

van Henten, Jan Willem, and Friedrich Avemarie. 2002. *Martyrdom and Noble Death: Selected Texts from Graeco-Roman, Jewish and Christian Antiquity.* London: Routledge.

Voosen, Paul. 2016. "Anthropocene Pinned to Postwar Period." *Science* 353, no. 6302 (August 26): 852–853.

Waszink, J. H. 1979. "Tertullian's Principles and Methods of Exegesis." In *Early Christian Literature and the Classical Intellectual Tradition: In Honorem Robert M. Grant,* edited by William R. Schoedel and Robert L. Wilken, 17–31. Paris: Editions Beauchesne.

Weaver, J. Denny, ed. 2014. *John Howard Yoder: Radical Theologian.* Eugene, OR: Cascade Books.

White, Lynn. 1974. "The Historical Roots of Our Ecological Crisis." In *Ecology and Religion in History,* edited by David and Eileen Spring, 15–30. New York: Harper and Row.

Wilken, Robert L. 1995. *Remembering the Christian Past.* Grand Rapids: Eerdmans.

Williams, Rowan. 2005. *The Truce of God.* Grand Rapids, MI: Eerdmans Pub. Co.

2005. *Why Study the Past? The Quest for the Historical Church.* Grand Rapids: Eerdmans Publishing Company.

Wink, Walter. 2003. *Jesus and Nonviolence: A Third Way.* Minneapolis: Fortress Press.

Woods, Mark. 2007. "The Nature of War and Peace: Just War Thinking, Environmental Ethics, and Environmental Justice." In *Rethinking the Just War Tradition,* edited by Michael W. Brough, John W. Lango, and Harry van der Linden, 17–34. Albany, NY: SUNY Press.

Yoder, John Howard. 2009. *Christian Attitudes to War, Peace, and Revolution,* edited by Theodore J. Koontz and Andy Alexis-Baker. Grand Rapids, MI: Brazos Press.

2002. *The Christian Witness to the State.* Scottsdale, PA: Herald Press.

1985. "A Critique of North American Evangelical Ethics," *Transformation* 2, no. 1 (January): 28–31.

1956. "Farming among Mennonites in France." In *The Mennonite Encyclopedia* 2, 306–7. Hillsboro, KS: Mennonite Brethren Publishing House.

1996. "How H. Richard Niebuhr Reasoned: A Critique of *Christ and Culture.*" In *Authentic Transformation: A New Vision of Christ and Culture,* edited by Glen Stassen, D. M. Yeager, and John Howard Yoder, 31–89. Nashville: Abingdon Press.

2008. *The Jewish-Christian Schism Revisited,* edited by Michael G. Cartwright and Peter Ochs. Waterloo, ON: Herald Press.

1970. *Karl Barth and the Problem of War.* Nashville: Abingdon Press.

2010. *Nonviolence: A Brief History,* edited by Paul Martens, Matthew Porter, and Myles Werntz. Waco, TX: Baylor University Press.

1994. *The Royal Priesthood: Essays Ecclesiastical and Ecumenical.* Grand Rapids, MI: Eerdmans Press.

Index